THE BRUNELS
FATHER AND SON

THE BRUNELS
FATHER AND SON

ANTHONY BURTON

PEN & SWORD
TRANSPORT

AN IMPRINT OF PEN & SWORD BOOKS LTD.
YORKSHIRE – PHILADELPHIA

First published in Great Britain in 2022 by
Pen and Sword Transport
An imprint of
Pen & Sword Books Ltd.
Yorkshire - Philadelphia

ISBN 978 1 52678 699 9

A CIP catalogue record for this book is available from the British Library.

Typeset in 10.5/13.5 pt Palatino
Typeset by SJmagic DESIGN SERVICES, India.
Printed and bound in the UK by CPI Group (UK) Ltd, Croydon, CR0 4YY.

Pen & Sword Books Ltd incorporates the Imprints of Pen & Sword Books Archaeology, Atlas, Aviation, Battleground, Discovery, Family History, History, Maritime, Military, Naval, Politics, Railways, Select, Transport, True Crime, Fiction, Frontline Books, Leo Cooper, Praetorian Press, Seaforth Publishing, Wharncliffe and White Owl.

For a complete list of Pen & Sword titles please contact

PEN & SWORD BOOKS LIMITED
47 Church Street, Barnsley, South Yorkshire, S70 2AS, England
E-mail: enquiries@pen-and-sword.co.uk
Website: www.pen-and-sword.co.uk

Or
PEN AND SWORD BOOKS
1950 Lawrence Rd, Havertown, PA 19083, USA
E-mail: Uspen-and-sword@casematepublishers.com
Website: www.penandswordbooks.com

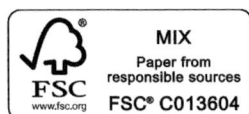

FSC
www.fsc.org

MIX
Paper from
responsible sources
FSC® C013604

CONTENTS

PREFACE

The name 'Brunel' is instantly recognizable by most people in Britain, but they usually only think of one man, Isambard Kingdom Brunel. I remember a song that was written for a Mikron Theatre Company based on his life:

I'm Isambard Kingdom Brunel
That's a name that you know very well
But I'll wager not one
Knows all that I've done.
I'm Isambard Kingdom Brunel.

The song is true on both counts. I learned a great deal more about the man very many years ago when I read L.T.C. Rolt's masterly biography – a book that inspired me to take an interest in and eventually write about the history of technology. Later, I became personally involved in writing and talking about Isambard; on television when presenting the BBC series *The Past Afloat* and then in a program marking the 150th anniversary of the Great Western Railway. But up to then, I had only had a passing interest in his father. That first began to change when I was asked to participate in a BBC Radio 4 series on underground Britain. This involved going to Wapping tube station in the early hours of the morning to wait until the last train had gone, and then walking into Marc Brunel's tunnel beneath the Thames and being aware for the first time just what a large and complex structure it was, something one never appreciates when rumbling through on a train. Then I began researching for my book *Rise and Fall of British Shipbuilding* and visited Marc Brunel's blockmaking mill at Portsmouth. It was then that I began to get really interested in the father as well as the son.

The more I read about Marc, the more interesting I found him. I also came to realise what a huge part he had to play in his son's life and how much he contributed to his early successes. I felt that this was a subject that had not really been fully explored. Even after Marc's death, Isambard was still making use of ideas that had been first explored and developed by his father. That led me on to more reading and research that eventually led to this book. It does not pit one against the other: but celebrates their single and joint achievements.

Anthony Burton
Stroud
2022

Chapter 1

MARC BRUNEL: THE EARLY YEARS

Marc Isambard Brunel was born in Hacqueville, between Paris and Rouen on 25 April 1769, the latest in a long line of Brunels, whose ancestry can be traced right back to 1490 when Jean Brunel was born in the same village. It has never been much more than a hamlet; today the population is under 500, but it is surrounded by rich farming land, and it was on that land that generations of Brunels had made their living as tenant farmers. The farmhouse itself is still there, a large and comfortable building that speaks of a certain prosperity. Although they were tenants not landowners, they were substantial members of the community and they traditionally held the position of Maître des Postes, which was remunerative as at that time the hamlet stood on the main road, though it is now bypassed. This set up a pattern of family life. The eldest son would inherit the farm and the next to arrive would usually be expected to enter the church. This would ensure the incumbent a good deal of prestige and a comfortable way of life. It was not considered necessary to have a vocation to enter the Church. Some may have been zealous, others might do little more than conduct the occasional service. That depended on the individual, but one thing was clearly understood in the family: that becoming a priest was a great blessing for the second son. So it was assumed from birth that Charles the eldest would get the farm and Marc would take holy orders and that he would be suitably grateful. Things did not exactly go as planned.

Although the Brunel family had the gift of the church living, so that there would be no problem in establishing him, it was still essential that the potential priest received a classical education and his father, Jean Charles, ensured that he got one. The process started seriously at the death of his mother, when the boy was seven. Marc did not prove to be an enthusiastic scholar, in spite of his father's efforts. Reports of those early days say that he showed more enthusiasm for watching the local wheelwright at work. This is not too surprising, since, for any child with a practical bent, there are few jobs more fascinating. There is the intricate carpentry of creating the wheel, but the real joy comes at the end, when the iron tyre has to be put on the wheel. Fired up to red-heat, the metal is placed over the wooden rim which

The village of Hacqueville in France, the birthplace of Marc Brunel. The entrance to the Brunel farm can be seen to the right of the picture.

promptly catches fire and is then dowsed in water, with its ensuing cloud of steam, to shrink the iron to the wood. For Marc, this was a great improvement over conjugating Latin verbs. Marc's father, however, seems to have been convinced that all he needed was discipline and the learning would follow. The standard punishment was to shut him up in a gloomy room with rather forbidding portraits of his ancestors, one of whom always seemed to be looking at him with a disapproving gaze. Young Marc became so depressed by the sight of this one particularly grim portrait, that he dragged a table to the wall, put a chair on top, clambered up and sliced out the offending eyes with his pocket-knife. After that, home tuition came to an end, and at eight he was sent to the military college at Gisors, some 20km away from home.

The college was much more to Marc's liking as the boys could strut around in uniform like little soldiers with powdered wigs and swords at their side. He was good at mathematics and drawing and in the holidays he would go out with his sketchbook, visiting interesting locations. One of his favourites was the great medieval fortress of Chateau Gaillard, built by the English king Richard I then also the Duke of Normandy, on a promontory overlooking the Seine at Les Andelys, just a few kilometres from his home. He also developed a taste for music and began learning to play the flute. He was later shown a harpsichord and was intrigued by the mechanism. According to legend, he promptly set about inventing a model musical instrument that could produce the sounds of both harpsichord and flute. If the story is true – and many stories surrounding boys who became famous later in life are not – then he must have been extraordinarily gifted. His instrument would have to incorporate both a keyboard attached to a mechanism to pluck the strings and a blowing device for the flute. True or not, the boy was still showing a reluctance to study for the church and an enthusiasm for mechanical objects. His father made one last attempt to set him on what he regarded as the sensible path and he was sent for religious instruction to the seminary of Sainte Nicaise in Rouen.

For young Marc, the move was not welcome in the sense that he was now required to spend ever more time on the subjects in which he had little or no interest. On the other hand, Rouen was a busy city and an important inland port, able to take a variety of sea-going ships as well as river barges. Everything about the docks fascinated him and he was kept busy sketching everything from cranes to ships. One day, he saw two large iron cylinders being unloaded and, asking what they were, was told they were part of a 'fire engine'. This was not a machine for putting out fires, but an early form of steam engine for pumping water based on a design by Thomas Newcomen in England. The system was quite simple. An overhead beam pivoted at the centre had pump rods suspended from one end. Just as in the village pump, someone has to move the handle up and down to get water, so a force was needed to raise the rods. Newcomen suspended a piston from the other end of the beam, that fitted tightly into a cylinder. Steam was admitted below the piston and then condensed by a cold-water spray, creating a partial vacuum, at which point air pressure forced the piston down, lifting the rods. Marc was intrigued and declared that one day he would like to visit the country that made such things. He could never have guessed how important a part steam power would play in the lives of himself and the son he would have many years later.

Marc now had a change in his fortunes. The principal of the seminary recognised that the boy had great talent, but no vocation for the Church. He informed Marc's father of his views, and at that point a distant cousin of Marc's stepped in. Mme Carpentier's husband had retired from a life of seafaring and was now American Consul in Rouen. The family offered to take the boy in and arrange for private tuition from a friend of theirs, the resoundingly named, Vincent François Jean-Nöel Dulague. The friend was, in fact, the Professor of Hydrography at the Collége Royal in Rouen, and author of two standard textbooks on navigation. Surprisingly for such an eminent man, he agreed to take over the job of tutoring the boy, who was just entering his teenage years.

This was just what the boy needed to encourage his talents and give them direction. Trigonometry can seem a sterile subject, but when taught in terms of its application, then it can inspire. After just three lessons, Marc had grasped how the subject could be used to measure things which would have otherwise prove difficult. The theodolite is a surveying instrument that can measure angles. If you want to know the height of something, then if you can measure the distance from the base to the point where you've set up the instrument, then by using the theodolite to measure the angle between the base and the top of the object you are calibrating, you can create a triangle that will give you the height. Marc was so impressed with his new-found knowledge that he built his own basic theodolite and measured the height of Rouen Cathedral. This combination of natural ability and eagerness to learn so impressed Dulague that he decided to do what he could to secure Marc a career in the French Navy.

Thanks to Dulague's prestige, he was able to arrange an introduction for his pupil to the Marquis de Castrie, who, after a distinguished military career, was now Secretary for the Navy. As a result, Marc was accepted as a Volontaire d'Honneur in the French Navy in 1785 and was assigned to a frigate. While waiting to set sail, he was far from idle. He saw that one of the officers had a Hadley's quadrant, a navigational instrument that was used for measuring the angle of the sun to the horizon to determine the ship's latitude. He at once set about making a similar instrument for himself. As the illustration on p.5 shows this was quite a complex device and the fact that he succeeded and used it throughout his time in the navy is a mark of his ingenuity and technical ability. In 1786, he boarded the *Maréchal de Castrie* and in 1786, as a 17-year-old cadet, he set sail for the Caribbean.

We know very little about his years at sea. There is a drawing of a coffee husking machine, marked Guadeloupe 1790, but there is no evidence it was

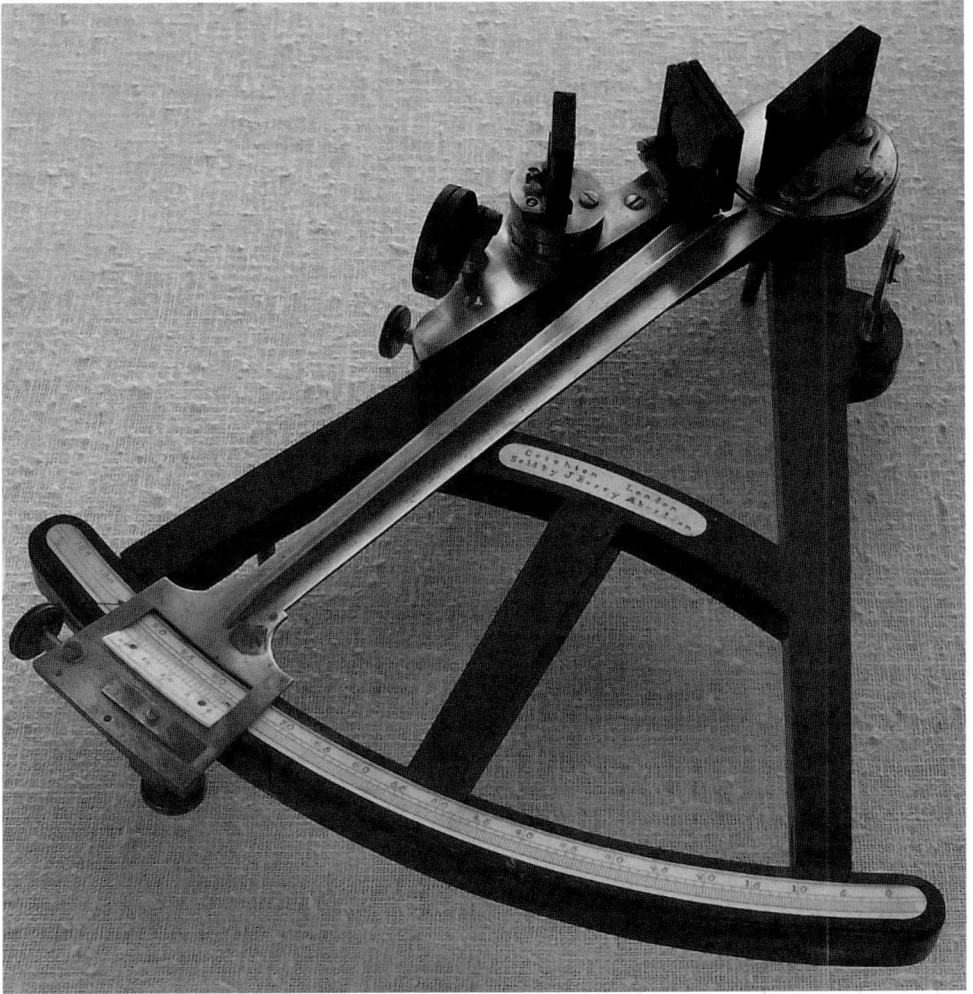

A Hadley quadrant. This was the type of instrument that the young Marc Brunel made for himself with the help of a local carpenter.

ever built. We do know that in the course of his travels he acquired a good working knowledge of English. He returned to Rouen in January 1792 and found a very different France from the one he had left six years ago. On 14 July 1789, the Bastille had been stormed, marking the start of an ever more radical series of demands for reform of the old feudal system. In 1791, a new constitution had been agreed, with the king as a constitutional monarch, though still with the power to veto legislation. Such moderation was short lived. The aristocracy had already been stripped of their powers; soon they would also lose their heads. On 25 April 1792, shortly after Marc's return, the guillotine claimed its first victim. He was, like most of the prosperous farmers of Normandy, a staunch royalist – a position that was rapidly becoming extremely dangerous.

Marc was once again staying with the Carpentiers in Rouen. One suspects the young man had a certain recklessness about him at this time; after all, he had almost certainly encountered many dangerous situations during his time at sea. The Revolution entered a new phase in August 1792 when a mob stormed the Tuileries Palace and imprisoned the king. The citizens of Rouen, who supported the king, set up a National Guard, which Marc promptly joined. After the sacking of the Tuileries, the defenders, including some of the Swiss Guard, made their escape and arrived in Rouen, expecting to be safe. But they were recognised and faced with a large band of sans culottes. Marc tried to intervene to plead for them, but the crowd was becoming more and more enraged. As he wrote in his diary:

'We could not have escaped had they closed in on us, but they were intimidated by the sight of a few of the National Guard coming down the Cours Dauphin.'

It was all very well declaring one's royalist sympathies in Rouen, but now he and François Carpentier decided to visit Paris. Here Marc could not refrain from expressing his views and told a crowd that he thought Robespierre's rule would soon be ended. Paris was not the place to express such opinions and the two men were lucky to escape, holing up in an inn until they could make their way back to Rouen. They were just in time as the following day the barricades went up around the city.

The Carpentiers were soon to have another guest. Sophia Kingdom, usually known as Sophie, who was just 16 years old when she arrived in Rouen. Her father, William Kingdom, had lived in Plymouth where he was agent for supplying both the Navy and the Army. She was the youngest of sixteen children. At that period, French manners and fashions were still highly regarded in Britain, and any young lady hoping to enter society was expected to know all about them and preferably have at least a smattering of the language. So young Sophie was sent to France with two friends, M. and Mme. Longuemar. Quite why anyone thought it was sensible to send a young girl into a country of bloody turmoil we will never know, but the party duly arrived at Le Havre in December 1792. The visits did not last long. The Longuemars heard that two of their friends who were known royalists had been killed, and they scuttled back to England. Sophie, however, was ill and unable to travel, so they left her with friends, the ever accommodating Carpentier family. It was there on 17 January 1793 that Marc met her for the first time.

By now it was obvious even to the impetuous Marc that the times were dangerous for Royalist supporters and that he needed to stay out of sight. His enforced isolation was made considerably more agreeable, as it was shared by a beautiful young girl, about to celebrate her 17th birthday. On her part, she must have been enthralled by the tales he had to tell – no doubt suitably embellished – of his adventures around the world. The result was that the young couple fell in love. But they could not stay together forever. Marc simply had to get away.

Once again, the Carpentier connection proved invaluable. François was able to arrange with the American Vice Consul for Marc to be provided with a passport for a journey to America. The reason given was that he was to arrange for grain shipments to come back to France, as the country was suffering a severe shortage of bread. Marc set off, but he had not gone far when his horse stumbled, throwing him and leaving him unconscious by the side of the road. When he came to, there was no sign of the horse, but a coach stopped and the occupant enquired where he was going. Marc replied that he was going home to Le Havre. The occupant offered to take him. So, the ardent young royalist was helped on his way by the Republican Navy Minister Gaspard Monge. On 7 July 1793, Marc was on board the American ship *Liberty* and ready to set sail for New York. It was only then that he discovered that he had either lost or forgotten the essential passport. It could have been a calamity, but he borrowed a passport from another passenger and set to work forging one for himself. He was obviously an expert counterfeiter, which was just as well; they had scarcely left port before they were stopped by a French frigate and all passengers were ordered to muster on deck for their documents to be checked. The fake was passed without query and he was safely on his way.

Back in Rouen, Sophie's life was becoming increasingly difficult. In October, a decree was passed calling for the immediate arrest of all English nationals. Sophie was taken away in a cart by armed men and, because the prisons were all full to capacity, she was taken to a convent at the port of Gravelines on the north coast. The nuns were reduced to extreme poverty, sleeping on bare boards with little to eat but a rough bread made out of a little flour mixed with straw. It was a terrifying place. It became overcrowded, but the authorities found a simple solution. They set up a guillotine, and prisoners were removed at regular intervals for execution. With each head that was removed, space was made for a new occupant. Petitions were sent for her release on the grounds that she had been very useful in France, teaching English to good, reliable republican families. None of this had any effect, but then, to everyone's surprise, the doors were opened and everyone was told they were free to leave. Robespierre had fallen. Sophie made her way back to the Carpentier family in Rouen, where she was given a warm welcome, and they arranged for her passage back to England. The days of terror were ended for the young Englishwoman, but she did not forget the young Frenchman with whom she had shared the dangers.

Chapter 2

MARC IN AMERICA

Marc landed in New York on 6 September 1793, found temporary lodgings and then started to worry about how he would earn a living. Two of his fellow passengers had talked about setting up a survey of land in the north of the country up to Lake Ontario on behalf of a French company. They were to be based in Albany, some 150 miles north of New York. He made his way there and met two ex-shipmates, Pierre Pharoux and Simon Desjardins, who agreed that he could join the expedition to map an area of over 200,000 acres of wilderness. They set off with two tents, axes and four Native Americans as guides. Richard Beamish, in his *Memoir of the Life of Sir Marc Isambard Brunel*, published in 1862, recalls discussing the trip with Marc Brunel, but received very little real information about what must have been a difficult journey. We do know that they used a boat as their means of transport, almost essential in a country with no roads of any sort. But it would have been an arduous journey, often having to lift the boat from the water for portages, carrying it round falls and rapids, as they made their way up a network of rivers to the Great Lakes. Two anecdotes did emerge from their conversations about his travels. They were journeying upriver when they heard children's voices shouting, 'Viens papa – viens Maman, voila un bateau' – Come on father and mother – there's a boat. They had come upon a family of French settlers, who made them welcome. The other simply states that Marc killed a rattlesnake on Rattlesnake Island; the name might have suggested that it was not the healthiest place to visit.

Marc Brunel and Pharoux returned to New York by sea, and during the voyage began talking to an American merchant, Mr Thurman, described by Marc as an 'homme sage'. He had become interested in the idea of developing a canal system that would ultimately link New York to the Great Lakes. He was, however, proposing a more modest start, a line from the Hudson River to Lake Champlain, which could later be extended to the St. Lawrence. According to Richard Beamish, Thurman 'is still remembered with reverence in New York'. Sadly, that reverence has not lasted through to the present day, and it has been impossible to find any more about the gentleman who can be said to have altered the whole direction of Marc Brunel's life. The two surveyors set off on the task of finding a route for the canal, but it seems that although Pharoux was originally in charge, he soon allowed Marc Brunel to take the lead in the work. They duly produced a report, but nothing was done. It was not until 1817 that work actually began on the Champlain Canal, which proved such a success that it was greatly improved over the years, and the old locks have now been replaced by massive new ones, 10 metres long by 13.7 metres wide. It seems that the reason the Brunel scheme was rejected was largely financial, but it has also been suggested that the survey itself was sound and used as the basis for the actual construction. In the course of his work, he also invented a floating mechanism for removing obstacles such as rocks and tree trunks from riverbeds. On one boat there was a winch from which a rope or cable rose to the top of what was in effect a set of shear legs fixed to a second boat, and from that the cable reached down to a drag.

A lock on the Champlain Canal, the first survey for which was carried out by Marc Brunel.

Pharoux was principally an architect rather than an engineer, and when a competition was announced for a design for what would be the Capitol building in Washington, he submitted a proposal. Marc also submitted his own design, which was extremely grand and said to be based on the Palace at Versailles, perhaps not the happiest choice for a new republic. The proposed building looks rather like a many tiered wedding cake with the main entrance approached by a pair of sweeping, curved stairways. It was considered by far the best design, but once again finance got in the way of execution. It was rejected in favour of a cheaper model. Brunel had, however, found an enthusiasm for architecture and now put in plans for a theatre for New York, the Park Theatre. The first proposal had something of the elaboration of the Capitol design, but once again his enthusiasm overtook the budget and he was forced to move to an altogether plainer design. This at least was accepted and built. Brunel had learned a lesson that probably most young architects need to learn; there is no good designing a magnificent building if the client can't afford to pay for it. Unfortunately, the building burned down in 1848.

Beamish has an anecdote about a joke played by Brunel and an unnamed friend at the grand opening show. A windmill, complete with turning sails, appeared on the stage, and from it a voice emerged making some outrageous comments about New York and well-known New Yorkers. There were howls of disgust from the audience, who seemed to be ready to attack the offending device and whoever was inside it. But it was wheeled over a trapdoor, and Brunel and his friend made their escape. The fate of the offending windmill is not recorded.

In 1796, Brunel formally became an American citizen and was appointed Chief Engineer for New York. He was very active in his new role. One of his most impressive achievements was the design of a cannon works, but sadly we

Brunel's design for the Capitol building for Washington DC. It was widely admired but proved too costly to build.

have very little information about the establishment. It was considered to be a very advanced factory and was widely admired, but whether Brunel designed all the machinery himself or with help from experienced armourers is a mystery, and we have no clue as to the methods used in making the cannon. It is unlikely that he designed everything from scratch and must certainly have made use of whatever technical information was available in the existing literature. He designed a number of commercial buildings and made great improvements to the waterfront in New York. It was a busy and active time, only marred by the news that Pharoux had died in an accident while on a surveying trip on the Black River, swept away while trying to cross dangerous falls.

Among Brunel's friends at this time was Alexander Hamilton, who had been Washington's aide-de-camp during the War of Independence, a gentleman who would probably be astonished to know that in the twenty-first century he would be best known as the subject of a musical. On one occasion, among the guests was an M. Delagibarre, who had recently been visiting Britain. The talk turned to news of recent British naval victories in the French Revolutionary wars, and especially the victory over a far larger Spanish fleet at Cape St. Vincent. At some point, Delagibarre mentioned the trouble the Admiralty had in acquiring the number of blocks they needed for their ships. It was estimated that the Navy needed 100,000 a year. They were used for everything, from manoeuvring the guns below deck to moving the spars on the masts. This may seem a large number, but a single frigate, defined at that time as a warship carrying at least 28 guns, carried around 1,500 blocks. He then went on to describe the block-making works set up by Walter Taylor at Southampton. Given the importance of blockmaking in Brunel's career, it is worth looking at what Taylor had already achieved.

Walter Taylor was born in 1734 and apprenticed to a block maker called Messer in Westgate Street, Southampton. When Messer died, Taylor and his father took over the business. Up to this time, blocks had been made individually by craftsmen, but they transformed the business by breaking the processes down into individual parts and producing each block to a specific size and pattern. At first, their new machinery was all hand operated, but as the business grew, they moved to nearby premises in Bugle Street, where the new machinery was literally horse powered – a horse walking a circular track, turned a shaft, which could be used to transmit power to the different machines. When his father died in 1762, Walter continued the business on his own, making many improvements to the system, including halving the size and weight of the blocks. As a result of a fire at a naval yard that destroyed many blocks by 1770, he had a contract as supplier to the Navy to make good the deficit. He was later joined by his son, Samuel. The works were later moved to Swaythling, Southampton, where Taylor also built a sawmill. These were the works that Delagibarre had visited and which he described in detail during the dinner party at Hamilton's house. Marc was at once interested in the fact that there was a shortage of blocks and began thinking of ways to improve their manufacture. He left various notes on his thoughts at this time. He wrote:

'My first idea for the block machinery came to me when I was dining with General Hamilton, the second, when resting in the forest under a tree in which I cut certain initials in the bark. The curve of one of the letters (S) struck me – "This is it," I cried, "my pulley shall have this curve".'

We can safely assume that the other initial he carved was a K. He also wrote: 'The shaping machine I conceived while I was roaming on the esplanade at Fort Montgomery.' He was clearly thinking hard about the blocks, but he had unfinished business for New York.

He had undertaken to design defence works to protect the Narrows, the stretch of water between Long Island and Staten Island. Once that was completed, he resigned his position as engineer for New York and planned to leave for England. Hamilton encouraged him and gave him an introduction to Lord Spencer, the Secretary to the Navy. On 7 February 1799, he joined the packet *Halifax* and 28 days later the ship made landfall at Falmouth, then sailed on to Plymouth, where Marc Brunel disembarked. As a young boy he had expressed his wish to visit this country: he had finally arrived, and it was to be his home for the rest of his life.

An illustration from the Taylor patent for his sawmill. The horses turn the disc marked 8 attached to a crank that pulls the saw backwards and forwards.

Chapter 3

A NEW LIFE

Marc soon made his way to London and at once went to see Sophie Kingdom. When they parted, she had been a pretty teenager, but now she was a beautiful young woman, who must have had admirers over the years. If she had, then they received short shrift; she remained loyal to her Frenchman and they were married at the church of St Andrew on 1 November 1799. They had been apart for many years, but neither had any reason to regret the wait. Theirs was a happy marriage that lasted until Marc's death.

Meanwhile, Marc had a living to earn, and he was relying on his own ingenuity. His first invention was what he called a 'Polygraph', a machine for duplicating writing or drawings. It was an ingenious and compact device. The master quill was held in the writer or artist's hand and was coupled to a second quill, which duplicated the movement of the first, writing at the same time and dipping in the inkwell simultaneously. The paper was mounted on a sliding base, which could be moved as each line was finished. It was the first of many inventions he patented in Britain. It was a device he used himself throughout his life. At the same time, he invented a machine for winding cotton into balls, which he never patented – a fact he came to regret. Later in life, he visited Jedediah Strutt's cotton mill in Belper, where he found several machines based on his design in profitable use. A lady remarked to Brunel that, although she found his cotton balls useful, she would have been much happier if he had invented something that would make hems without her having to do endless stitching. He took the hint, and in 1802 took out a patent for 'Trimmings and Borders for Muslins, Lawns and Cambric'. Sometimes, one feels, he invented things for the sheer pleasure of solving a problem. At about this time he devised a machine for shuffling cards – not perhaps something the world was desperately in need of. But his main concern was block making.

He began producing working drawings of the different machines he had in mind. The Kingdom family had always had strong connections with the Navy, and Sophie's brother, who was Under Secretary to the Navy Board, agreed to help Marc. The obvious place to start was with the Taylor family, well established as the leading block makers to the Navy. Kingdom wrote on

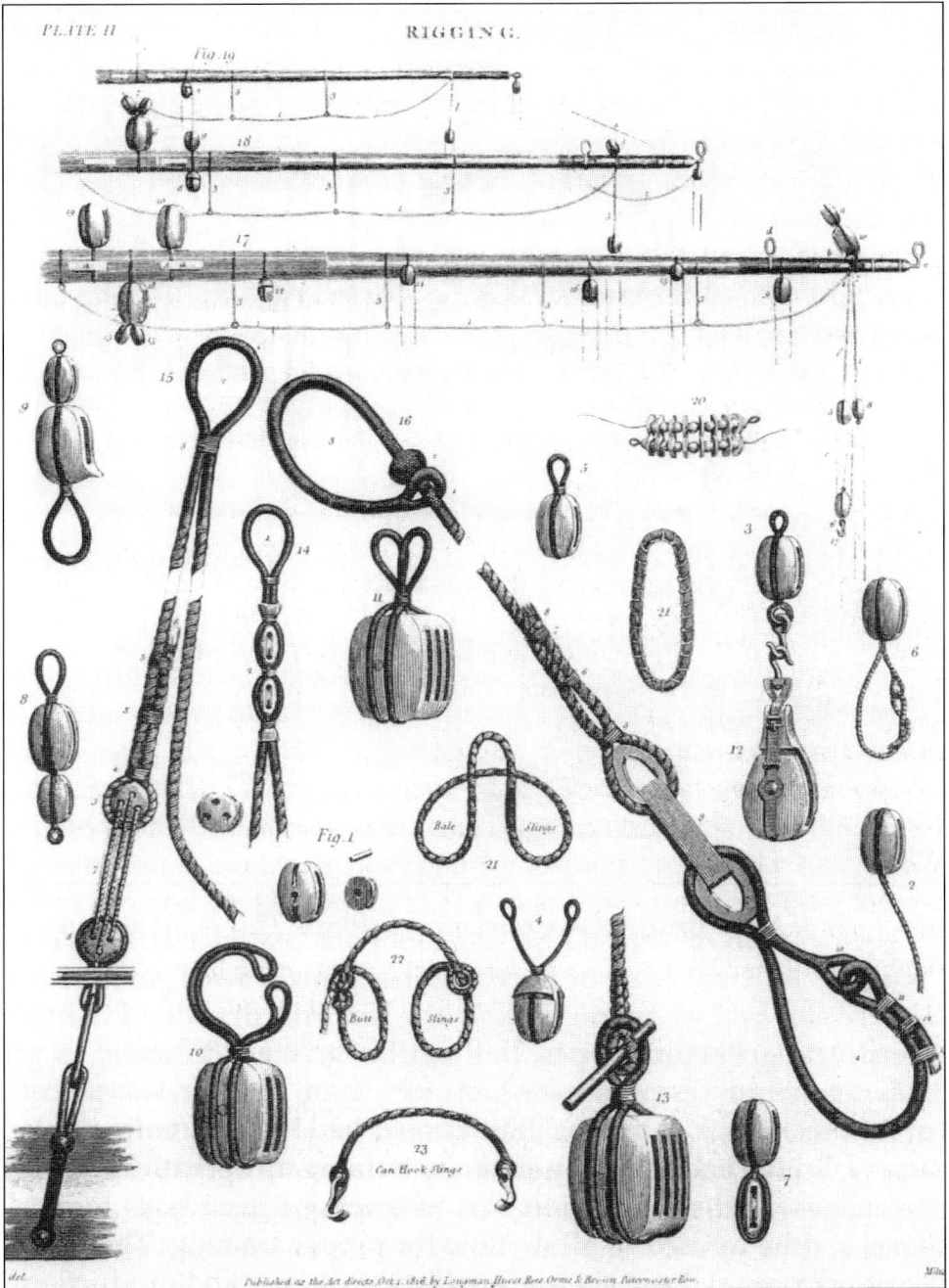

Examples of the many types of blocks I use on a sailing ship from *Rees's Cyclopaedia* of 1809.

Marc's behalf and got a distinctly frosty reception. After explaining how their company made blocks, Samuel Taylor ended his letter:

'My father has spent many hundreds a year to get the best mode, and most accurate of making the blocks, and he certainly succeeded, so much so, that I have no hope of anything ever better being discovered, and I am convinced there cannot. At the present time, were we ever so inclined, we could not attempt any alteration. We are, as you know, so much pressed, and especially as the machine your brother-in-law has invented is wholly yet untried. Inventions of this kind are always so different in a model and in actual work.'

This was a setback, but Marc was to be fortunate to meet two men of remarkable ability, and together they were to make his dream a reality.

In early 1800, he was introduced to a mechanical engineer who had recently set up business on his own in London. Henry Maudsley was born at Woolwich in 1771 and by the age of 12 was already set to work in the arsenal there. He soon showed himself to have far more than average ability. His fortunes changed when he was recommended to Joseph Bramah, who had invented a new, improved form of lock, but was having difficulty machining the parts. Bramah must have felt that very little could be expected of an 18-year-old boy, but soon recognised his exceptional talents. A year later Maudsley was put in charge of the works. Together they began developing a variety of machine tools, including the slide-rest, the screw-cutting lathe and the planer. At this time, Bramah also began developing the hydraulic press, for which he became famous. How much credit should be given to Maudsley in helping with these developments is impossible to unravel. But it is generally agreed his contribution was considerable. Bramah, however, refused to pay him more than 30 shillings a week, just under £140 at today's values. It was at this point that Maudsley left and set up on his own.

Between them, Brunel and Maudsley began the serious business of designing a full set of machines for block making. At this stage, the next important figure steps onto the scene – Samuel Bentham. He was the brother of Jeremy Bentham, the originator of utilitarianism, a reformer who argued for equal rights for women, decriminalisation of homosexuality and many other causes. He helped found University College, London, where his preserved body is still displayed. Samuel was always, it seems, rather more concerned with practice than theory. Born in 1757, he left school to became a naval apprentice at the Woolwich Arsenal and then to Portsmouth Naval

College. After some years at sea, he spent time in Russia, where he travelled widely and reorganised the factories that were being overseen by Prince Potemkin. He built guns that fired shells instead of round shot, an innovation that played a large part in the Russian victory over a Turkish fleet. The biggest problem he faced was the lack of skilled mechanics, and he became interested in the idea that much of the work in the factories could be carried out by comparatively unskilled workers, given suitable machinery. When he returned to Britain in 1791, this was one of the ideas he brought with him. In 1796, he was appointed Inspector-General for the English Navy dockyards and at once began making many improvements, including developing a better system for operating dry docks. As an innovator himself, he was more than ready to listen to Marc Brunel and his new ideas.

In 1802, the Admiralty authorised the construction of the block mills. Between 1802 and 1807, the mill was constructed, two steam engines installed for power and a total of forty-five machines constructed and installed. There were four classes of machinery. The first was used to saw the timber into appropriately sized blocks. The next set of machines was used for boring holes, shaping the block, cutting grooves by morticing, scoring the outside to take the ropes. The third set worked to produce the sheaves, the pulleys inside the block, which were made out of lignum vitae together with the brass lining, and boring holes for the pins, etc. The final group of machines was used for forging the metal pins for the sheaves. It is not necessary to describe every machine in detail, but as an example we can took a look at the morticing machine, if only because that was the one Brunel chose to have shown as part of his portrait. He was obviously particularly proud of it.

The morticing machine is illustrated on page 18. Basically, the machine needs to cut an accurate grove in the block, which involves an up and down movement of the cutting head, combined with a backward and forward movement of the wood. It has a large flywheel at the back and, like all the machines, was driven by a belt from overhead line shafting. The pulley that conveys the drive is attached to a cone clutch M and a shaft D. At the front of the shaft is a crank, which as it turns raises and lowers the cutting head. The block being chiselled out is mounted below the cutting head and is moved backwards and forwards by a feeding screw. When the cut has reached the required length, the carriage is returned by hand. The machine worked at a hundred strokes a minute. Although the mechanism is quite complex, the actual operation is very straightforward, simply because so many of the essential movements are automatic. As a result, unskilled men could be

The morticing machine designed for the Portsmouth block mill; the belt drive is not shown.

employed and trained to use two or more of the machines at the mill. Some, such as the shaping machine, could handle as many as ten blocks at the same time. This was the most complex machine in the works, yet it seems that Marc came up with the idea with very little trouble: 'the shaping machine

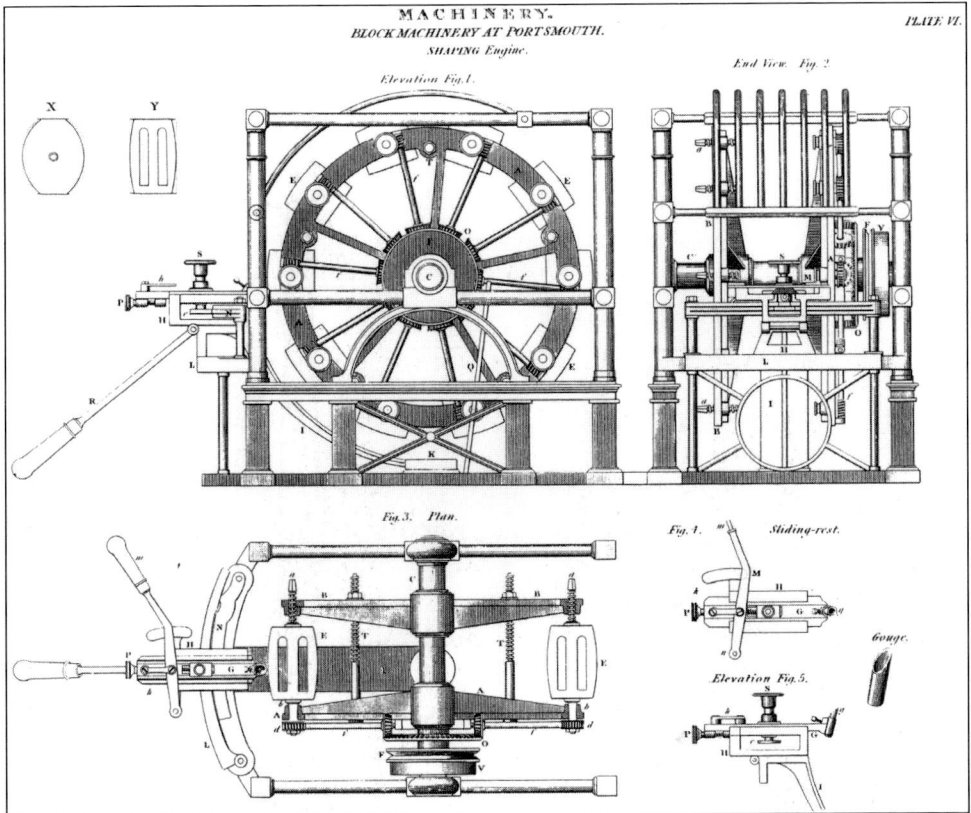

The shaping machine: this was the most complex machine in use at the block mill.

I conceived while I was roaming on the esplanade of Fort William'. Where once a hundred men would have worked in a block mill, the whole system could be worked by just ten, each operating several machines. By 1808, the mill was turning out 130,000 blocks a year for the Navy. As well as the blocks described, the mill also made deadeyes, with no moving parts, used as part of the standing rigging. In their day, the mills were famous. Nelson himself made a visit, just before setting off for his fateful voyage to Trafalgar, and Queen Victoria came as a teenage girl as part of her education. Today the mill is still there, but inside is somewhat forlorn, with almost all the machines removed, though the line shafting is still in place. A boring machine has been restored and is on display in the Portsmouth Historic Dock Museum.

Having agreed to the establishment of the block mill, one might have expected that the Navy officials would do all they could to make sure things went as smoothly as possible. In practice, this never happened. On the contrary, they seem to have gone out of their way to make things difficult. There was a hearty dislike of anyone outside the Service having control of anything, and to have a Frenchman in charge was twice as bad. Instead of allowing Marc Brunel to take full responsibility for supervising the training of men to work the machines, they put a manager called Burr in charge, who seems to have been illiterate and a poor mechanic. To Brunel's great vexation, he kept inviting people to come in and watch the work in progress, getting in everyone's way and being a thorough nuisance. Then Burr decided that instead of men, he would bring in young boys to work the machines, without consulting Brunel, and there was inevitably trouble. The inexperienced boys were quite unable to manage, and soon machines were having to be repaired. To add to Brunel's troubles, his greatest ally, Bentham, was suddenly removed from Portsmouth and sent to St Petersburg. At one point, the Navy Board even tried to make Burr the senior manager at the mill, over Brunel, at which point the latter threatened to resign.

A very good example of the sort of problems he had to deal with can be gauged by a letter to Bentham on 7 January 1805:

'The block-making has hitherto been managed so very badly, that it is not possible to ascertain exactly the price of every part, so as to determine the piecework of the labourers.

'This bad management is entirely owing to the want of a steam engine keeper conversant with the parts, and capable of foreseeing accidents and guarding against them.

'The present keepers are stopped by the least difficulty, and cannot point out the cause. The person who gives orders for pumping is the manager of the steam engine. Owing to his absolute ignorance, particularly in the management of the steam engine, the keepers are not able to point out any defects, and keep on till it stops entirely.'

Given the difficulties, it is amazing that anything got completed and that the works were so successful.

Marc Brunel was a great engineer but a poor businessman. At the start of the whole project, he worked on the assumption that he would be adequately repaid for his work, but never signed a contract. He wrote to the Admiralty in June 1802:

'I beg to inform their Lordships that the invention and execution of models, and of machines on a large scale, have been attended with considerable expense; and that my time for the *last two years*, has been almost entirely employed in bringing them to their present state of perfection. I will trust to their Lordships' liberality to decide on the remuneration which they may deem adequate to the merit of discovery.'

He received no reply, and it was only when Bentham intervened that anything was done. And although the Admiralty had approved the project, the Navy Board was reluctant to pay anything. Bentham insisted that Brunel should be treated fairly, and the Admiralty instructed the Board to pay Brunel at a rate of a guinea a day. Even then, when the works were completed and the blocks were being made in vast quantities, the Board proved reluctant to cough up the money due. He became increasingly desperate, and the problems at the works and the lack of money began to affect his health, and he wrote in some despair in July 1808 that 'engaged as I have been lately, merely in the pursuit of information on the fate of my late application respecting my renumeration for my past services, I find that the best part of days and weeks are wasted away without any appearance of success.' He finally received a reply a month later, but instead of the payment of some £17,000 which was due they offered him £1,000 'on account'. It took two years and much pressure from powerful allies of Brunel's before the £17,000 was paid. It was the first – but would not be the last – time that a Brunel found that dealing with the British Navy was a painful and exhausting experience.

Brunel's achievement is remarkable. He designed new machines, and although much of the practical work of turning those designs into working models was down to Maudsley, he took personal responsibility for their installation and satisfactory working. Breaking down the manufacture of an object into its different parts was not entirely new. In the eighteenth century, Josiah Wedgwood had done that in his pottery, setting up a simple production line, in which for example one worker would make the cup part of a teacup, a second make the handle, and a third stick the two together. But at the Wedgwood works, the main work still required skilled craftsmen. At the block mill, the machines could be managed by men with only a little basic training, and they would be producing identical block after identical block with great accuracy. He demonstrated that this form of mass production was efficient, saved money, with an end product that was more reliably uniform than the old hand-made blocks could ever have been. Bentham and Brunel had both shown that there were huge improvements that could be made in all naval dockyards to the great benefit of the Navy. The Lords of the Admiralty, however, were firmly wedded to tradition, and preferred old well-tried ways to modern innovation. As we shall see later, this attitude lasted for many, many years.

Marc's concern for getting money for his work is very understandable. He had already paid out over £1,000 to Maudsley, he had an enlarged family to support. While the blockmaking works were being established, he had taken a house in Portsea, within walking distance of the docks. The street has changed a great deal since those days, but old photographs show terraces of three-storey houses. His first daughter, another Sophia, was born here in 1802, followed by Emma in 1804, though the exact date of her birth is not known. Sophie gave birth to a boy, on 9 April 1806, who was named Isambard Kingdom.

Throughout this period, although the block mill was his main preoccupation, he was soon turning his inventive mind to new ideas. One problem that was hampering work at the block mill was the irregular supply of timber. Brunel's answer was to design a new, improved saw, which he patented in 1805. This was for a circular saw, which in the patent was to be five feet in diameter and made up of interlocking segments. The timber was to be locked onto a movable carriage, running on rails in the saw pit. A steam powered saw, made by Maudsley, was installed at the docks in 1806. He had obviously been giving a great deal of thought to working with timber, for the circular saw was only one of a number of devices he designed at this time. He came up with a new way of bending timber. This was done by steaming it to make it flexible, but Brunel concluded that, once it was removed from the steam chest, 'It is obvious that the fibres, strained by this operation, and receiving no further assistance from the emollient effect of the steam or water, are exposed to separate, and even to break.' He proposed a system in which the timber could be bent to shape 'without being removed from the place during the operation'. He then went on to devise a machine that would cut thin strips of wood for veneers, and another for cutting staves for barrels. The latter was particularly valuable for the Navy, as barrels were essential for storing food and water for long voyages.

He understandably wanted to gain more independence, to be his own master and not be subjected to the capricious nature and reluctance to pay that had marked his time with the Admiralty. He decided to invest all his money in a sawmill of his own. He began negotiating for a riverside site on the Thames at Battersea. The negotiations were complex, but a deal was eventually reached, and Brunel went into a partnership with a gentleman called Farthing, who probably put up most of the capital, and they began to equip the new premises. The Navy was not the only customer for blocks, and Brunel was able to report that representatives of the vastly important East India Company had visited Portsmouth and approved the block making machine. Supplying their merchant fleet would be a very profitable business indeed.

In 1806, the family moved to Lindsey Road, Chelsea. Originally, this had been Lindsey House, built in 1674 for the 3rd Earl of Lindsey, but converted into four separate houses in 1775. They lived in the centre section, now No. 98 Cheyney Walk. The situation was ideal, as the Thames was crossed near the house by the Battersea bridge, built in the late eighteenth century – the last wooden bridge to be built across the river, which was replaced by the present bridge a century later. The house was, and is, a handsome building with a garden giving access to the river, where the young Isambard learned to swim. Fortunately, the river was comparatively clean in those days, but was still dangerous – it is still tidal this far upstream. Shortly after moving house, the family also received a considerable boost to their income in 1808.

It was not just the Navy who called on Brunel's expertise. In 1808, the Army requested him to supply designs for saws at Woolwich Arsenal. Brunel's reply is modest, not claiming too much for his own ideas, but explaining where those ideas had originated:

'They are the result of experience, and not merely copies of what I have already executed; but are mostly original ideas peculiarly calculated to answer for the service of the gun-carriage department … Although I cannot claim the merit of original invention in the saw-mills, I would beg leave to observe, that saw-mills, such as those used on the Continent and in America, are confined to a uniform work, and entirely to fir. They could not be used with any advantage in the service of the carriage department, for which elm, ash, and oak timber, varying in size, length, and form, are indiscriminately used, and to be converted into scantling of different dimensions.'

At the same time, he adapted the machine used for making pins for blocks to use for axles for gun carriages. The whole scheme was a great success, and the new saws were rated as cutting timber at the rate of ten to twelve feet a minute with just a single operative. The cost of cutting was reduced to one sixth of the previous rate. As a result, Brunel was awarded a grant of £4,500 for his efforts, which today would be the equivalent of around £4 million.

Brunel was never a man to simply sit back and enjoy the fruits of his earlier labours. He was constantly looking for improvements and trying new ideas.

The house in what is now Cheney Walk, home to the Brunel family.

He devised a way of cutting rabbets – also known as rebates – in wood. A rabbet is an open sided groove, as seen for example in window jambs. Previously, the wood that was removed by chiselling was simply waste, but Brunel was able to devise a way of removing the timber in a single piece, that could then be used for other purposes. When working with expensive woods such as mahogany, this represented a real saving. Not all his inventions were equally successful. In 1810, he took out a patent for 'Improvements in obtaining Motive Power'. In essence this involved using an Archimedes screw to force air through cold water to cool it and then pass it through hot water to heat it. This resulted in the air expanding, providing a usable force. There is no evidence that this unlikely contraption was ever made.

In spite of his previous experiences with the Navy, he was still interested in Naval contracts. He sent an impressive set of statistics to the Navy Board in November 1811. Most sawing was done using saw pits. The timber was placed above the pit, and was cut by a two-handed saw: one man had the unpleasant job of working in the pit, pulling the blade down, and covering himself in sawdust, while the top man pulled the saw up. Although the bottom man had the worst job, he also received the worst pay. According to Brunel's figures, the top man got 3s 6d a day, the bottom man 2s 10½d a day. He estimated that the Navy was then employing 300 pairs of sawyers. He then went on to work out in detail, the output from sawmills compared to that of the saw pits and the relative costs. His conclusion was that the Navy could save £14,400 a year.

There was inevitably opposition to Brunel and his sawmills. Some of it, not surprisingly, came from the sawyers who would lose their jobs and partly from others who felt aggrieved that the British army and navy were being supplied by a Frenchman, a citizen of the country's traditional enemy. One argument was that there were British engineers who had produced equally efficient sawmills – and probably even more efficient. In particular, John Rennie, the eminent civil engineer, was cited, who had built mills in Scotland. When a Rennie sawmill was constructed at Rotherhithe, it was possible to make a direct comparison. The Rennie mill cost £9,300 and contained a ten horsepower steam engine, driving four frames and turning out 9,500ft of sawn timber a week on average. The smallest Brunel mill at Woolwich cost £12,000 but was better built, had a twenty horsepower engine, driving six frames and turning out 10,000 to 12,500 ft a week. The comparison was enough to convince the authorities that the man to build a new sawmill at Chatham Docks should be Brunel.

He set about the job with enthusiasm. One of his first tasks was to work out the most efficient way of getting imported timber from the dock to the sawmill. He estimated that 8,000 loads a year would be arriving. A load was roughly defined as the amount a single horse could pull in a cart. To put this into perspective in terms of ship building, Nelson's ship *Agamemnon* was only a medium sized warship, but that required 2,000 loads of timber. The timber had to be stacked for surveying to check the amount and quality and then dragged to the sawmill. This was costly and inefficient. He saw a solution. Beamish has a story that he heard from Marc Brunel himself, about his visit to Chatham in the company of a naval officer.

'After a careful examination of the ground, he suddenly exclaimed, "that hill must be bought!" "Oh yes," replied the officer he had before addressed, "Government has been so recommended, but the cost of removal of so great a mass of earth has deterred them." "Remove! Take away that noble hill – the most valuable bit of ground in all the yard!" replied Brunel; "No, no! but buy it – buy it as quickly as possible."'

The hill in question was roughly 2,000 by 200ft and the top was 38ft above the Medway. Brunel's idea was to sink a shaft down from the hill to the level of the riverbed, and from the shaft, drive a tunnel to the river. This would enable the timber to be floated to the bottom of the shaft, without being dragged through the dirt and grit of the yard. It could then be raised up to the top of the hill using a water-balance lift. This would consist of two caissons, into one of which the logs could be floated. This was counterbalanced by a larger caisson which, when filled with water, would outweigh the other. As a result, as the heavier caisson dropped, the smaller rose. The scheme was accepted, but as so often happened when Brunel worked with the Navy, they preferred to supervise the actual construction process themselves. Brunel had designed the tunnel with a segmental arch and sloping sides: it was built with an elliptical arch and straight sides. The result was disastrous; the arch collapsed, killing one man and injuring ten more. He also experienced problems with the chimney for the sawmill. He expressed doubts about its stability, which were ignored by the authorities, who declared the whole structure to be perfectly safe, soundly built on firm foundations. It was only when cracks appeared in some parts and bulges in the brickwork in others, that his advice was finally taken. The chimney was buttressed and reinforced with wrought iron hoops. The result was satisfactory, and the chimney still stands firm today.

The logs that emerged at the top of the shaft on the hill could then be taken down a sloping railed track to the sawmill. Inside were eight saw frames, powered by steam, and running at a rate of eighty strokes per minute. It was an undoubted success. As the need for timber reduced and the wooden ships eventually gave way to vessels of iron and steel, the sawmill became largely redundant. But it survives and has resumed its old function. In 1988, North Kent Joinery moved in and saws are again at work, no longer cutting timber for ships, but making a variety of bespoke products, ranging from staircases to window frames. Brunel would, one imagines, be delighted.

The war against Napoleon was not going well. The British force that had been sent to Spain to prevent the country falling to the French found themselves in a desperate situation. The Spanish they had been sent to help had, in effect, been completely overrun. The British, under Lieutenant General Sir John Moore,

The sawmill at Chatham: the buttressed chimney is a prominent feature. The sawmill is still in use, run by a private company.

had initially planned an attack against the French, but instead they were forced into a hasty retreat in terrible winter conditions. They made their last stand at Corunna and in the final battle, Moore was killed. Relief ships eventually arrived, and the demoralised British troops were brought back to England. A contingent arrived back at Chatham in February 1809, where they were given a hero's welcome. They did not look like heroes, bedraggled and wretched. Brunel was there and was horrified to see that many were shoeless, with blistered and bleeding feet. He soon discovered that the fault lay with the disgracefully inadequate boots with which they had been issued. He at once decided something needed to be done – and that he was the man to do it. He set about designing machinery for making boots and shoes. By 1810, his work was completed and he took out a patent the following year. The manufacture was largely automated. The upper leather was stretched over an iron last: the soles were cut to size, and the two were then united by means of an awl, worked by a treadle that created a hole, through which a nail was driven. The last moved round until the whole of the sole and upper leather were attached. A work force was recruited from soldiers who had been injured in the war and invalided out. Once the factory was in full production, it was capable of turning out 400 pairs of boots a day. He was supplying all the army's needs and everything was going well. Then, in 1815, Napoleon was defeated at Waterloo; the war was over. Soldiers were no longer needed and without soldiers, the army no longer needed boots and shoes. Brunel was left with huge stocks and no customers. He struggled on for a time, but in 1819 he felt it necessary to apply to the Chancellor of the Exchequer, Nicholas Vansittart, to ask for help.

It is a sad litany. Once again, Brunel had acted in the public good and had expected officialdom to respect his efforts and reward him appropriately. He received praise for his work and acknowledgement that the shoes previously supplied to the army had scarcely lasted a day's march, while his were far more durable. He received encouragement from the Foreign Secretary, Viscount Castlereagh, who, according to Brunel, said to him, 'When you are ready to make any number of them let me know.' But as had happened in the past, there was never anything formally agreed in writing. As a result, by July 1815 he was incurring expenses of £200 a week and receiving no income. His debts were mounting, and he was assured by no less a person than Palmerston that all would be well. The assurances were of little value. When peace came, the best the government could offer was to take half the stock off his hands at less than two fifths of the previous price. He had lost something like £3,000 and was still having to pay £400 a year for the works. The help never came.

Chapter 4

FINANCIAL DISASTER

So much of Brunel's energy had been expended on the Chatham sawmill that he had neglected the Battersea works. This was not a problem while Farthing was keeping a watchful eye on the works and an even more acute gaze on their finances but, in 1812, he retired from the business. We do not know why he left, but he does not seem to have fallen out with Brunel, as the two men remained on good terms. We know so little about him that it is idle to speculate, but one reason that has been put forward is that he had simply made enough money from the enterprise to retire in comfort. It is too often the fate of inventive geniuses to fail to match their considerable talents in business acumen. A few, such as James Watt, found a partnership with an equally brilliant entrepreneur, in his case Matthew Boulton. Others, such as Richard Trevithick, never make such a connection and failed to profit from their efforts. Brunel, unfortunately, falls very much into the latter camp. Without Farthing, Brunel's lack of business sense was storing up troubles that would soon all but overwhelm him.

In spite of his difficulties, 1814 started off well. He was made a Fellow of the Royal Society, the highest honour that Britain awards to its scientific community. That year he also received a request from the Duc de la Rochefoucauld to design a steam engine for the Conservatoire des Arts et Métiers in Paris. It never materialised, but the ideas of working with a new steam engine obviously interested him. The early nineteenth century had seen the rise of a new phenomenon, the seaside resort. One of the most popular was Margate, which by 1810 had forty bathing machines that allowed visitors to change into their bathing costumes – or not – and dive straight into the sea. Package boats took the visitors from London on a regular basis. Brunel thought that it was time to update the travel arrangements. He designed a double-acting steam engine which was installed in a packet boat, converting it into the paddle steamer *Regent*. The maiden voyage was a success as far as he was concerned but caused dismay among the owners of the old sailing packets. Brunel wrote to Beamish on 14 September 1836, when he was surveying for a railway from London to Margate.

'Today, by mere chance, I am at the *York Hotel,* for my arrangements were at another hotel. It is at *this same hotel* that in 1814 I was refused a bed because I came by a steamer, and every one of the comers met with a very unfriendly reception. If they knew at this moment that I came to carry off the cargoes of the steamers to Ramsgate, I might probably have the same fate.'

The owners of the old packets were right to be worried; there was soon a regular steamboat service operating between London and the south coast resorts and, by 1841, Margate had six companies competing for the tourist traffic. It is worth noting at this point that Marc Brunel was involved in designing an engine for a paddle steamer and successfully starting up a regular passenger service two decades before his son became involved in ship building. The *Regent* was, in fact, to continue in service for many years.

When he was not engaged in invention and designing new machines, Marc took delight in his family. Although he had deep affection for all the children, much of his attention was centred on Isambard, particularly when the boy started showing an interest in machinery and practical subjects. He encouraged him to draw, just as he himself had done as a boy. Marc regarded an ability to draw an essential part of any engineer's training – and the surviving drawings by Marc show that he was well qualified as a teacher. We do not know if he also tried to instil in him the necessity for writing a clear, legible hand. If so, he failed, as anyone, including myself, who has had to struggle to read Isambard's letters and other handwritten documents can testify. There was always a strong practical element to Isambard's education. It seems that Marc chose the cartwheel as an example of a good practical design and showed the young boy just why it was so perfect for the job. It is a good choice, because what might at first glance seem to be simply a piece of wood that goes round and round, it is in fact more complex, involving skilled craftsmanship in accurately creating curves and complex joints. Watching a wheelwright at work had inspired Marc and he no doubt thought his son would be just as enthusiastic. By the age of six, Isambard was already coping with problems in Euclidian geometry. After a short period at a local day school, Isambard was sent to Doctor Morrell's Academy, a boarding school at Hove. Although all the attention was on Isambard's training with the aim of following his father's profession, Sophia also showed an equal affinity to practical work. It was just that at that time, the idea of a woman training as a professional engineer was literally unthinkable.

Isambard was certainly precocious: not many young boys of his age would write home to their mother to say they enjoyed reading Horace, but preferred

Virgil. In the same letter, he also describes how, just as his father had done at Rouen, he was making plans of the town and drawing the most important buildings.

> 'I have also taken a plan of Hove, which is a very amusing job. I should be much obliged if you would ask Papa (I hope he is quite well and hearty) whether he would lend me his long measure. It is a long eighty foot tape; he will know what I mean. I will take care of it, for I want to make a more exact plan, though this is pretty exact, I think. I have been drawing a little. I intend to take a view of *all* (about five) the principal houses in that great town.'

Everything seemed to be going well for the Brunels, until 30 August 1814. That evening, a serious fire broke out in the city of London and all available fire engines were rushed to the scene. Later that same evening, by a most unfortunate coincidence, a fire also started at the Battersea works. As a result of the city blaze, only two engines were available to fight the flames at the Brunel works, and as the buildings were stocked with timber, the fire soon took hold and only one wing and the steam engine survived the wreckage. Brunel was not dismayed. One can only presume he had taken out insurance – and if he hadn't, it is almost certain the more prudent Farthing would have done. Consequently, the engineer simply saw it as an opportunity to rebuild with even better machinery than before. He was quite ready to invest his own money in the enterprise, but when he came to evaluate his bank balance, he discovered that though it had stood at around £10,000 a year before, it had now reduced to less than a thousand. Where had it all gone? He had no idea, but a great deal had been spent on developing his ideas and on projects, such as fitting out the paddle steamer, and a good deal less time spent on ensuring that he was getting a proper return for his investment. There was, however, one event to cheer up the family the following month; a third daughter, Harriet, was born.

Marc now had to try and sort out his affairs to enable the sawmill business to be set back on a profitable footing with new machinery in new buildings. According to a report in the *Gentleman's Magazine* at the time of the fire: 'the fruits of six years of exertion and ingenuity, attended with an expense of above £20,000, were destroyed.' Brunel sought the help of a banker called Sansom to try and sort out his affairs, who made it clear that he thought the business side of the enterprise had not been well run, but was optimistic for the future, assuring Brunel that he could expect a rebuilt Battersea works to yield £8,000 to £10,000 profit a year. But sorting out the affairs was not easy, not least because the accounts for the saw mill and the boot business were horribly entangled, as Sansom wrote to Brunel on 7 January 1817:

'It was a most extraordinary jumble, which you certainly have not understood, and I would have wondered if you had. I should hardly have been more surprised than I am if one of your saws had walked to town.'

In spite of Sansom's efforts, the business side of the different enterprises continued in a state of confusion, in part because those who Brunel relied upon were inefficient, but also because he took too little interest in that side of the business. He was too busy pursuing new schemes.

Later that year, he received an invitation from an English company to visit Paris to devise a system for supplying the city with clean water. It was an ideal opportunity to introduce his children to their father's homeland, so the whole family joined him. All went well until the voyage home, when the ship was caught in a severe gale. The Captain insisted that the best course was to head for Dover, but the entire crew opposed him, fearing that rather than reach harbour they were more likely to founder. The Captain was adamant, but was prepared to take a bribe, and handed over the command to former French naval officer, Marc Brunel, who safely steered the vessel into Deal. The situation was saved, but the trip turned out not to have led to any further work. In spite of the project having the support of Louis XVIII, it was not adopted.

Having taken his steamer to the seaside, he now planned to use it to demonstrate to the Admiralty how steam power could be used to the navy's advantage. There were various tasks in which a steamer could be employed. It could reach vessels that were foundering in high seas, taking out cables and anchors. There was a recurring problem with all sailing ships, the difficulty in leaving harbour when the wind was against them. In the open sea, a ship can tack, but in harbour there is no room to manoeuvre. Up to this time, the only solution was to tow the ship out using rowing boats with large crews. The advantage of having a steam tug to tow the boat out would seem obvious. The proposal was to adapt *Regent* and then lease it to the Admiralty for a modest sum as an experiment. After months of deliberation, the idea was rejected. That conservative body seems to have shied away from anything as 'modern' as steam power, though three decades had passed since the first successful experiment with a steamboat on a lake in Scotland. But if one scheme failed to materialise, Brunel would always turn to something new.

So far most of his inventions had been involved with the military and working in wood, but he had applied his genius to a wide variety of other ideas as well. In 1814, he took out a patent for 'rending leather durable' by means of a machine that would insert small pins or nails. The intention was to improve the lasting quality of boot soles and heels. He then went on in 1816 to invent a knitting machine for making tubular knitwear that could be used to make woollen stockings. It was not a success. The stocking frame for knitting hosiery had already been in use for more than a century and although his version might have been an improvement, the demand for woollen hosiery had declined in the face of the increased supply of cotton stockings from the mills of Lancashire. New opportunities to exercise his ingenuity, however, soon appeared.

In the early part of 1814, Tsar Alexander I had visited Britain and taken a great interest in the block mills. He had met Brunel and the meeting had gone well as the Tsar was fluent in French and he had shown his appreciation of the engineer by giving him a gold and diamond ring. Now an invitation came from the Tsar, suggesting he might wish to design a bridge to cross the River Neva in St. Petersburg. Brunel set to work on drawing up plans. He proposed a timber arch of 880-foot span, from which the actual roadway would be suspended by vertical ties. This type of bridge is usually known as a bowstring bridge, for the very obvious reason that if you turn it sideways, it looks like a bow with the arch as the bow itself and the roadway as the string. It is also known as a tied arch bridge. The best-known example of this type of construction is the Sydney Harbour bridge, though there is an equally good example nearer home in the Tyne bridge at Newcastle. These, however, were all constructed a century later, so Brunel's design was innovative. He faced problems. The first was the lack of technical expertise in Russia, though there was a long tradition of building in wood. He therefore chose timber as his building material. The second problem he faced was the river itself, which froze in winter and in spring was a mass of floating ice. This made traditional building techniques, involving constructing piers and then assembling centering for any arches, extremely difficult. He explained his plan in simple terms:

'The bridge should be constructed in some convenient locality, sheltered from frost, and when completed and the river free, floated into place. Four pontoons of dimensions proportional to the magnitude of the structure would easily form the platform; for, independent of the reasons which suggest this expedient, it will be found really less costly and more certain than any other.'

There was one other problem to be overcome. The river needed to be navigable by tall ships. He proposed solving that difficulty by having the central section of the roadway as a bascule bridge, which could be raised to let ships through – though it has to be said that in the sketch (see below) it looks to be a remarkably narrow opening that would test the navigation skills of any ship's captain.

The bridge was destined never to be built. The Tsar himself had studied and approved the plans but had reluctantly come to the conclusion that the country could simply not afford to build it at that time. In a letter from Count Nesselrode to the Russian ambassador in London, it was made clear that Alexander had for a long time had the highest regards for Brunel as an engineer and hoped that perhaps when the situation improved, Brunel might come to St. Petersburg. It was all very fine receiving praise, but it hardly compensated for the fact that what should have been a very welcome fee would not be coming Brunel's way. But, being Brunel, he already had new ideas to put into practice.

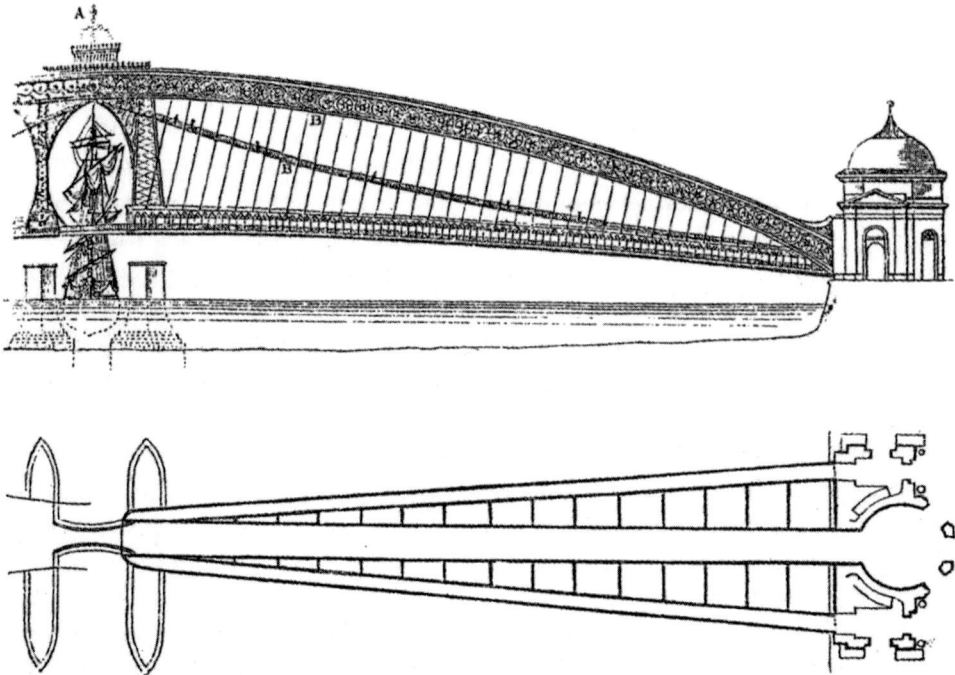

Marc Brunel's design for a bridge over the River Neve at St. Petersburg; the central section could be lifted to allow ships to pass through.

One thing that stands out in looking at this period of Marc Brunel's life is the way in which his mind seems to leap between totally different ideas for new developments with no apparent connecting link. In 1818, he turned his attention to tinfoil. This time he had a new partner, Samuel Shaw. The idea was to produce what he called crystallised tinfoil, which would shimmer with different colours. In the process, a very thin sheet of tin, no more than 1/600 of an inch thick, was laid on an iron plate which was then heated until the tin was almost molten, and the tin was then smoothed out to remove any air bubbles. Once that was achieved, a hot flame was passed over the tin and in Brunel's words, the result was a 'large, varied and beautiful crystallisation'. The foil was finally treated with acid, then covered with a thin varnish for protection. It was intended for use in decorating all kinds of objects from lamp stands to urns. It was very popular, but the idea was soon being pirated, much to Shaw's disgust. He wrote to Brunel in May 1818.

> 'I am so sick of the vexatious occurrences and disappointments at Battersea, that I should be glad to get rid of the whole concern altogether. Others are making fine profits by the invention applied to tubes alone, of which, as I told you, 500 were supplied by one man … I feel no inclination to incur fresh expenses by going to law; indeed, the uncertainties of the whole concern do not appear to me to justify it.'

But a month later, when sales seemed to be looking up, with exports to India booming and good profits seemed possible, he was writing gleefully 'Brunel for ever!' But by then the engineer had already been working on a new way of treating tinfoil to create a colourful wrapping material, which he patented. The optimism of June did not last long. As so often in this story, the lack of business acumen meant that the inventor got far less from his innovation than he expected or that he would have done if affairs had been better managed.

In spite of all this, there was still time for an active social life and often he and his family visited the Hawes family at their home at Barge House, Lambeth. The Hawes family owned the largest soap factory in London, then run by Benjamin Hawes senior. His eldest son, also Benjamin, was soon attracted to the good-looking, intelligent Sophia Brunel. The result was that in 1820 they were married and moved into Barge House. Benjamin was to have a successful political career as MP for Lambeth and was later knighted. He was to play a valuable part in supporting the Brunels, both father and son, in various enterprises that we shall come to later. Meanwhile Isambard's time in

Hove was coming to an end, and his father decided that if he was to have an education that fitted him for the life of an engineer, he would be better off in France than in England. He was sent first to Caen then the Henri Quatre Lycée in Paris. Britain was not noted for its technical education at any level. Sir John Rennie was to recall his own father's views on higher education:

> 'After a young man has been three or four years at the University at Oxford or Cambridge, he cannot, without much difficulty, turn himself to the practical part of civil engineering.'

A near contemporary of Isambard, Robert Stephenson, did go to Edinburgh University, where he enjoyed himself for a while but soon left when he realised he was learning nothing that would help him in his career. Marc also had a poor opinion of the practical advantages of a British University education, and hoped that in France, things would be different.

1820 ended on a high note. Brunel had become interested in printing and in particular ways in which the steam powered press invented by König and installed at the offices of *The Times* in 1810 could be improved. It used rollers for inking, geared to the movement of the platen that carried the actual print. He wished to devise a better system that would involve providing curved stereotype plates to fit round a cylinder for printing. In traditional printing, once a piece of work had been printed, the type had to be taken out of its forms, so that it was available for the next job. But if it could be reproduced as a stereotype, then the problem was solved. He took out a patent, but he was far ahead of his time. Cylindrical presses of this type were developed later, but Brunel's system was never used. He did, however, at the same time design a portable duplicator. It was a box with a lever on top. The box opened up and a sandwich was created with the original manuscript at the top, then a sheet of thin, transparent paper, calico that was kept permanently damp and oiled paper at the bottom. When the lever was pushed down, it created an impression on the thin paper, but as a mirror image. However, because the paper was transparent, it could be read from the other side. It was manufactured by Taylor and Martineau who had a well-established business, so that for once there seemed to be every chance that a real profit might be obtained.

The following year began well, with a proposal that he should visit Rouen in order to build a new bridge across the river. He was drawing up plans when news reached him that his bankers, Sykes, had come to grief and closed down. Very soon the creditors moved in and on 18 May 1821, Marc and Sophie were both arrested for debt and sent to the King's Bench prison. It was

Portrait of Marc Brunel by James Northcote, painted in 1812. He is shown holding drawings of block making machinery.

a disaster that might have been prevented had Brunel been more cautious in his affairs, but even he could not have foreseen the collapse of his trusted bankers. It was a dark time in both their lives and especially for Sophie. She had endured prison once in France and had never expected to be imprisoned again in England.

Chapter 5

RECOVERY

Marc Brunel had worked tirelessly in improving the efficiency of the naval dockyards and many a soldier must have been relieved to find he had a pair of boots that did not wear through by the end of the first day's long march. It might have seemed to him, given the problems he had met in trying to get paid for these services to the state, that those in authority had not really valued his efforts. However, he began appealing for help. He wrote to James Bandinel in the Foreign Office in June, shortly after his imprisonment. His letter began:

'If I had been indifferent on the score of attachment for this country, I should long ago have accepted the flattering offers I have had of employment abroad, and, indeed, it is not without just ground if I had so done. I beg you will consider that for the last four years I have had nothing to do for Government, consequently no pay – no tie whatever – and that I have been subject to many vexations.'

He went on to explain that he had received tempting offers from Russia. His case was pursued by his son-in-law Benjamin Hawes and apparently the affair had already been discussed with another government official, a Mr. Arbuthnot. The whole situation was summed up very precisely in a letter from Bandinel to Hawes, written on 18 June 1821:

'Mr. Arbuthnot has told me that it is the intention of Government to do something immediately with a view to relieve Mr. Brunel from his present difficulties. He added that a report was current, that Mr. Brunel would, on being released, go to Russia, and that, if such were to be the case, Government would not relieve him; for the step they now take is more in liberality than absolute justice; and they have the right to hope for the benefit of his future services. I answered that I had, in the first instance, made it my business to come to a distinct understanding on this point with Mr. Brunel, who had told me that it was not his intention to go to Russia if he could get employment here; that upon his relief from his difficulties, he should apply to Government for employment. If they would not give an immediate answer, he should still wait, and if in the mean time a distinct offer came from Russia, he then should go to the Government and say: I applied to you for employment – you gave no answer – here is an offer from Russia. I must starve, or get employment here, or go to Russia. You cannot expect me to starve; will you give me employment, or shall I go to Russia? and then only should he, upon further declining to give him employment here, go to Russia.'

The whole affair deeply depressed Brunel, and he wrote rather plaintively to Lord Spencer: 'My affectionate wife and myself are sinking under it.' But he did not have to endure the prison for long. In August, the government made him a grant of £5,000 to acknowledge his work for the navy and the army. On 10 August, he was able to write to the Prime Minister, the Duke of Wellington, to express his thanks and to say how much he appreciated this recognition of his work. He ended by hoping that he would soon be working for the government again. He was indeed offered a job quite quickly, but one which offered very little in the way of excitement or scope for ingenuity. He was asked to advise on setting up sawmills, first in Trinidad and then in Bernice. He was not required to go there himself, but as so often in his dealings with government, found that his advice was about to be ignored. He had proposed installing circular saws, but the authorities thought otherwise and proposed using hand saws. Brunel at once wrote to expound the advantages of the powered saw. He used the sort of argument best designed to impress a government department – the money that would be saved. He set out a table showing the relative costs of hand sawing against different thicknesses and types of wood, starting with comparisons for a two inch thick timber of oak, that would cost by hand sawing 11½ pence but only 1½ pence by circular saw, and similar savings were made for fir and for timbers up to 20 inches thick. This was the British government's only offering at this time, but a much more appealing proposition soon appeared from the French government. He was invited to design two bridges for the island of Bourbon, now renamed Réunion. This was a French possession to the east of Madagascar.

Brunel was made aware that strength was all important, as the island was subjected to tropical storms with winds of 100 miles an hour and more. He at once set to work and produced an elegant design for suspension bridges, which would be prefabricated in Britain and then shipped out in sections for erection on site. The design was unusual in that there were two separate

Marc Brunel's design for suspension bridges to be built on the Island of Réunion in the Indian Ocean.

roadways consisting of teak platforms, suspended by chains from a central tower. Chains beneath the platforms braced them against any high winds. The French approved the design and in July 1822 gave Brunel a contract for £7,000 to be paid in four instalments. It seems that initial experiments were carried out in an iron works in Bradford, but the actual construction was entrusted to the Milton Ironworks in Sheffield. The work did not go smoothly.

By December, the work was not finished and the following month was so cold that several castings were broken. It was April before the completed bridges were examined by a French expert and declared satisfactory. Things should then have been completely straightforward; all that had to be done was to dismantle the bridges and send them down to London for forwarding to the island. But at this point, the Milton company demanded a further payment of £500 before they would send the material on. Brunel objected and after a lengthy negotiation, everything was ready for despatch. Brunel sent one of his own men, Thomas Mathews, to Sheffield to check everything out. He was not pleased with what he found, and suspected that everything was not as it should be, or to put it in his own plainer words: 'I told 'em of all the jobs I ever had been at, I never saw such goings-on as these'. When the parts reached London, Brunel felt compelled to carry out a thorough check. He found that the under chains were short by 800 feet and 200 of the flat links for the suspension chains were missing. These were eventually made good, but the bridges were not finally shipped until October. The contractors withdrew their demand for extra payment, and when at last the job was complete, the engineer received his final payment.

While all this was going on, Isambard had left the Lycée and had been taken on as an apprentice by Louis Breguet, acknowledged as the finest maker of timepieces and scientific instruments in France. This was an excellent training in precision engineering as watches and chronometers were among the most complex mechanisms being manufactured at the time. Mastering such techniques were to serve him well throughout his later life. After two years, which Isambard seems to have thoroughly enjoyed, he had hoped to join the Polytechnic in Paris for further technical education, but in spite of having a French father, he was not allowed in as he had been born in Britain. So, at the age of eighteen, he returned to England to work for his father, who shortly afterwards moved in to a modest office at 29 Poultry in the City of London. During his time at home, Isambard was able also to make several visits to the Maudsley works in Lambeth, adding yet more practical information in his chosen field of engineering.

Marc Brunel had time once again to think about new ideas and inventions. He had got rid of both the boot and tinfoil concerns and had passed over half the sawmill to a new partnership, Hollingworth and Mudge – it is likely that the latter was related to his wife. He hoped that the new arrangement would ensure that the works would be well managed and financially successful but, as usual, took little interest in checking how the financial side of the business was being run. As a result, he was regularly cheated by Hollingsworth, while Mudge appears to have been totally ineffective. Now he returned to an earlier interest and began to think about marine steam engines and how they might be improved. He came up with a new design that he patented in 1822. The engine consisted of two cylinders in a V formation, acting alternately on a crank, which was extended to form the drive shaft for the paddle wheels. The exhaust steam was condensed, providing a supply of fresh water that could be used for feeding the boiler. The engine was controlled by means of a spring activated governor that worked regardless of any pitching or rolling of the ship. The boiler was kept full of water, with a dome to collect the steam. The V formation was to appear some years later in the SS *Great Britain*. Brunel was also consulted about ways for improving the performance of paddle wheels. The steamers suffered from problems that were intrinsic and difficult to solve. There was an optimum depth below the surface for the lower part of the wheels, but ships could be either lower or higher in the water, depending on how heavily loaded they were. At sea, another problem occurred. If the ship was rolling, one paddle wheel would be deep in the water and the other almost raised up into the air. The difficulties would always remain no matter how ingeniously paddles could be organised.

Over the next few years, Marc was to be involved in a bewildering variety of projects. It would seem that with the grim memory of prison very much in his mind, he was reluctant to turn down any job that was offered him. There was one exception and a curious one. He was invited to design a steamship that could cross the Atlantic to the West Indies. He declined, stating that he did not consider it possible; his son was later to prove him wrong. It may have been a rather hurried decision as he was heavily engaged in a project of his own which he was convinced would be an outstanding success. He called it a gas engine, but it was not a gas engine in the same way as the engine developed later in the century.

In May 1823, Marc recorded a meeting with Sir Humphry Davy, who told him of Faraday's experiments with liquefying gases. He had treated ammonium carbonate with sulphuric acid to produce carbon dioxide, which he had then passed into a freezing mixture, where it turned into a liquid. It was found that on heating the liquid to 112°F, the gas could be produced at a pressure of 450 pounds per square inch (psi). Brunel recognised that this was a far higher pressure than being used for any steam engine then in service and was convinced that if only he could find a way to harness it, he could create a new type of efficient engine. He spent a great deal of time finding a suitable metal to contain the carbon dioxide – the metal used for steam engines, cast iron, proved too porous – but he eventually found a form of gunmetal that did the job. He developed a system by which the gas was condensed in vessels called receivers which were connected with others, called expansion vessels. With cold water passed through thin tubes in one vessel and hot water through tubes in the other, a pressure difference was developed and it was thought that the expanding gas could then be used to work a piston in a cylinder. There was great enthusiasm for the idea, and he managed to receive some financial backing and was sufficiently confident in his work to take out a patent in 1825 covering Great Britain, Ireland and France. There were years of experiments, but in spite of encouragement from Davy and Faraday, the two most eminent scientists in the country at the time, the whole project came to nothing. A great deal of money had been spent on apparatus, so that it was as well that other projects came along that offered guaranteed financial rewards.

He worked on a number of commissions including suspension bridges for the Huddersfield Canal Company and another to cross the Thames at Kingston. He designed new coal docks for the Grand Surrey Canal Company and more docks at Bermondsey. He planned an underground aqueduct to provide water to Hampstead from the Thames at Hammersmith. All these schemes were developed in 1824, but none came to fruition. The following year, he had more diverse projects to occupy his time. He was consulted over the construction of a new bridge across the River Dee at Chester. At the opposite end of the country, he was asked to draw up plans for a ship canal that would link Fowey on the south Cornish coast with Padstow on the north. The main engineering feature was to be a tunnel through the high ground round Lanhydrock. The plans were accepted but the cost estimated at £450,000 was considered too high – and as canals rarely came in at anywhere near their estimated budget, this was a wise decision. Brunel was later to have one successful canal scheme to his credit. The early years of canal construction were dominated by James Brindley and among the canals he engineered was the Oxford which ran from that city to join the Coventry Canal at Hawkesbury Junction, as part of a through route connecting Birmingham to the capital. Brindley always preferred to go round obstacles rather than through them or over them and as a result his canals tended to wander all over the countryside. At the end of the eighteenth century, a new, improved canal was built from London, the Grand Junction. It joined the Oxford at Braunston. But it was apparent that the old Brindley Canal was no longer adequate to take the increased traffic. In 1828, the Oxford Canal Company called in Marc Brunel to devise a new route. He laid out a plan for a straight line canal that would cut right through the sweeping curves of the old, reducing the distance by over 13 miles. His plan was accepted and he was paid £512 for his work, though the actual construction was left to others.

He received an invitation from the Duchess of Somerset in September 1825 to visit her at her home in Berry Pomeroy, which resulted in a commission to build a bridge across the Dart at Totnes. He submitted a design but the bridge that was eventually built was the work of a local architect. The next invitation came from Liverpool in August 1826, asking him if he could design a landing stage that could be used at high and low water. He was asked to visit the site as:

> '… it would be almost impossible to explain, by any plans, or description, the inconvenience the public at present labour under from the number of steamboats which frequent this port, and the frequency of their arrival, as also the immense number of passengers which each boat brings.'

He made the journey to Liverpool, saw the problem for himself and designed a floating pier and approach ramp. A model was made and taken to Liverpool by Isambard, but once again the project was not followed through. He had been very busy but had little to show for his efforts. That was about to change dramatically.

Chapter 6

THE THAMES TUNNEL

In 1805, Parliament passed an Act authorising the newly formed Thames Archway Company to raise £140,000 in £100 shares, with facilities for raising another £60,000 if needed in order to construct a tunnel under the Thames at Limehouse. Because of the busy shipping that was constantly using the river below the old London Bridge, a tunnel was the only practical way of providing any sort of crossing on the Lower Thames. One of the early enthusiasts for the scheme was a Cornish engineer, Robert Vazie, who had bought shares, and so seemed the obvious man to take over the job of running the project. He took the route that any experienced mining engineer would have followed – dig a shaft on the shore and then work out from the bottom of it, much as a level would have been created in a tin mine. Vazie's competence was soon called into question. After the first year's allocation of funds had been spent, all that was to be seen was an incomplete shaft some hundred yards from the riverbank. It was suggested that a new man should be brought in to work with Vazie, and the man chosen for the task was another Cornish engineer, Richard Trevithick, builder of the world's first railway locomotive. He reached an agreement to construct a drift, rather than a tunnel to its full working size, to test the ground. He was to be paid £500 when it reached halfway and another £500 when he got to the opposite bank. He was ever the optimist, and cheerfully wrote: 'I think this will be making a thousand pounds very easy.' The optimism proved to be wholly misplaced.

The partnership proved successful in as much as work progressed far more rapidly than before. By October 1807, the drift had been advanced 394 feet. At this point, the directors decided that the improvement was entirely down to Trevithick's influence and sacked Vazie, who now became, as a shareholder, a vociferous critic of everything his ex-partner did. And Trevithick soon found that he was not going to make easy money after all. At one point they hit rock, and because the drift was close to the riverbed, the normal mining technique of blasting a way through with gunpowder was far too risky. There was no option but to hack away manually. After that they met the opposite hazard – quicksand. And it soon became apparent that the drift was not so far beneath the bed as they thought: they found oyster shells embedded in the roof. In January 1808, the drift had just passed the 1,000-foot mark, when the roof collapsed and water flooded in. The roof was patched, the drift drained and work recommenced. The criticism became more intense, and the company, although they declared their confidence in Trevithick, decided to bring in experts – though as no one had attempted to dig a transport tunnel below a river before, it is difficult to say what expertise they might bring. Work continued in fits and starts, with more problems. Then on 26 January 1809, the roof collapsed again. Trevithick was in the drift himself at the time and waited, deep in flooding water, until the last workman was out and eventually emerged minus his shoes, which had remained stuck in the mud. Trevithick put forward several suggestions for continuing the work, but the company kept calling in more experts, who failed to agree on anything. The upshot was that the whole project was simply abandoned. It was decided that building a tunnel beneath the Thames was impossible. One director, I.W. Tate, however, never lost faith. He heard reports of another engineer who had devised a new and improved way of constructing tunnels. That man was Marc Brunel.

Brunel had taken out a patent for a new system for 'Forming Tunnels or Drifts under Ground'. He had earlier considered the idea of a tunnel under the Neva as an alternative to the bridge, and now he was thinking of ways in which tunnelling could be improved. The first method he described was, he wrote, suitable for a tunnel of large dimensions. He went on to describe the proposal:

'In the formation of a drift under the bed of a river, too much attention cannot be paid to the mode of securing the excavation against the breaking down of the earth. It is on this account that I propose to resort to the use of a casing or a cell, intended to be forced forward before the timbering which is generally applied to secure the work…. The workman thus inclosed and sheltered may work with ease and perfect security.'

In a diagram to accompany the patent, he showed the 'cell' as a circular construction inside which the workman could hack away at the ground in front of him. As the work advanced, so the whole cell would be moved forward by hydraulic jacks.

The second idea was based on his observations of *Teredo navalis*, the famous, or rather infamous, shipworm that can bore its way through a ship's timbers. It was the scourge of shipping until the idea of sheathing the hulls in copper sheets was invented. He felt that its action could be imitated in a tunnelling device that would act like auger. Tate got in touch with him and urged him to develop his ideas with the view of another attempt to create a Thames tunnel. By the end of 1823, Brunel had his plans ready and declared that the project seemed feasible. The proposal was for a tunnel from Wapping on the north bank to Rotherhithe on the south, and a meeting of interested parties was held in February 1824, when it was agreed to form a company, authorised to issue 4,000 £50 shares. By June, Parliament had passed the Act authorising the construction with no opposition. Work could go ahead and Marc was appointed chief engineer for the project at a salary of £1,000 per annum for three years. He got to work.

Among the first tasks was to check whether the project was feasible by taking test borings to discover the nature of the riverbed. That task went to Francis Giles, an engineer who had already worked on surveying for a number of different canal companies. A total of thirty-nine borings were made and according to the official report, all they had found was 'a stratum of strong blue clay of sufficient strength to insure the safety of the intended tunnel.' At the same time, borings were made on the bank at either end of the tunnel, by Sir Edward Banks and a Mr. Joliffe. They were able to report reaching a 'strong bottom' at a depth of forty feet. At the same time, Brunel was to be paid £5,000 for the use of his patent when the tunnel had reached both banks, and a further £5,000 when the first passenger paid a toll to use the tunnel. If all went well, Brunel would be receiving a total of £13,000 over a three-year period. It seemed that the family fortunes were once again on the rise. He began making plans, and he and his family moved to a new home in Blackfriars.

His first task was to rethink the design of what he had first called the 'cell', but which was later known as the tunnel shield. He recognised that a more effective version would be straight-sided rather than circular. The tunnel was divided into two sections. It was originally intended for use by horse-drawn vehicles as well as pedestrians, so in effect this created a dual carriageway that would avoid collisions. This was very sensible, as it appears that when first planned, all kinds of users were envisaged; the officially approved charges for use varied from 2d for foot passengers to 2s 6d for a carriage and six horses, but there were also rates for a whole menagerie of livestock – cattle, sheep, geese, ducks and turkeys. There were two shields, one for each arch, and between them they contained a total of 12 frames with 36 compartments, each of the latter being about 7 feet high and 3 feet wide. The miners worked at the face, while at the rear of each compartment, a platform was extended to be used by bricklayers facing in the opposite direction, working on the lining of the excavated section. Above the top compartments there were pivoted metal plates, known as 'staves', that supported the roof of the excavation and other staves protected the sides. Within each compartment was a set of heavy oak boards, known as 'poling boards'. These were held in place by 'poling screws'. The workman would remove one board and cut away the ground behind it to a depth of 4½ inches. He would then replace the board, screw it back into position, remove the next board, and continue until the whole area had been excavated. Behind the shield there were arrangements for filling trucks with spoil that could then be wheeled to the shaft and raised to ground level for disposal. The whole shield was steadily moved forward as the work advanced. And progress was indeed steady, almost snail-like, but it ensured that only a small part of the excavation was unprotected at any one time. A section of the shield can be seen in the drawing from Beamish's biography on page 48. It would be reasonable to say that this was Marc Brunel's greatest invention, variations of which are being used to this day.

The first stage was to construct a shaft at the Rotherhithe end of the tunnel, 140 feet from the riverbank. This was an immense undertaking, 50 feet in diameter and to be sunk to a depth of 42 feet. The tunnel was to be worked outwards from the foot, but when everything was completed, the shaft would provide access to the tunnel – as finally built there would be a grand staircase snaking its way from the surface to the bottom of the shaft and the actual tunnel entrance. Creating a shaft of this size was a major undertaking. The first step was to form a great cast iron hoop 2ft 6in deep, the lower edge of which was brought to a point. The hoop was built up in sections, and a timber curb was laid on top of it. Piles were attached and driven down by a pile driver with a 296lb weight. The metal rim dug into the earth and once it was stabilised, work began on building a brick tower on top of it. On 9 March 1825, the first brick was laid by the chairman, William Smith MP, the second by Marc and the third by Isambard. Work could now begin on sinking the shaft. As the earth was excavated under the iron curb, the whole structure sank under its own weight and a bucket system brought spoil to the surface. Once the shaft had reached the full depth and had been lined with brick, timbers were placed at the bottom to support the shields as they were lowered down. A steam engine was installed above the shaft that would be used for pumping out water that was then to be collected in a specially constructed reservoir. Brunel wanted to build a drift from the reservoir to run directly under the tunnel, much as Trevithick had proposed in his failed attempt. The directors

The shield developed by Marc Brunel for excavating the tunnel under the Thames.

declared it was far too expensive and the idea was dropped. Had it been built, it would have acted as an efficient drain and might well have proved worth the money. Now, with everything in place, tunnelling could begin. But it all had been a great strain for Marc Brunel, who was basically working seven days a week. The shaft was finished on 21 November and the following day, Marc became ill: 'On getting out of bed I was taken with giddiness and sickness'. His doctor was called and applied the nineteenth century cure-all for most afflictions – he was bled by leeches. He soon recovered and was back in charge. He appointed William Armstrong as the Resident Engineer, with the young Isambard, some years later, as one of his assistants.

Everything went well at first, and soon the tunnel had advanced as far as the riverbank and would now be under the Thames itself. But as the work advanced it became clear that though the first report had cheerfully described a uniform thickness of 'strong blue clay', reality was quite different. There was indeed clay at first, but after the first 250 feet that gave way to a mixture of silt, patches of quicksand, gravel and in places hard rock. Tunnelling was going to be a lot more difficult than anyone had expected and hoped. Water was a constant problem and scores of men had to be employed to operate bucket pumps, but even then the water at the bottom of the tunnel was often knee deep. To describe Thames water at this time as less than pure would be a masterpiece of understatement. Raw sewage flowed into the river, in theory to be washed away on the falling tide. In practice, it simply moved down on the one tide and much of it returned on the next rising tide. As a result of the foul conditions in the tunnel, many of the men became ill.

Things were not proceeding as smoothly nor as rapidly as everyone hoped, and Brunel had to face some criticism, mainly from William Smith who seemed unreasonably eager to see a return on his investment, regardless of any other concerns. For him, everything was wrong: the shield was an unnecessary expense; the brickwork was wasteful – and it was all Marc Brunel's fault. Fortunately, the other directors backed their engineer, but there was a constant background murmur of discontent, which could only have put more strain on all those involved. The main problem that the tunnellers had to cope with – apart from the water – was the constantly changing nature of the ground through which they dug their way. In April 1826, Armstrong became so ill from a combination of stress and the foul conditions in the tunnel, that he resigned. The new Resident Engineer was Isambard, still just twenty years old. He too had had problems, when earlier in the month he had damaged his leg, which had been hit by a collapsing timber, but he was a young man of huge vitality. Whenever he had time off from the tunnel, rather than resting he had a highly active social life – which included flirting with several young ladies. He wryly wrote of one that he had made a fool of her and she had made a fool of him.

There were difficulties ahead, some of which were unavoidable, while others were brought on by the insistence of the directors that everything needed to be speeded up. Their first move was to change the payment method for the workers from wages to piece work. This was seen as an incentive for everyone to work faster – the bricklayers pressed the miners to speed up and they in turn laid bricks as speedily as humanly possible, but not necessarily as carefully as the job demanded. Marc wrote in his journal for 21 August 1826:

'A work of this nature should not be hurried in this manner. Fewer hands, enough to produce 9 feet per week, would be far better than the mode now *pursued from necessity but not from inclination,* on my part. Great risks are in our way, and we increase them by the manner the excavation is carried on.'

Then it was decided to bolster the company's finances by allowing visitors in to view the workings at a shilling each. A barrier was erected to keep them away from the shield and the scene was lit by oil lamps. It only added to Brunel's worries and although he opposed the idea, he was overruled. At a later stage, he was persuaded to increase the size of the platform on the shield so that more work could be carried out, which put extra stress on the whole structure.

The problems with the changing nature of the ground became ever more apparent as the works progressed. It soon became clear that, far from being driven through good, solid clay, they were meeting loose gravel. By 1826, Richard Beamish had joined the team supervising the works and in his biography of Marc Brunel, he has left us with some detailed accounts of the dangers that were ever present. On 8 September 1826, water began to seep into the workings followed by a flood of silt and water. The gaps were plugged but as the frames were moved, more and more silt appeared. Wooden boards and clay were forced up to fill the gaps. Eventually, the flow of silt was stopped and only water appeared that could be removed by the pumps. The whole affair that had begun on a Friday lasted right through to the following Tuesday, during which time Beamish and Isambard were constantly in demand, grabbing whatever moments of sleep that they could. It was only the first of a number of such incidents. The pressure told on Beamish and Isambard, both of whom were laid low. They were not alone; at the time seven per cent of the miners and bricklayers were off sick. The tunnel was not a healthy place to work.

Early in 1827, it was clear that the ground above the tunnel was far looser and far less secure than everyone had hoped. Marc Brunel managed to persuade the directors that it was essential to find out exactly what the situation was and was given permission to hire a diving bell. The result was alarming. There was a depression in the river, and the material was so loose that when an iron rod was pushed down through the riverbed it hit the top of the shield. It was not an encouraging result. On 11 May 1827, Marc wrote in his diary:

'During the preceding night, the whole of the ground over our heads must have been in movement, and that, too, at high water. The shield must, therefore, have supported upwards of six hundred tons! It had walked many weeks with that weight, twice a day, over its head! Notwithstanding every prudence on our part a disaster may still occur. May it not be when the arch is full of visitors!'

His forebodings of disaster were soon to prove all too accurate. Beamish was on hand and has left a vivid account of the events that were to happen just a few days later.

At 2 o'clock on the morning of 18 May, Beamish took over the role of superintendent from Isambard and there were soon ominous signs that all was not well. At five, 'as the tide rose, the ground seemed as if it were alive'. There were a few gushes of water and silt and the morning shift were nervous and reluctant to start the day. In spite of all this, a party led by Lady Raffles was allowed down in the afternoon. After they had left, Beamish changed from the smart clothes and shoes he had worn to greet the aristocrats into waterproof clothes and boots, anticipating trouble. It soon arrived:

'The tide was now rising fast. On entering the frames, Nos. 9 and 11 were about to be worked down. Already had the top polings of No. 11 been removed, when the miner Godwin, a powerful and experienced man, called for help. For him to have required help was sufficient to indicate danger. I immediately directed an equally powerful man, Rogers, in No. 9 to go to Godwin's assistance; but, before he had time to obey the order, there poured in such an overwhelming flood of slush and water, that they were both driven out. A bricklayer (Corps) who had also answered the call for help, was literally rolled over on to the stage behind the frames, as though he had come through a mill sluice, and would have been hurled to the ground, if I had not fortunately arrested his progress. I then made an effort to re-enter the frames, calling upon the miners to follow; but I was only answered by a roar of water, which long continued to pound in my ears. Finding that no gravel appeared, I saw that the case was hopeless. To get all the men out of the shield was now my anxiety. When this was done, I stood for a moment on the stage, unwilling to fly, yet unable to resist the torrent which every moment increased, till Rogers, who alone remained, kindly drew me by the arm, and, pointing to the rising water beneath, showed only too plainly the folly of delay. Then ordering Rogers to the ladder I slowly followed.'

As he got down from the frame, he had to make his way down a flooded tunnel, in which timber, boxes and crates were floating around, making progress difficult. He was able to make his way to the west arch, which was the one used by visitors, and was at least not full of dangerous debris. Even so, the water was now up to his waist. Eventually he reached the bottom of the shaft, where he was met by Isambard. They turned back to look at the scene of devastation.

'The spectacle which presented itself will not readily be forgotten. The water came on in a great wave, everything on its surface becoming the more distinctly visible as the light from the gas-lamps was more strongly reflected. Frequently a loud crash was heard. A small office, which had been erected under the arch, about a hundred feet from the frames, had burst. The pent air rushed out; the lights were suddenly extinguished, and the noble work, which only a few short hours before had commanded the homage of an admiring public, was consigned to darkness and solitude.'

Beamish reached the surface, when it was discovered that someone was still down the shaft. Isambard grabbed a rope and slid down an iron tie. The rope was passed round the man and he was safely brought to the surface. It turned out to be 'old Tillett the engine man', who had been caught when he had descended to look after the pumps. After that there was a roll call and, to everyone's relief, every name was answered. Now all that remained was to pass on the grim news to Marc. He was out dining with friends, but when he got the news late that evening, he at once sat down to write a letter to *The Times* to tell the world what had happened and exactly what he intended to do about it.

The first thing that needed to be done was to find out exactly what had happened, so once again a diving bell was brought out to enable the damage to be assessed. A hole was discovered, with vertical sides, but there didn't appear to be any great collapse of gravel into the workings. Local watermen explained what they were sure had happened. The hole was right beneath a spot where colliers – the sailing vessels bringing coal from the north east, had anchored. Over the years, the anchors had bitten deeper and deeper into the riverbed, and that, combined with dredging operations, had resulted in the hole. It seemed that all that needed to be done was to plug up the hole, pump out the water and then operations could restart. Beamish rather nonchalantly noted that by almost getting out of the bell, it was possible to put a foot on top of the iron frame. Operations with the bell were always dangerous. On one occasion when Isambard was in the bell and Beamish was supervising operations on the surface, he was horrified to see one of the floorboards of the raft float up to the surface. For a moment he feared the worst, but it turned out that the man with Isambard had attempted to stand on the river bed, which gave way and he had to be hauled up, breaking the board in the process. Both men returned safely to the surface.

As the frame had been discovered to be in place and apparently more or less intact, it was decided to start getting ready to reopen the workings. Marc Brunel arranged to have sacks filled with clay interlaced with hazel twigs to be dropped into the hole to fill up the space. As so often happened, the company directors had their own ideas which they insisted Brunel follow. Their idea this time was to construct a 35ft square wooden raft, load it with 150 tons of clay and then lower it into the hole. There was always a danger that this cumbersome structure would damage the frame, but work went ahead. Soon the pumps were at work. The raft was soon found to be useless. The rising tide got underneath it, tilting it dangerously, so, having with some difficulty lowered it into place, there was the more difficult task of raising it up again, while working in the middle of the busy river. It was eventually removed and the task of filling in the hole with clay and gravel was resumed; by 11 June, almost 20,000 cubic feet of this material had been thrown in. A fortnight later, the pumps had worked so well that the shaft was now clear. Beamish was able to go down into the tunnel and approach the frame by boat. To his great relief, apart from the cells being filled with silt, there was no great damage done.

Two of the directors, Martin and Harris, insisted on seeing the site for themselves. The company directors had been a constant irritation, but no more than an inconvenience most of the time. This time was to be very different.

Inspecting the damage in the flooded tunnel using the diving bell.

William Gravatt, one of the engineers on the project, took them down with two miners, T. Dowling and Samuel Richardson. It did not start well; the directors insisted on sitting together in the stern, which dipped close to the water. As they progressed further in, more and more water slopped over the stern, at which point Martin stood up, banged his head on the tunnel roof, fell on the others and in a moment the boat had overturned and they were all plunged into deep water. Unfortunately, only Gravatt and Dowling could swim. The two directors tried to cling to Gravatt, which would have dragged them all under. He dived down, dislodging them and left them clinging to the edge. Once Gravatt was able to swim to the shaft, he got another boat and went to the rescue. The two directors were saved, but there was no sign of Dowling – his body was retrieved later. It was a tragic accident, that could and should have been avoided.

By the beginning of November 1827, the hole had been plugged, the pumps had done their work and men were back in the shield. There was still nervousness, both among the workforce and the investors. Marc was ill, so Isambard took it upon himself to organise an event that would both celebrate the success in getting work restarted and be a show of confidence – there would be a banquet in the tunnel. It was a sumptuous affair, with crimson drapes, gas-lit candelabras and the band of the Coldstream Guards playing suitably patriotic airs. Although not recorded as having been played on this occasion, this was probably also the first performance of the specially written *Tunnel Waltz*. Some years ago, I was a contributor to a Radio 4 series on underground Britain which included visiting the tunnel in the early hours of the morning. A researcher at the BBC actually managed to find a recording of the waltz to accompany the programme. Apart from the lavish meal for invited guests, there was also a more modest feast for the tunnel workers – and where the grandees toasted the King and the Duke of Wellington, the workers toasted their tools. A painting of the main banquet done by one of the guests, shows Marc and Isambard in the foreground, although Marc was not actually there. No doubt, the artist felt he really needed to be in the picture and made use of that handy device, the artistic licence.

The celebrations were well meant but premature. It was clear that the hole that had caused the major flood was not the only irregularity in the riverbed, and that at times the top of the frames was dangerously close to the water. There was an urgency about the work, and Isambard in particular was keen to push on as fast as possible without, according to Beamish, taking the necessary safety precautions. On the morning of 12 January, Isambard was

The banquet given in the Thames tunnel to celebrate the resumption of work. Marc Brunel can be seen portrayed in the bottom left hand corner, though he was not actually there on the day.

below ground with two workmen, Ball and Collins, removing the wooden shoring from one of the frames, when the earth seemed to swell outwards, then collapsed and a deluge of water rushed in. One of the timbers was swept along and fell over Isambard's leg, but he extricated himself and made his way to the foot of the shaft. He found the staircase blocked so made his way to the bottom of the visitors' staircase. No sooner had he reached the foot of the shaft than he was met by a great surge of water that swept him up and threw him clear out of the top. He was doubly fortunate; Beamish, realising what was happening, had opened up the locked doors of the visitors' entrance. Had he not done so, Isambard would have been carried back down and would never have survived. As it was, other workmen were less fortunate and six of them died in the flood, including Ball and Collins.

Isambard had several internal injuries as well as a damaged leg, so was laid up convalescing. As a result, Marc stepped in to take over the duties of resident engineer to see what could be done to get the works reopened as soon as possible. Now it was his turn to take to the diving bell to assess the extent of the collapse, and soon discovered that the hole was far larger than before. He at once ordered the same treatment to start that had cured the earlier problem, dumping clay into the gap, but this time in far larger quantities. The directors, however, were not happy. They invited the public to send in their solutions to the problem – which they did in their hundreds. They were, without exception, entirely impractical, but Marc now had the job of sifting through them all on top of his other responsibilities. The work of plugging the hole and pumping out the water continued, until at last the workmen were able to go down again and begin clearing away the wreckage that had followed the flood. But then a new, and more damaging gap appeared – there was a hole in the finances. There was only £12,000 left in the kitty, not nearly enough to finish the work.

Inevitably, there were those who criticised Marc for extravagance and at this point Francis Giles, who had earlier carried out the survey of the river bed, proposed doing a new, more extensive survey to ensure that no more unforeseen problems would occur in the future. William Smith was the man behind the idea of using Giles. He had never really given his support to Brunel, doubted if the shield was actually needed and hoped that if Giles was allowed to do test borings, he might soon afterwards take over the whole works. So an agreement was made between the company and Giles. Isambard had a chance to view the contract and wrote scornfully that it was 'the most childish collection of absurd and contradictory clauses, grasping at petty rights which they know they can't make use of, and in fact, a humbug.' More worryingly, Giles was proposing driving 100 piles down into the riverbed at a depth which threatened to break through the existing roof of the tunnel. Not surprisingly, Marc Brunel objected strongly to the idea. It was now a question of who was really in charge of operations, Giles or Brunel? Isambard came to the rescue, canvassing supporters of Marc's leadership to subscribe funds and he was able to present cheques for £8,358 on the condition that Marc remained in charge. Smith's schemes were scuppered, and Giles retreated from the project.

The money was never going to be enough. At this point, the Duke of Wellington stepped in and proposed raising a further £200,000 and he himself promised his own contribution. But there was no immediate possibility of raising the whole sum and three weeks after subscriptions opened, a paltry £9,600 had been invested. There was now no option. On 9 August 1818, work was abandoned and the tunnel entrance bricked up. What had been a source of pride had become an object of ridicule. *The Times* labelled it the 'great bore' and Thomas Hood wrote a satirical poem suggesting that it should be turned into a wine cellar.

'Stick up a sign – the sign of the Bore's Head
I've drawn it ready for thee in black lead.'

With work on the tunnel ended, if only temporarily, the Brunels had to find new works to keep themselves occupied.

Chapter 7

A WAITING GAME

With work on the tunnel ended at least for a time, father and son were kept busy looking for other work. Marc had already begun his survey of the Oxford Canal and he also had an amount of work in surveying for the Grand Junction Canal Company, improving the Medway Navigation and providing plans for docks at Woolwich. Much of his time, however, was still taken up in dealings with the tunnel. The Duke of Wellington had indicated that the government might well be interested in providing the funds necessary for completion. The big question that remained unanswered was – would the work be given to Brunel or to another engineer? Smith, as always, was all for getting rid of Brunel and he had a new candidate for the job, Charles Vignoles. He wrote a scathing article in the *Mechanics' Magazine* in which he claimed that the flooding could 'only have arisen from the grossest negligence, or the grossest mismanagement; from an utter want of calculation, or utter want of thrift. Mr. Brunel may take his choice of either view of the case as he pleases.' He then went on to suggest that the Duke of Wellington 'would not, to befriend Mr. Brunel or anyone else, open the public purse wider than necessary'. He then went on to repeat his criticisms to the shareholders. Brunel was incompetent and a spendthrift, and in particular had wasted money on the entirely unnecessary tunnelling shield.

On 30 June 1829, Smith called a meeting of the tunnel shareholders, where he presented them with the Vignoles plan. This was scarcely new. It involved driving a drift from the Wapping bank out to the existing tunnel to act as a drain and would be continued under the tunnel itself. This was what both Trevithick and Vazie had proposed at one time, but now it had to deal with an existing work. Smith showed the plans to the Duke of Wellington, who pointed out that if the drift flooded, it would inundate the tunnel. Smith replied that they had thought of that and an iron door would be used to close off the drift, to which the Duke wryly remarked that it might keep out the water, but it would shut in the engineer and the workers. The Duke, at least, continued to have faith in the engineer who had worked so hard and so long on the project.

Marc felt compelled to send a detailed rebuttal of the charges against him. He began by looking at the charge that he had been hopelessly uneconomic. He produced comparisons between the costs involved in excavating the original Thames driftway when Trevithick was in charge. He showed that the 1809 excavation had cost £12 17s 6d per cubic yard, whereas the cost of the present Thames tunnel to date had only been £4 5s 0d per cubic yard. He continued by making the case for the shield. He pointed out that two experts – William Jessop and Dr Charles Hutton – had been consulted and declared that 'effecting a tunnel under the Thames by an underground excavation in the old mode was impracticable'. Yet that was exactly what Vignoles was proposing. In a long letter, he also went over his old bugbear, the interference of the committee of works and the committee of finance. 'I am not aware of any proposition having proceeded from them by which any material saving was effected.' Piece work had been introduced against his advice and had resulted in work being hurried, suggesting that this had been a major factor in causing the disastrous flood. His final point was that when it came to the actual digging of the tunnel, the ground had proved totally different from that which had been expected from the test borings.

It was a frustrating time for Marc. He had thought that, given the advice of so many experts, that all ideas of accepting the Vignoles proposal had been set aside. Yet, the following year, the directors were bringing it out again for discussion. It was all too much for Brunel. He resigned, causing great consternation. The directors may have waffled, but deep down they knew that everything depended on the loan being secured from Parliament, and that loan depended on the backing of the Duke of Wellington – and Wellington had already made it clear that he had a very low opinion of the Vignoles scheme. They needed Brunel. But discussions dragged on with nothing being decided, one way or the other.

While all this was going on, Isambard was making his own way in the world. With his energetic nature, he was quite prepared to go anywhere that offered the likelihood of an engineering job. His first opportunity came when he was invited to devise a drainage scheme for Tollesbury on the Essex coast, a small port best known for its oyster fishery. Isambard consulted Cornish engineers about the latest development in pumping engines, before having a model made in brass by Maudsley. Satisfied, he then ordered the engine, but had difficulty arranging its transport round the coast to the port. He was to have other commissions in those years, after the tunnel closure. In 1831, he was invited to submit plans for improvements to the harbour at

Monkwearmouth on the River Wear, Northumberland. There was to be a tidal basin, and an inner harbour protected by lock gates. He drew up elaborate plans, but they were rejected by Parliament. He applied for a job as engineer for the Newcastle and Carlisle Railway that had received the approval of Parliament in 1829. He did not get the job which went to, of all people, Francis Giles. However, he made good use of his time in the north, travelling widely. He went to see the suspension bridge, which had been built for the Stockton & Darlington Railway, and was unimpressed – it shook alarmingly whenever a train crossed and was soon replaced by a more solid iron structure.

He also went to see the newly opened Liverpool & Manchester Railway. He wrote, perhaps prophetically, of the 'shaking' he received and wondered if one day he might travel by rail and be able to drink a cup of coffee while travelling at 45 miles an hour. Not all his travels involved looking at engineering works. He went to look at Beverley Minster, which he greatly admired, and was equally enthusiastic about Durham Cathedral. There was one rather curious comment. He praised the elegance of the Grosvenor Bridge across the Dee at Chester. Was he aware that this was a bridge for which his father had submitted a design which had been rejected?

Marc Brunel was also being approached with offers of work. At the end of 1829, he and Sophie had gone on a brief visit to France, and when they returned Marc found two new possibilities for bridge construction. One was from Warsaw for a bridge across the Vistula, the other from Bristol for one across the Avon Gorge at Clifton. Marc decided that he would be the one to look at the Warsaw proposal, while Isambard would take the other. In the event, the Warsaw scheme came to nothing, so both father and son concentrated on Bristol.

The city of Bristol was expanding in the eighteenth century, and more and more wealthy citizens were making their homes in Clifton, a development that stretched to the edge of the Avon Gorge. This gave rise to an interest in finding a way across to Leigh Woods on the opposite bank, but there was the usual problem of keeping the Avon open for shipping. One public minded citizen, William Vick, a wine merchant, bequeathed £1,000 to the Merchant Venturers, with the instruction that, once sufficient interest had accrued and the capital had reached £10,000, the money should be spent on a bridge. The initial bequest was the equivalent of around £153,000 at today's prices, so a considerable sum of money. Vick died in 1754 and forty years later the first proposal for a bridge was put forward by the appropriately named W. Bridges. It was an extraordinary extravaganza of a structure that almost filled the entire gorge. There was a central archway that reached the full height of the gorge to allow ships to pass, and either side of it, instead of the normal abutments, there were five floors of accommodation, that could have been used as apartments, offices or shops. Needless to say, it was not built. By 1829, however, the Vick bequest had reached £8,000 and it was decided to make a start on finally getting a bridge by purchasing land at Leigh Wood. But it was clear that the money would never be enough, so an Act of Parliament was obtained allowing them to raise extra money and charge tolls for use of the completed bridge. Now all that was needed was an appropriate design. It was decided to hold a competition and invite leading engineers to submit designs.

Although this was always referred to as Isambard's bridge, and Marc never attempted to take any credit for it, there is ample evidence that it was more of a joint project. This is hardly surprising, seeing that only Marc had any previous experience in bridge design. There is a telling incident quoted by Beamish, which demonstrates just how astute the engineer's understanding of bridges, and suspension bridges in particular, was. He was looking at plans for a chain bridge over the Seine, designed by Clause-Louis Navier, the Inspector General for roads and bridges in France.

> '"Look here," exclaimed Brunel, as he examined the drawings. "You would not venture, I think, on that bridge unless you would wish to have a dive."
>
> "No," he added, "that will not stand – that will tumble into the river."
>
> I observed that M. Navier had a high reputation for his mathematical knowledge and his skill in arithmetical computations.
>
> "Ah, well!" replied Brunel, "maybe; but this time he has left out the last nought in his calculations."'

In fact, shortly afterwards the bridge had to be demolished; the chains had proved too heavy and the abutments were starting to crack.

Marc was constantly firing off letters to Isambard with suggestions – sending a drawing of an improved way of passing the chains over the head of the bridge to allow for expansion and suggesting ways of securing the anchoring points for the chains. Altogether, there were twenty-two sets of plans submitted, four of which were from Isambard. His designs were for spans that varied from 760 feet to 1,160 feet. The committee felt themselves unqualified to judge between them, so they called in the help of the most respected engineer of the day, Thomas Telford, to judge the entries. He would have seemed to be ideally qualified as the man responsible for the great suspension bridge across the Menai Straits. To the committee's dismay, the great man rejected every single entry. At this point, they suggested that perhaps Telford might provide them with a design of his own. He agreed, but the result was not at all what they expected.

Over the years Telford has been criticised for turning down the original ideas – especially the Brunel versions. But in his defence, it should be pointed out that he had first-hand experience of the difficulties in stabilising the deck of the Menai bridge, which led him to the conclusion that it would be unwise and probably unsafe to build anything longer than 600 feet– and all the Brunel designs failed to meet that requirement. That explains his decision to reject the young engineer's plans but does not excuse the grotesque design he produced himself. To reduce the width of the span, he submitted a design which had the cables suspended from towers rising over 300 feet from their foundations on the river bank. And these were not plain, unadorned towers, but elaborate structures in the newly fashionable Gothic style, which Telford had rather taken to in his latter years. Whatever the committee might have thought, public opinion violently opposed the design, and it was all too clear that the citizens of Bristol would never provide funds for the 'monstrosity', as it was known. There was nothing for it, but to mount a second competition. This time there were twelve sets of plans submitted, Telford's amongst them. These were then whittled down to just five for serious consideration and the great old engineer's design failed to make the cut. At first, Brunel was only the second choice, but there were objections to all the designs. In general, apart from Brunel's, all the designs had chains that were too heavily stressed. The objection to Isambard's version was that he had used long links connected by a single pin, as opposed to long links connected by shorter links as Telford had done at Menai. However, when Brunel explained the reasoning behind his decisions, in which he pointed out that this system was as safe as the others, but far lighter and therefore less expensive, the two judges were convinced and changed their minds about the order of preference. On 19 March 1831, the official announcement was made: Isambard was appointed chief engineer for the Clifton bridge.

The original design that Isambard had presented was for two tall towers, described as 'in the Egyptian style'. They would have been elaborate affairs, decorated with cast iron representations of the work during construction. He had also been forced to compromise by reducing the length of the span to 630 feet, which involved building out an abutment at the Leigh Wood side. This was an expensive operation that was really unnecessary, and it

Thomas Telford's design for a gothic suspension bridge across the Avon gorge at Clifton: it was rejected.

was money that could profitably have been spent elsewhere, especially as subscriptions for the building fund were coming in more slowly than hoped and expected. The official ceremony to mark the start of construction was held on 18 June 1831. Stones had been excavated and laid in a ring. Isambard picked up one and handed it to Lady Elton who made a short speech, at the end of which cannon were fired and the national anthem was played by a band at the foot of the gorge. There were more speeches and it was all over. The truth was, however, that there was not really enough money to justify any major works. It was decided to make a fresh appeal in October. The timing could scarcely have been worse.

The House of Lords had just thrown out the second Reform Bill, which would have abolished the rotten boroughs, of which Old Sarum was the most extreme example. Back in Norman times it had been a place of great importance with a castle and cathedral, but by the nineteenth century it was home to just one farm, yet still returned a Member of Parliament. Bristol on the other hand, with a population of over 100,000, had only 6,000 citizens entitled to vote. There were disturbances in Bristol and when the magistrate Sir Charles Wetherell arrived to open the new assizes and announced that protestors would be arrested, the crowd turned on him and he fled to the Mansion House in Queen's Square. It marked the start of three days of rioting during which much of Queen's Square was demolished and buildings burned. In the early stages, the Riot Act was read and the troops called in, but no action was taken to prevent the destruction. Colonel Brereton in charge of the 3rd Dragoons ordered the troops back to Keynsham. With the military removed, the rioting became ever worse and leading citizens were recruited to act as Special Constables, among whom was Isambard, who had come down from Clifton to find out what was happening. It was all very chaotic and at a later hearing, Isambard described how some of the rioters had themselves been made constables and when he had taken a rioter prisoner, a group of these newly recruited officers released him. Events came to an end when the Dragoons finally came in to quell the riot. They did so with such ferocity that four of the crowd were killed and eighty-six injured. Any hope of raising funds for the bridge were left in abeyance, which left Isambard with time on his hands and the towers standing alone and unadorned.

Marc was still wrestling with the tunnel committee and was pessimistic about the chances of the Clifton bridge progress ever moving forward:

> 'They have resolved to draw a prospectus, and to go round with it to invite the public to subscribe. It may fairly be inferred that the project is sinking in public estimation. Coupling the state of things in Bristol with the prospect of the trade with the West Indies, we may pronounce at once and unhesitatingly that the scheme at Clifton bridge is gone by.'

But, as always, Marc had new ideas to try out. This time it was for a better method of constructing arches for bridges. The traditional method of constructing an arch was to make a centering, a wooden frame on top of which brick or stone could be laid. Once the arch had been completed, the centering was removed. He felt that the system used in the tunnel lining of combining bricks with iron ties could be used more generally. He experimented with a variety of bonding materials, and eventually decided to build an experimental arch in the tunnel yard. He used a foundation of cement and iron ties. He originally had intended to build a double arch but found there was not enough space. This might only have been an item of passing interest, were it not for the nature of the arch. In the event, he built a single arch with counterweights for stability. It had a span of sixty feet. If, like

A dramatic representation of the brutal force used to quell the Bristol riots; an illustration from *Bristol Past and Present*. (1882)

bridges in the past since Roman times, it had been built with semi-circular arches, it would have meant a rise of thirty feet to the crown. But this arch had a rise of just ten feet six inches. This was entirely new and the idea of the low arch was to be developed by Isambard some years later when he came to build his railway bridge across the Thames at Maidenhead. That great railway enterprise, however, was not yet even close to becoming a concrete proposal.

Isambard was still occupied with Bristol projects in 1832, notably on improving the floating harbour. Until the end of the eighteenth century, ships had approached Bristol on the tidal Avon and laid up alongside quays on that river and on the Frome. But with growing competition from Liverpool for the Transatlantic trade, Bristol needed docks where ships could be berthed in non-tidal waters. The great canal engineer, William Jessop, devised the scheme which involved construction of a dam at Hotwells, and a diversion of the water into a new enlarged dock area, secured behind lock gates, the

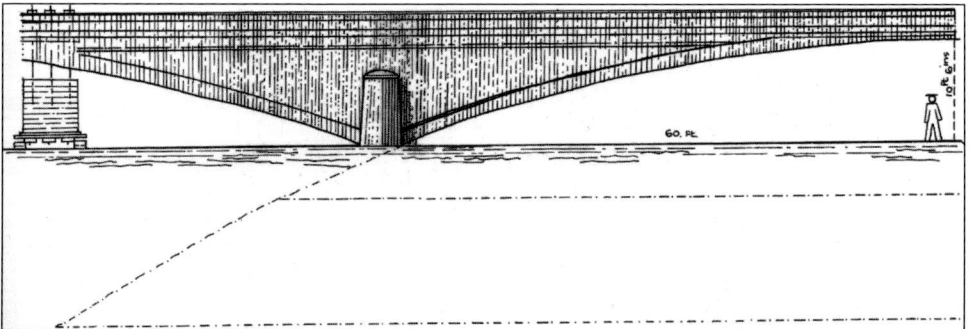

Marc Brunel's experimental flat-arched brick bridge that he constructed at the tunnel works.

Cumberland Basin. The whole area got the name 'floating harbour' because now vessels could be kept afloat even at low tide. However, there were problems caused by silting in the basin. Isambard was invited to investigate the problem. He proposed repairing and increasing the size of the dam to divert more Avon water into the harbour, building a stop gate by Prince's Street and using a drag boat to scour the harbour. The riots that had stopped work on the bridge now seemed to have stopped work on the harbour as well. But instead the work was put in hand early in 1833, with Isambard in charge, and proved successful. A drag boat *Bertha,* based on the Brunel design, was built in 1844 to scour the Bridgwater docks and has survived. This is a steam-powered vessel, in which the on-board engine was used to pull the vessel along chains reaching across the dock. A vertical metal sheet reached down to the bed of the harbour, scraping away the collected silt to the sides. The old vessel is now in Bristol but is not, at present, on public display. During his work on the Bristol harbour scheme, Isambard had become friends with the Quay Warden, Captain Christopher Claxton. He was to remain a lifetime friend and was to play an important role in many later developments.

Both father and son were in limbo. Marc took the opportunity to have a holiday in Ireland with his wife, which they both enjoyed, while Isambard scrambled to find more work. Both, however, would soon be back in harness, working full time on major projects – one old, one new.

Chapter 8

RETURN TO THE TUNNEL

The petition for the government loan should have been presented to the Commons on 29 April 1834, but mysteriously it seemed to have been lost. It looked as if further delays were inevitable, but fortunately, the Chancellor of the Exchequer, Lord Althorp, stepped in and gave his assurance that the money would be available from the Treasury. With that reassurance in place, Marc decided to use the time before work recommenced to make a visit to his old home town Hacqueville, where he went to see Penchon, the joiner who all those years ago had helped him make his octant. Penchon was delighted to see him – 'Ah, c'est Monsieur Marc! Mais comme il est change!' Indeed, he had changed. The lively young man was now a somewhat careworn gentleman of sixty-five. On his return to England, he had now to wait until the funds reached the tunnel company, so that work could restart.

The government approved a loan of £240,000 with the first instalment of £30,000 being available immediately but with the condition that the money 'should solely be applied to carrying on the tunnel itself, and that no advance should be applied to the defraying any other expense, until that part of the undertaking which is most hazardous shall be secured'. Ideally, Marc would have preferred to have restarted work with sinking the second shaft at the Wapping end, then working towards the damaged flooded section, but the government ruling made that impossible. Quite why they insisted on this way of working is unclear, unless they were concerned that the gap could never be closed. It was with some reluctance that Marc undertook to carry on at all, especially as he no longer had Isambard at his side to help. The young man was far too busy now with projects of his own. As a result, Richard Beamish was now appointed resident engineer, with five assistants.

When work started, the first job was to remove the old shield. It weighed eighty tons and was to be replaced by a far more robust shield, weighing 140 tons, made up of 9,000 separate parts. It had several improved features, including slings between the frames, which kept the whole thing steady when moving forward, and strengthened top and side members. As usual, there were some of the directors of the company who thought the task was impossible, and one volunteered 'to eat any part we dared remove'. It was as well that no one took him seriously, for he would soon have faced a very indigestible meal. The first requirement was to drain away the flood water. It was decided to dig reservoirs, six feet square, at a distance of 25 feet from the shield. Bore holes were dug to test the ground, but at between 8 and 10 feet, they hit quicksand. As a result, the piling for the reservoirs had to stop a few inches above the sand. The piling itself occupied three sides of the reservoir and a drift was dug from the fourth side to carry away the water. Pipes from the reservoirs could then be used to carry the pumped water to the surface. Once this was complete, work could be done on excavating a space for the removal of the shield. The ground had to be dug clear, and supported by 1,656 feet of supports, using 300 metal piles.

By November 1835, the whole of the old shield had been taken away and the directors, who had been sceptical that it would ever be possible, demanded to be allowed below ground to see the excavation for themselves. They took just one look at the vast hole under the river and scampered back to the safety of the shaft and the open air. The new shield had been constructed at the Rennie ironworks near Blackfriars Bridge. It was brought to the site, but assembling the vast, complex structure was difficult and time consuming and was only in place and ready for use by March 1836. Removing the old shield and replacing it with the new had been a remarkably successful operation, and in spite of the dangerous conditions, there were no major accidents and no loss of life.

This time, Marc was not to be hurried. The consequences of trying to move ahead too rapidly had been demonstrated all too clearly, and he wished to be ready for any emergency. The nature of the ground above the excavations remained as much an unknown quantity as it had been at the start of the whole enterprise and there was no reason to think that another sudden flood of water could not appear at any time. It proved a wise policy. On 21 June 1836, water did indeed rush in at high tide, and with such power that the pumps could no longer keep pace. However, everything held and at low tide, the flow began to ease. The new stronger shield stood firm and suffered no damage. All that remained was once again to let the pumps do their work and to fill in the riverbed with clay and gravel as they had done before. Work was resumed, slowly at first, but by the end of August, the shield had moved on and passed the midpoint of the river. It was all going well in one sense, but the conditions underground took their toll on the health of those involved. Beamish, who had been such a stalwart supporter of both Brunel father and son, was forced to retire. His place was taken by Thomas Page.

Inevitably, the good rate of progress could not last forever. Familiar problems returned, of bad, loose ground. In September 1836, the work moved forward by roughly twenty feet, by November that had reduced to just under 7 feet in the month and January the following year saw them advance by a single miserable foot. Obviously, the expenses did not change from month to month as the work progressed, but as the progress slowed so it became increasingly clear that the overall costs were rising. There was nothing for it but to apply to Parliament for more money. Fortunately, the sensible view was taken that with so much work done, and so much money already spent there was no point in refusing the request, otherwise all the effort and investment would be wasted. It was a worrying time for Marc, but his life was briefly brightened by the marriage of his younger daughter to the Rev George Harrison. But it was no more than a respite, for life in the tunnel was no easier and progress just as difficult.

Flooding was a constant problem. The water broke in in August, November and again in March 1838. As work advanced, it seemed that every time a poling board was removed, there would be a sudden inrush of water. Brunel realised that the problem was the saturated ground beyond the shield and came up with a solution. He ordered the whole shield to be forced forward by the screws, compressing the earth behind it. With that problem more or less solved, another soon appeared. For too long, the Thames had been treated as London's main sewer and now springs were bringing contaminated water and stinking mud into the workings. The air was filled with the foul smell of hydrogen sulphide and the engineers tried to overcome it with disinfectants, which proved useless. The air was so bad that the men could only work short shifts, but even so they suffered with eye infections, sickness and on occasions simply collapsed at their posts and had to be helped out into the fresh air. The engineers in charge were just as vulnerable but somehow managed to carry on. Then a new danger appeared, one all too familiar to coalminers and known to them as fire damp – methane. Alarmingly, there would be sudden bursts of flame above the shield, but nothing worse.

It seemed that everything that could go wrong had gone wrong. Then on 4 April 1840, when the tunnel had reached the low water mark, the ground above the shield was suddenly seen to sink. The hole grew ever bigger, until it was a massive crater thirty foot across and thirteen foot deep. Underground, the effect was dramatic. Air rushed in, described as sounding like thunder, blowing out all the working lights. Many of the workmen fled in panic, but some of the older hands, who had witnessed so many dangers, held their ground. They were waiting to see if water followed the explosion of air, if not then there was nothing to fear. As it turned out, all was well. Repairs were quickly made, and yet another hole in the riverbed was filled in.

As the tunnel slowly edged towards the shore, it was time to start sinking the shaft at Wapping. The company was, as always, short of cash and as a result had to find the cheapest, available site – which turned out to be one surrounded by dilapidated buildings that looked as if a strong wind might push them over. Yet it was next to these that the great shaft was to be dug, and if any did collapse, then the company would have to pay compensation. Work began in October 1840 and as the metal curb bit into the ground, it was discovered that the workings had met an old ship breaker's yard. The first obstacle was a wooden floor, supported on metal piles and after that all kinds of ships' timbers and boat wrecks were encountered, none of which helped speed up the work. Inevitably, the directors grumbled and urged Brunel to move faster and save money. And, as always, the engineer refused to go at a rate that would endanger the whole enterprise and risk men's lives. As a result, thirteen months after work started, the shaft was complete and no lives had been lost – and none of the surrounding buildings had tumbled, probably to the dismay of their owners who would have welcomed the compensation.

At this stage, work on the tunnel itself was brought to a temporary halt. The tunnel was just sixty feet away from the shaft, and at this point a drift was constructed to connect the two, which completely drained the shaft. For the first time, there was a continuous passageway under the river. The job was almost complete and Marc, who had been harangued and pestered for so long by so many, now received royal recognition for his achievements. Just before tunnelling restarted former French refugee, plain Marc Brunel, became Sir Marc Brunel, knighted by the Queen.

In July 1841, tunnelling resumed and on 15 December, a poling board was removed and showed, instead of earth, a solid patch of brickwork. The tunnel had finally reached the shaft. There was still work to be done. The water was still determined to get into the workings, but gradually the flow was eased and shaft and tunnel united. In May 1847, the water flow was so reduced that it was clear the end was in sight. The strain upon Marc had been immense and, in Beamish's words, 'Brunel's sensitive mind began to exhibit itself in the dreaded form of paralysis', although but slightly affecting his speech and features or, as we would now say, he had a minor stroke. Fortunately, he made a good and swift recovery, and was able to attend the great event that took place on 25 March 1848: the official opening of the tunnel.

Advertisement for the opening of the Thames tunnel in 1848.

The event was every bit as grand as the banquet in the tunnel, with two marquees for junketing – one for the directors and one for lesser mortals, but Sir Marc had the gratification of being roundly cheered by a watching crowd. He then walked through the tunnel, with the other guests, following the band of the Coldstream Guards. It was a great curiosity and a wonder, and in the first twenty-five hours after it opened, 50,000 Londoners passed through the tunnel. Within fifteen weeks, a million pedestrians had made the

THE THAMES TUNNEL.

Length 1300 feet. Width 38 feet. Height 22 feet. Width of each Archway, including footpaths 14 feet.

Projected, and Commenced in 1825 by M. Brunel Esq.ᵗ To whom this Plate is most respectfully inscribed, by The Publishers

A somewhat idealised version of pedestrians in the Thames tunnel. In reality the alcoves were filled with a variety of disreputable characters.

journey. Not everyone was enthralled. The *Illustrated London News* was quite critical, declaring the view from the top of the shaft down the staircase as 'frightful', complaining that the tunnel itself felt damp and that the 130 gas lamps produced an unpleasant glare. Nevertheless, that did not deter the royal family; Queen Victoria and Prince Albert made a visit, which threw the staff into a flurry of excitement. Unfortunately, Brunel himself was unable to be there on the day. J.A. Hoy – a name understandably absent from most poetry anthologies, wrote these verses after the Queen's visit:

Have you seen the tunnel? Allow me to enquire
This most noble structure all the world must admire
It is well ventilated and lighted with Gas.

And no smoking allowed by any class.
The Tunnel's constructed like unto a cave,
By stairs you descend its shaft under the wave.

Some thousands of persons to the Tunnel have been,
A visit was paid by our most Gracious Queen;
At the Tunnel Bazaars, too, stalls there are many'
You may buy what you please, admission one penny.
The Tunnel's constructed like unto a cave'
A subterranean passage right under the wave.

But in spite of royal patronage, once the initial excitement of taking a walk under the river had died down, the crowds dwindled. As the ditty quoted above indicates, it had become home to cheap stalls and it appears some less savoury attractions. It soon became well known as the haunt of prostitutes. One of the problems was the depth of the tunnel. It was all very well going down, but there was a long trudge up the stairs to get out again. The idea of having ramps that would allow it to be used by carriages and livestock had been abandoned at an early stage, and the income from pedestrians was never enough for the company to make a profit. There had been talk of installing steam-operated lifts, but nothing came of the plan. It must have been a relief to the directors when, in 1865, the East London Railway Company bought the tunnel to make a rail connection between the Great Eastern Railway at Liverpool Street to New Cross and the London, Brighton and South Coast Railway. The penny bazaar and pedestrians gave way to steam locomotives for a time, before electrification. Today it carries the Wapping-Rotherhithe section of the London Overground network. Although it has become part of a system that Marc Brunel could never have envisaged, it is still very much his tunnel. Having been fortunate enough to spend the early hours of one morning walking through the great tunnel, it was fascinating to see that all the old original features, the arches dividing the two walkways, are still there. It remains a remarkable piece of engineering that has remained in daily use for more than a century and a half.

Sir Marc Brunel was 73 years old when the great work was finally completed, and he was able to take a well-deserved holiday with Sophie, staying at Chilcompton, a village on the edge of the Mendips, south of Bath. He was there when the letter arrived telling him of the Queen's visit to the tunnel and he felt greatly disappointed at not being able to welcome her personally to what he referred to as 'his domain'. While on holiday, he celebrated his 74th birthday. There was also another great event to attend in Bristol during their stay, which we will return to later. On their return, they settled into a new house in Park Street near St. James's Park in London. Any chance of taking on more work disappeared when Marc had a second stroke, which left him paralysed down his left side, at which point he at once set about learning to write with his left hand. His spirit was undimmed. He had not much longer to live, but now it is time to turn back the clock to see what had been happening in these years in the life of his son, Isambard.

Chapter 9

THE GREAT RAILWAY SCHEME

While Isambard was busily engaged with the Bristol dock scheme in 1832, leading Bristol citizens were discussing a new idea. There was growing concern that while their city was languishing, the rival Liverpool was prospering at their expense. That port now had a rail connection to the equally prosperous and burgeoning heart of the cotton industry, Manchester. Bristol could perhaps go one better, with a link not to another provincial centre but to the capital. The group of railway enthusiasts was led by Thomas Guppy, a wealthy businessman, who was not only a partner in a local sugar refinery, but was also an engineer himself, having served his apprenticeship with the highly prestigious company of Maudslay, Sons & Field. He was destined to play an important role in Isambard's life. To understand the issues that the group faced it is as well to take a brief survey of how the railways had arrived at the position they were in by 1832.

The first rail system had been the tramways, usually connecting a navigable river or canal to a mine or other industrial site. Throughout the eighteenth century, they had all relied on horses for power, and as a result the simple cast iron rails were mounted on parallel rows of square stone sleeper blocks, leaving a clear path down the middle for the horses. Because they were all short, independent, privately owned tracks, there was no need for any sort of conformity when selecting the gauge. One such tramway was the Bristol & Gloucestershire Railway, a modest affair of just ten miles joining the harbour to the local collieries. An important event occurred not far away in South Wales in 1804, on the Penydarren tramway, linking the Samuel Homfray ironworks at Merthyr Tydfil to the Glamorganshire Canal. It was here that Richard Trevithick gave the first fully documented demonstration of a steam locomotive running on rails. It was a success in that it succeeded in pulling the trucks, but a failure in that it proved too heavy for the brittle cast iron rails. Trevithick went on to try and raise investment money in London, by running a locomotive called Catch-me-who-Can, but there was no interest. He was soon to go to Peru to install pumping engines in a silver mine and was not to return for another eleven years.

Nothing more was heard of locomotives until 1814, when the Napoleonic Wars had raised the price of fodder to a point where alternatives suddenly became attractive. The Middleton Colliery near Leeds had a tramway leading to the Aire & Calder Navigation, and the manager, John Blenkinsop, together with the engineer Matthew Murray turned again to the locomotive. The problem with the rails had not gone away, and they realised that the only solution was to try and work with a much lighter engine. The trouble was that an ordinary light locomotive would not have enough power for the job. Their solution was to convert the track to a rack and pinion system but paid for the use of the Trevithick patent for the locomotive. The experiment was a success, and other engineers began building engines. Among the early pioneers were the Chapman brothers and William Hedley, all of whom built locomotives for colliery tramways. They were soon followed by a mining engineer who built a locomotive for the Killingworth colliery tramway – George Stephenson.

Stephenson was famously chief engineer for the Stockton & Darlington Railway, the first to be authorised as a public railway using steam locomotives. That might suggest that it was just like the system we know today, but it was really just a somewhat larger colliery line, for although the coal trucks were hauled by steam, passengers had to make do with an ordinary horse-drawn coach, specially fitted with flanged wheels. The Killingworth tramway happened to have a 4ft 8in gauge track, and that seemed to work well, so he kept the gauge for the S & DR. Then, when he was put in charge of the first intercity line, the Liverpool & Manchester, he used the same gauge, though somewhere in the planning or construction an extra half inch was added. But even after two decades of development, the steam locomotive was not yet seen as essential. The directors of the Liverpool & Manchester were undecided. Some, looking at the slow, cumbersome colliery engines, wanted a system that involved a series of stationary engines, that would haul carriages and trucks by cable, from one to the next. Others felt that the locomotive was capable of being developed to do the job. The issue was settled at the Rainhill Trials of 1829, designed to see if an engine could haul a train along a distance equivalent to a return journey between the two termini at an average speed of 10mph. In the event, it was *Rocket* 'designed by Robert Stephenson' that carried the day, easily meeting and surpassing the target set for qualification. With its multi-tubular boiler, exhaust from the cylinders being sent up the chimney to increase the air blast to the firebox and angled cylinders, it set a pattern for further development. So, the pattern of locomotive design was clearly set out, but there was still a good deal to be done in planning the routes and improving the track. Even the Liverpool & Manchester had to rely on cable haulage to overcome a steep approach at Liverpool. One thing, however, was not yet being questioned to any great extent – was the somewhat arbitrary 4ft 8½in the ideal gauge for a modern rail system?

The first stage for any potential railway company was to get an Act of Parliament to authorise construction and the necessary land purchase and for that to happen the company needed to present parliament with detailed plans of the proposed route. This was not a mere formality as George Stephenson discovered when he had to give evidence for the Liverpool & Manchester Railway. He had handed most of the survey work and planning to subordinates and they had not done the job well. The result was that he was examined and humiliated and the Bill was thrown out. The errors were eventually rectified and, at a second attempt, the revised plans were approved. But the story shows just how important it was to get the initial survey carried out thoroughly. So, the first job of the committee set up to push the railway plan forward was to appoint an engineer to take charge of an initial survey for the potential investors.

There were originally two main candidates, Henry Habberley Price and William Brunton. Price had already put forward a scheme which had not impressed. Brunton had been among the locomotive pioneers looking at ways in which engines could be constructed that would have traction and not damage the track. He decided that the best solution was to get rid of the wheels altogether and design an engine that would 'walk' on two legs. At each stroke of the piston, one 'leg' moved forward and the other back. At the trials for this unlikely device the engine blew up, killing the crew. It was not exactly a great testimonial to his reliability and common sense. Nicholas Roch, who had been a member of the Dock Committee and who had been impressed by Isambard's abilities, suggested he should also become a candidate.

In the event, the surveying was put in the hands of W.H. Townsend, a professional land surveyor who had laid out the route of the little Bristol & Gloucestershire Railway. Isambard was also appointed to help with the work. The agreed fee was £500 for the whole survey. A Bristol solicitor called Osborne who was on the committee was dubious about Townsend's abilities to take on the bigger task and made his views known. Isambard wrote: 'Osborne was of the opinion that unless I took the whole management and only left T– the nominal surveyor and a little bit at this end of the line we would never get through it.' Townsend himself soon recognised that he was not quite up to the task and Isambard became in effect, if not in name, in charge of the whole operation. On 7 March, he received the welcome news that he had now been officially appointed as chief engineer, with Townsend as his assistant. It was far from a unanimous decision – there was just one vote in it.

The two men set out to start the task on 9 March 1833, Isambard tartly noting that Townsend 'as usual was late'. Not surprisingly, Townsend wanted to start by heading north out of Bristol, following the line of his old tramway, and then heading east along the line of what is now the A420 to Wick, before dropping down to Bath. Isambard was unimpressed – 'dreadfully hilly country', which indeed it is. He returned to Bristol via the lower road down the Avon valley, which he considered a far better route, and began to think of a terminus at Temple Mead to the south of the city centre. The following Monday he was off again, this time looking at the route beyond Bath. The Kennet & Avon Canal had been built in the previous century to link the two rivers in its title, and to provide a link at Reading down to London via the Thames. John Rennie, the canal's engineer, had managed to provide a long level section as far as Bradford-on-Avon, but only by means of a flight of seven locks to lift the canal from the river to the rim of the Avon valley. This was not an option for a railway, unless an incline was used, using a stationary engine for haulage, which was not an idea that appealed to Isambard. He set out to investigate the possibility of squeezing the line into the narrow Avon valley. He found the conditions difficult, not helped by the poor condition of the canal at the rim of the valley. The man in charge of the canal, Blackwell, was described by Isambard as being 'bigoted and obstinate'. He should not have been surprised by his obstinacy – as the canal manager, he would not have welcomed the competition for trade. Isambard went on to Corsham, where the road from Bath curved up over Box Hill and afterwards made his way to London, where he recruited an assistant surveyor called Hughes, who seems not to have been quite as good and efficient as Isambard had hoped. His diary for 18 April recorded having to go on a hunt for the assistant and eventually found him 'on the wrong track'. Losing Hughes proved a recurring theme in the diary.

It was a punishing schedule for Isambard. He would have to take coaches as and when he could get on board, grab a few hours' sleep and then ride off on horseback to survey the next section of the proposed line. Gradually, the plans began to fall into place. The first decision was whether to go south or north of the Marlborough Downs. He looked at the line through the Vale of Pewsey that had been recommended by Price and an alternative, more northerly route through the Vale of the White Horse and Swindon to Reading. He found the latter to be the better choice. He had to provide a number of alternative routes into London, depending on where the London terminus was going to be sited. There was also the crossing of the Thames to be considered, which was originally thought to be likely to be near Kingston. By the end of July, ideas had crystallised to the extent that it was possible to hold a public meeting in Bristol to present the plans to the public. Brunel had to speak – not something he enjoyed doing. Public speaking was, he wrote, 'like playing with a tiger, and all you can hope is that you may not get scratched or worse.' This was followed by a London meeting on 27 August, which was again greeted with less than wholehearted enthusiasm by Isambard, and he was not impressed by the worthies who made up the London committee – 'rather an old woman's set'. He soon found, however, that the secretary, Charles Alexander Saunders, was far from old womanish, and he was to become a friend and supporter. At some time in the proceedings, what had until then been simply known as 'the Bristol railway' now had a new name. Up to then, railways had usually taken their names from their destinations – Liverpool & Manchester and so on. This one would be different; it would be The Great Western Railway. There is no evidence to confirm who coined the name, but it would be typical of Brunel to make such an extravagant claim that a railway would indeed be great, even before any work had begun or indeed been authorised.

With the outline plans approved by the two committees, things were now moving forward quite rapidly, and Isambard had to make arrangements for his own role in the next phase. Up to then, he had been sharing his father's office in London, but now he needed one of his own and he found just what he wanted at 53 Parliament Street, Whitehall, conveniently situated for what were bound to be several meetings with the Parliamentary Committees, who would oversee the passing of the bill – or its refusal. Isambard was confident of success, and realised that as well as a new office in London, he would be spending a great deal of time out in the country as the work progressed. In the course of the initial survey, he had had far too many frustrating times, waiting for public coaches, which too often turned out to be booked up already, and then having a frustrating wait for the next vehicle and also too many nights in dingy hotels and inns. What he needed, he decided, was a britzka. This was a long four-wheeled coach in which the seats could be folded down at night to make a bed – the nineteenth century equivalent of a camper van. He designed his own version that could serve as travelling coach, mobile office and bedroom. In this long black vehicle, he was eventually to spend many days dashing around the country and it was to become known from its black colour as the 'flying hearse'. But before that was ready for use, he now had to produce a detailed survey, with all the information that would be needed to convince the committees of the Commons and Lords to approve the Bill and give the company the essential Act of Parliament.

Marc Brunel had found one of his biggest headaches in constructing the Thames tunnel to be the constant interference by the committee, a fact that Isambard would have been well aware of. Now he faced not one committee, but two, each containing twelve directors, one for London and one for Bristol. The Bristol men knew him, and he knew them, but the London men were a different matter. His first impression simply lumped them together as 'old women'. Now he made detailed notes on their characters – and not very flattering ones either.

> 'I think I can gain ground with Mr. Miles, he seems an amiable man but pig-headed. Fenwick I think is a friend, Gibbs will go with the Bristol Committee. Bettington is a jobber, but probably caring little about anything but his salary and shares, Grenfell must be humoured. Gower very doubtful – stupid enough and proportionally suspicious. Hopkins I hardly know. Simonds a hot warm tempered Tory, just another as K. Claxton i.e. warm friend but changeable and very capable of being a devil of an opponent.'

K. Claxton is presumably Christopher Caxton – who may have been known to friends as Kit – but from what we know of their later relations, he was always to be a good friend to Isambard and never a devilish opponent. By early September, Isambard had been appointed to carry out the necessary detailed survey and was given an extra assistant to help with the task. Unfortunately, the britzka was not yet ready, so there was no alternative but to return to the arduous routine of public coaches and trips on foot or by horse. During this time, he complained about how hard the life had become – 'I am rarely under twenty hours a day at it'. To add to his stresses he now found that Townsend was proving incompetent as Isambard noted in a diary entry for September, had been found working on a curve, but not at all on the correct line: 'could not make him understand the theory or rational'. But there were other problems that were looming that had nothing to do with engineering; the hoped-for investment was not coming in quickly enough. Estimates were always presented that implied an accuracy that was seldom, if indeed ever, forthcoming. For the GWR, the estimated cost was £2,805,330. The directors then gave their estimates of the revenue likely on completion, when the line was up and running. They expected an annual revenue of £747,752 from goods, cattle and passengers, which was, they assured investors, 'a total arrived at not on mere calculation founded on probabilities but deduced from careful inquiry into the facts'. In spite of the nicety of the estimate, the sum that the company hoped to raise was a round £3 million in £100 shares. It is interesting to note that they seem to have expected goods traffic to be more important than passengers, who appeared on the list after the cattle. Parliament would not even look at a Bill unless the company could show that they had a guaranteed 50 per cent of the working capital secured, and there was not nearly enough shares being taken up, in fact scarcely more than a quarter of the shares had been subscribed at the date when they had hoped to present the Bill. At this point, a rather bizarre decision was taken. They would go to Parliament with a proposal for constructing two lines – Bristol to Bath and London to Reading, with a promise to close the gap when funds were available. Isambard was instructed to temporarily abandon the survey between Reading and Bath.

There were various factions opposing the Bill. The obvious ones were the Kennet & Avon Canal Company and coaching lines, who both argued that the arrival of the railway would be their ruin, and landowners, who simply did not want a noisy, smoky railway anywhere near their property. As these arguments had all been used in opposition to the Liverpool & Manchester Railway Bill and been rejected by Parliament, there was no reason to believe that they would fare any better this time round. So it proved, but there was, of course, always the elephant in the room – the gap in the middle of the line. One of the lawyers for the opposition famously noted that the proposed line was neither 'Great', nor 'Western' nor even a 'Railway'. The whole thing was 'a trick' and 'a fraud'. But in spite of the ridicule, the Commons passed the Bill by 182 votes to 92. It was then sent to the Lords, where it was rejected by 47 votes to 30, mainly on the grounds that the finances were suspect. It was now obvious that the only hope was to raise more capital so as to be able to present a new Bill, covering the whole route from London to Bristol. By February 1835, there were sufficient prospective shareholders for a return to Parliament for a second attempt.

Isambard once again had his assistants out, surveying the proposed line, including the central section that had earlier been ignored when the decision was taken to only apply for permission to build the two ends. He wanted to make sure that there were no unexpected hitches and no unwanted complications, so he set out a set of clear instructions in a letter of 1834:

'In conducting this portion of the survey of the Great Western Railway entrusted to you it is particularly desirable that you should ascertain the names of the owners and occupiers of any land to be passed over and as early as possible obtain their sanction to the making of the survey. It will not of course very often be impracticable to obtain this information until you have actually entered upon the land but if you make the application as early as you can I think you will not find any vexatious opposition thrown in your way. You will at all time afford every information to persons interested in the property likely to be affected by the Railway and you will consult them as to the manner in which the line may be carried so as to be most advantageous to their property explaining to them at the same time if necessary any circumstances which from the nature of a Railway may render such a distinction difficult or impracticable in order that as far as consistent with the absolute requisites of a public work of this description the line ultimately selected may be adapted to existing interests.

'You will be particularly careful that all persons employed by you shall conduct themselves with propriety and civility, that no damage be done to the hedge or fences and that they do not unnecessarily encroach upon gardens or enclosed ground or otherwise annoy the inhabitants.'

The usual opponents set out their stalls again, but with little hope of faring any better this time round. Far more worrying was the opposition from the London & Southampton Railway Company who had earlier suggested that the GWR should join their line at Basingstoke. When that was rejected, they then decided to promote their own line from Basingstoke to Bath, which followed the southern route originally proposed by Brunton. Once again Francis Giles popped up in the story – this time as the surveyor for the southern route. Brunel dismissed it contemptuously, which infuriated Brunton, who took on the role as the main engineering witness opposing the GWR. Brunel, however, was able to draw on rather more heavyweight supporters, including George Stephenson who said of the proposed GWR route that he could imagine a better line but if so didn't know of one.

The opposition from the proposed London & Southampton extension to Bath proved rather feeble in the event. When it was pointed out that there were many heavy gradients on their line, they replied that as there were as many grades going up as there were going down, the whole line could be thought of as essentially level as they cancelled each other out. The Chairman of the Committee pointed out that using that argument the Scottish

Highlands should be ideal country for railway building. The reception their plans received in the committee room didn't prevent them holding a public meeting in Bath, where their ideas were demolished by Brunel.

Now, it seemed, there was only one contentious item, the proposed tunnel through Box Hill. The tunnel, at almost two miles long and with a gradient of 1 in 100, seemed to horrify several of the committee members. No one, they declared, could possibly be induced to go through such a thing; that the noise of trains passing in the tunnel would be terrifying and if anyone could be persuaded to make the journey once, they could never be persuaded to repeat the performance – even, presumably, if they had a return ticket. And the voice of science appeared to be on the side of the critics. Dr Dionysus Lardner was the Professor of Astronomy at University College, London and was best known for his numerous works of popular science as well as more scholarly textbooks on mathematics, so one might have expected a common sense view from him. That is not what he produced. He declared that if the brakes failed on the train, gravity would take over and it would hurtle down the slope, emerging eventually at a speed of 120 miles an hour, at which point the unhappy passengers would no longer be able to breathe. It was left to Brunel to correct the mathematician's maths. He simply pointed out that the calculations had omitted two factors: friction and air resistance. Put those into the equation and the exit speed was a more modest 56mph. Another opponent appeared in the shape of the Master of Eton College, who demanded that no railway should reach the town, lest boys should catch a train and head for the fleshpots of London – and if the railway did come anywhere near, it should be shielded from view by a ten foot high wall stretching for four miles. At least he had his way – the proposed line to Eton was abandoned and the nearest station would be at Slough. Thanks largely to Brunel's eloquent and clear testimony under days of cross examination, the arguments of the opposition were dealt with one by one, until the last remaining question had to be answered. Which would be the best route from Bath to London, the southerly Basingstoke and Bath or the northerly as proposed by Brunel? The committee came down firmly on the side of the northern route. Basically, the fight was now over: on 31 August 1835, the Bill for a railway from Bristol via Bath, Swindon, Maidenhead and Reading with branches to Trowbridge and Bradford-on-Avon received the Royal Assent. Work on the line could begin.

Chapter 10

MARRIAGE

Like many young men, Isambard was fond of female company and it seems quite flirtatious, but not, at the age of 21, particularly keen on settling down. His focus was very much on the great things he wanted to achieve. He wrote on 19 October 1827:

'Q. Shall I make a good husband? Am doubtful. My ambition or whatever it might be called (it is not the mere wish to be rich) is rather extreme but still I am not afraid I shall be unhappy if I do not reach the rank of Hero and Commander-in-Chief of His Majesty's Forces in steam (or Gaz) boat department. This is a favourite 'castle in the air' of mine. Make the Gaz engine answer, fit out some vessels (of course a war), take some prizes, say, some fortified town, get employed by Government contract and command a fine fleet – fight – in fact take Algiers or something in that style.'

Nothing in his daydreams seems to go very well with the idea of domestic bliss, though he also mentions that following his successful career he will, as a rich man, build his own house, and he had in fact already designed it. Why was he even considering the idea of marriage? It appears that he had several young ladies to whom he was attracted, but one in particular seems to have been a more serious attachment than any of the others. Ellen Hulme was a member of a family in Manchester that was friendly with the Brunels. According to a note of 17 November 1827, they had first met as teenagers.

'I have had, as I suppose most young men have had, numerous attachments, if they deserve the name. Each in its turn has appeared to me the true one. E.H. is the oldest and most constant, now, however, gone by. During her reign, nearly 7 years, several inferior ones caught my attention. I need only remind myself of DC, OS, and numerous others. With E. Hume [sic] it was mutual. The sofa scenes must now appear to her, as to me, rather ridiculous'.

The next section has been carefully cut out, and one can only speculate as to what it might have contained, possibly evidence of why the relationship had broken down or, perhaps, some intimate details that Isambard did not want to be seen by anyone else. It then continues:

> 'serve me right if I had been spilled in the mud – certainly a devilish pretty girl, an excellent musician and a very sweet voice – but I'm afraid those eyes don't speak of a very placid temper.'

It all provides an interesting insight into the young man's ideas at that time. We do not know what went wrong, or why he deserved to be 'spilled in the mud'. Of course, he never did become the dashing naval hero, and the gas engine never came to fruition. He was, however, already set on the path that would make him an engineering hero, whose name would be remembered long after his death. The note suggested that everything with Ellen was over, but only a month later, he was writing that it seems people always returned to their first loves – and that 'Ellen is still it seems my real love'. He had written her a long letter, expressing his love and was waiting for a reply, which would decide the fate of their relationship – and if she was uncertain then he would give it up. Rather curiously he wrote that they could have been very happy if only she had kept up her music practice and learned to play 'tolerably' – an unusual condition for a lifelong relationship. Days later, he was still waiting for a letter and he was concerned that she might send a 'quizzing' reply, that is one that was rather frivolous and jokey. He was worried, too, that he was not yet in a position, financially, where he could even contemplate marriage. There is no further mention of any reply, but months later, he could write that he thought he had dealt with the whole situation well and was now 'independent'. It would seem that he was the one who broke off the affair, and it seems unlikely that she left him for someone else as she never married.

At around the same time that the relationship with Ellen Hulme was coming to an end, Isambard was introduced by his brother-in-law to the Horsley family, with the rather unappealing address of 1 High Row, Kensington Gravel Pits. This was in fact a village just on the edge of London, very close to the site of the present Notting Hill Gate tube station – their house stood in what is now the smart Kensington Church Street. The Horsleys were an extraordinarily gifted artistic family. The father, William, was an organist and composer, whose works included three symphonies and many songs and hymn tunes, including the music for the popular *There is a Green Hill Far Away*. He was one of the founders of the Philharmonic Society of London in 1813. The Society was to promote musical performances in the capital and, in 1827, they invited Beethoven to visit London. He was too ill to come, so they asked him to provide them with a new work. He was quite poor at the time, so they sent him £100 (around £9,000 today) and in return received the famous *Choral Symphony*. William's son Charles followed in his father's footsteps and also became a composer. Another son, John, was to become a Royal Academician and is generally credited with designing the first ever Christmas card. Fanny was an artist but died young and Sophy was apparently a brilliant pianist who had the misfortune to live in an age where being a professional musician was not an acceptable occupation for a young lady. The eldest of the five children was Mary, who was always teased in the family for being rather haughty and was nicknamed 'the Duchess of Kensington'. There seem, however, to be no mentions of any great talents; perhaps her alleged haughtiness was little more than a failure to keep up with her brilliant siblings and a withdrawal into herself. She was, however, the family beauty and it was said that when she was presented at court, Queen Victoria was entranced.

The house saw a constant procession of world-famous musicians passing through its doors. Sophy kept an autograph book, which would be worth a fortune today as among the signatures are those of some of the greatest composers of the nineteenth century including Brahms, Chopin and Bellini. One of the most frequent visitors was the young Felix Mendelssohn, who might have been impressed by the talents of the younger sisters but was bewitched by the beauty of Mary. On returning from a visit, he wrote how he cherished a flower she had given him as something precious. Any romance between them, however, did not blossom. This was the household into which Isambard was introduced, but his first comments do not suggest that he was yet as enchanted as Mendelssohn, merely commenting, 'Went to Mrs. Horsley in the evening – much amused.' That was in February 1832 at much the same time that Mendelssohn was swooning over Mary.

Fortunately for Isambard, he was able to hold his own in this extravagantly gifted musical family, Marc, it should be remembered, had played the flute and as a boy made a model of a mechanical musical instrument. Isambard may not have played himself, but he loved music, and gifted performers are generally glad to welcome an enthusiastic and informed listener. L.T.C. Rolt in his excellent biography of Isambard describes Mary as a 'cold beauty' and described her features as seeming to 'lack animation'. This judgement is based on a sketch by her young brother John, and it is rather lifeless, but he was probably in his teens when the sketch was made. It seems a touch unfair to judge the model when the fault of lack of animation could equally be down to the artist. From all we know of Isambard, he was unlikely to fall for a young woman simply because she was beautiful – though, of course, many young men have done just that. Whatever the initial attraction to Mary might have been, an affection grew up between her and the young engineer.

Isambard had been reluctant to make any serious attachment to Ellen Hulme, in part at least because he had yet to make his way in the world. Things were different now. In the years between the failure of the first GWR Bill, and the presentation of the second, he had been far from idle. The citizens of Cheltenham were particularly keen on promoting a railway to what was becoming an increasingly fashionable spa. They promoted a line from Swindon, on the assumption that the London to Bristol main line would indeed be built. They appointed Isambard as their chief engineer. The line was to run to Gloucester as well as Cheltenham with a branch to Cirencester. Although railways were becoming established throughout the country, local gentry could still be a nuisance. Squire Gordon of Kemble House insisted that the line should not be visible from the parkland surrounding his house, so the company agreed to create a short tunnel to the west of his grounds. He also insisted that no station should be built on his land, so the current Kemble station was built at the far end of the tunnel. He also got a substantial cash compensation. There were others who had to be pacified, though sometimes with good reason. The proposed line from Kemble to Stroud passed through the village of Chalford. The railway would have cut off a large woollen mill and mill house from the main road, so the company agreed to install a signal box and a manned level crossing to provide access – and it is still there to this day and still manned. The mill itself has long since stopped working, but it is the only mill in the region to preserve its steam engine, though not alas the boiler, and a colleague and I make an annual visit to oil the old machine and polish its brasses ready for a public open day. This involves a ritual which may well be unique on the present rail system. On arriving at the crossing, I have to get out of the car and ring a bell, at which point a man emerges from the signal box, opens the gates and lets me through. This was not the only new line proposed during this period. The Bristol and Exeter Railway was also being promoted, once again with Isambard as the engineer – and here there were few problems with greedy landowners. Both these lines were approved and received their Acts in 1836.

Isambard was in the happy position of having not one but three important railway jobs, and several other engineering works, including the Clifton bridge. In December 1835 he moved into 17 Duke Street, London, near

St. James's Park, a handsome four-storey house, which was to be both home and office. He had an income and a fine home and could now think seriously of marriage. The affair seems to have taken the family by surprise. The family had all gone out for a walk, Isambard with Mary on his arm, walking far more slowly than the rest of the family. The story was taken up by Fanny Horsley writing to her aunt, in a lively, witty letter. The two younger girls had gone to bed, and when they heard Mary coming up the stairs, they called her into the room.

'"Well, what could you be doing lagging behind in that way?", said Sophy.
"Indeed, Mary," I said – but quite in fun, without any idea of the truth – "one would think he had been making you an offer."
"And what would you say if he really had?" said Mary in an awful, hollow voice which I shall never forget. Sophy and I immediately fell into such tremendous fits of laughing, that Mary said she must go away. It certainly seemed very unfeeling – and she, poor thing, with tears in her eyes – but so it was, and I must confess I was much the worse of the two. However, we soon got composed, and listened with delight to the little she had to tell, I mean little in quantity for such happy and excellent facts are great, if anything is."'

Isambard had proposed, explained to Mary that he had been attracted to her ever since they had first met, but had waited until he was able to propose marriage until he was in a position to offer her a comfortable life and a suitable home. She had accepted his proposal at once and the Horsley family were all delighted with the match. They were married on 5 July 1836 and afterwards set off for Capel Curig in Snowdonia for a two week honeymoon. After that, Isambard was back to the hectic life of a busy engineer.

Chapter 11

BUILDING THE LINE

We know that Brunel was less than delighted by his ride on the Liverpool & Manchester Railway, and to his mind the problem was obvious. The track was simply not smooth enough, nor firm enough and the rails were too close together. It might do well enough for some lines but was not up to the standard he wanted for the Great Western. As is well known, his first change was to move the lines apart to a seven-foot gauge, though in the event, the actual gauge was 7ft ¼ in. The rails were different from those then in use on other lines. Known as 'bridge rails' they looked in cross-section like a tall hat with rounded crown and wide brim. Originally, they were comparatively light at 55lb per yard, but later heavier rails were used, up to 75lb. We are all familiar with the railway sleepers of today, laid at intervals at right angles to the track. At the time, however, this was still comparatively rare. Most of the Liverpool & Manchester Railway had rails mounted on stone blocks, as in the old days of tramways, though some sections did use transverse sleepers. The stone blocks almost certainly accounted for the uneven ride that Isambard experienced, and he quite rightly thought there had to be better systems. The system he developed was totally different. The rails were supported on wooden baulks of timber, running the full length of the track, made of pine with a hardwood top. They were fastened together by cross ties, running across both tracks. These in turn were held in place by iron spikes driven into the earth between the rails, creating a rigid, three-dimensional framework. Once in place, the system was ballasted with stones. It all took up a lot of space; the total distance between the outside rails for a double track route was 21ft, with the vertical iron spikes 15ft apart. The expectation was that this would provide the smoothest possible ride thanks to its rigidity. In fact, it was if anything too rigid; there was no give in it. Also, there was always the problem of natural settlement of the ground and the shifting of ballast, which left the vertical piles exposed. Brian Morgan in his *Railways: Civil Engineering* (1971) suggests that Isambard may have based his seven-foot gauge on the track built by his father from the Chatham sawmill, but there seems to be no evidence to support this. On the whole, the idea that the Stephenson gauge was simply too mean seems to have been his inspiration.

A section of bridge rail used on the GWR, which is currently in use as a door stop by the author.

One other project was also demanding Isambard's attention. Funds had finally been raised that allowed work to restart on the Clifton bridge. The first requirement was to provide some sort of crossing of the gorge. A 1,000 foot long wrought iron bar had been fabricated, and the plan was to haul that across the gorge, and suspend a carriage from it. The bar was on the Leigh side, and it was to be pulled across by means of hawsers and a capstan on the Clifton side. The first attempt was made in August 1836. All went well until a hawser snapped and the bar fell into the river. It was retrieved but had been damaged so that it was slightly bent. Nevertheless, a car was slung

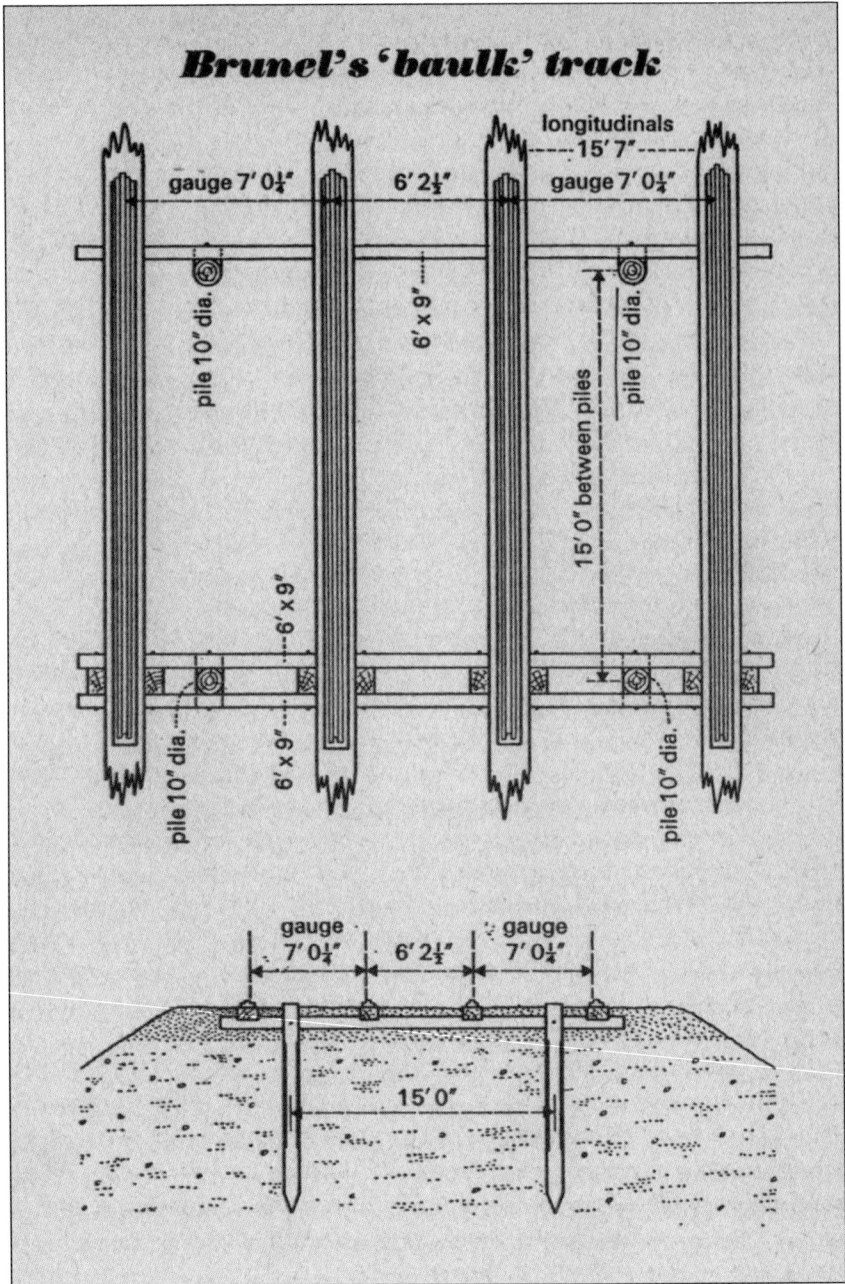

The system used in laying down a double broad gauge track, from Macdermott's history of the GWR.

beneath it, and a brave – or foolhardy – man decided to make an unauthorised crossing. As a result of the bend, the car stuck halfway and he had to be rescued. Isambard was furious – the bridge project did not need any more bad publicity. Later, a new bar was wrought, and it was Isambard himself who made the first ever crossing high above the Avon, with an anonymous companion. As they moved along, the bar bent under the weight of the simple carriage, which stuck halfway across, jamming the roller. Brunel simply climbed up the supporting cables, eased the roller back into place and continued the journey, calm and unharmed.

On 27 August there was a second official ceremony, this time for laying the foundation stone for the tower on the Leigh Woods side of the gorge. A huge crowd gathered, in spite of the fact that the event was scheduled for seven in the morning. Flags were flown, steamers on the river were bedecked and the ceremony was carried out by the Marquis of Northampton, who was visiting Bristol in his role as President of the British Association for the Advancement of Science. There were the usual fanfares and a number of objects were placed in a niche; representatives of all the coins then in circulation, from the double guinea to the farthing, together with a copy of the Act of Parliament and a china plate with a picture of the bridge, one of a set specially made for the official breakfast that followed the ceremony at the Gloucester Hotel. There was a new sense of optimism, though it soon received a setback when the contractors went bankrupt. The Trustees took over the responsibility of continuing the work themselves. Progress was depressingly slow, and it was not until 1840 that the abutment that would carry the tower on the Leigh side was in place – a massive piece of red sandstone, 100ft in height. Had the original Brunel plan been followed, this would not even have been needed. Three years later, the money ran out again. The piers on both sides were almost complete, but were left there and came to be known locally as 'Monuments of Failure'. The bridge would not be completed in Isambard's lifetime.

As work began on the Great Western Railway, a great mass of men had to be gathered, organised and controlled. Brunel was the man in charge: he decided where the line would run, where stations would be built; drew up plans for the major structures on the route; and in fact was responsible for the whole project. This involved long days and nights touring the line in the flying hearse. He could not see to everything himself, so he appointed his own young assistant engineers, whose job it was to help him in a variety of ways, but mainly to ensure that the work was carried out efficiently and well. The actual work was handed out to contractors who took on a certain section of

A polychrome picture of the Clifton suspension bridge, c.1900. It was only completed after Brunel's death.

the work at an agreed price. One of the tasks the engineering staff needed to keep an eye on was the way in which the contractors carried out their tasks. Their interests did not necessarily coincide. For those contractors, the sooner a job was completed, the sooner they got paid and the less they had to put out in wages. For the company, speed was less important than thoroughness. The contractors, in turn, employed the navvies who would do the actual hard work. It was a giant pyramid with Isambard Brunel at the top.

The first essential was to decide exactly where the line would be laid. There had been a good deal of discussion about the London terminus for the line. When the first Bill had been presented to parliament, the idea had been to end at Euston, already chosen as the terminus for the London & Birmingham Railway. Later, however, there were disagreements between the two companies, partly over the terms of the lease and partly over the decision to build the GWR to the broad gauge. In the event, the decision was taken to make a terminus on what was then the outskirts of London at Bishops Bridge Road, Paddington, to the west of the present station. The first station was not the magnificent terminus we see today, but a temporary timber structure, with little in the way of facilities.

As so much of the impetus for creating the railway had originated in Bristol, that end of the line was to get a far grander station than London, at least for a time. Brunel was not allowed to build within the old city walls, so a site was chosen on the meadows at Temple Mead. Brunel designed a structure in the Tudor revivalist style. The most striking feature was the train shed, with a mock hammer beam roof, and separate platforms for arrivals and departures. Passengers made their way between platforms through the undercroft, which

The first, very rough and ready Paddington station from *The Illustrated Guide to the Great Western Railway* (1852).

also contained waiting rooms. The company offices were part of the overall design. There was also a separate engine shed. It remains a splendid building, though it has long since been displaced by the present station and is now an events centre. It was completed and in use by 1841.

Once the detailed surveys had been completed and the route marked out, it was time to get down to the task of building a railway. Isambard had no engineers with actual experience of railway construction to draw on. There had, after all, been very few railways constructed up to this point, and those that had were mainly the work of the Stephensons, father and son, and their associates, such as Joseph Locke, and they continued to employ virtually every experienced man they could find. So Isambard was left with training up his own staff and keeping them on their toes. He was quick to praise and equally quick to blame when his standards were not met. One assistant received this letter, and when he had finished reading must have thought it was time to start taking an interest in the Situations Vacant columns of his newspaper.

'Plain, gentlemanly language seems to have no effect upon you, I must try stronger language and stronger measures. You are a cursed, lazy, inattentive vagabond, and if you continue to neglect my instructions, and

The original Temple Meads station at Bristol, designed by Brunel in a medieval style, complete with mock hammer beam roof.

to show such infernal laziness, I shall send you about your business. I have frequently told you, amongst other absurd, untidy habits, that that of making drawings on the backs of others was inconvenient; by your cursed neglect of that you have again wasted more of my time than your whole life is worth, in looking for the altered drawings you were to make of the Station – they won't do.'

It was not just his assistants who caused Isambard concern. Contractors blithely underbid each other in the hope of securing the work, only for a few to discover that they were unable to keep up the rate of work and were sinking under debt. Brunel supported them as far as possible, largely because of the huge inconvenience of having to change to a new man and a new crew. One example was Brunel's dealing with the contractor William Ranger, who had taken out a contract in 1836 for work on the Box tunnel. Progress was depressingly slow, and Isambard suggested sinking an extra shaft and putting in more men so that work could continue day and night. To encourage Ranger, it was agreed to advance him a further £1,000. In most contracts there were penalty clauses for not meeting targets. Ranger was soon paying out more in penalties than he was getting in through regular payments. He put in claims for more cash, and Brunel suggested paying up: 'Make it as a great accommodation afforded with considerable reluctance & not to be thought of again as a precedent.' Things staggered on for months, until finally Ranger admitted that he had been trying to extract more money than was legally his due. It was the end of his contract, and he admitted that he could have been sent to gaol.

It was the contractors who were responsible for hiring and firing navvies and once work was under way, the great navvy army had to be marshalled and set to work. The railway navvies have a popular image as being mainly Irish and prone to riotous behaviour and there is some truth in both assertions. Certainly, the navvies on the Great Western managed two particularly violent riots. The following account from *Felix Farley's Bristol Journal* of 28 April 1838 demonstrated just how seriously things could go wrong. It is worth quoting at length if only because it is a vivid picture of the events, but also shows what a mixed group the navvies were.

'On Monday last a number of navigators working on the Great Western Railway, amounting to upwards of 300, principally natives of the County of Gloucester, tumultuously assembled and made an attack on the workmen employed at tunnel No. 3 Keynsham, who are most of them from Devonshire,

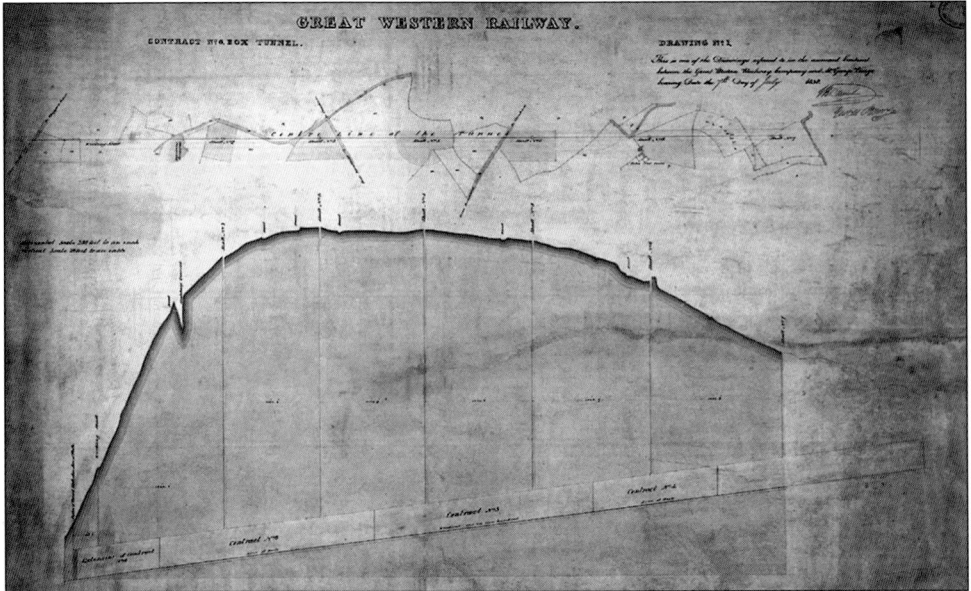

A working plan setting out the details for contractors working on the Box tunnel.

and the lower parts of Somerset. The ostensible motive for the attack was a belief that the latter were working under price; to this was added a local or county feud, as the rallying cry of onslaught was 'Gloucester against Devon'. The result was a regular fight with various dangerous weapons, ready at hand, such as spades, pickaxes, crowbars, &c – The contest was long and severe, in which several were most dangerously hurt, & one man was obliged to be taken to the Infirmary, but no one was killed. The insubordination continued for several succeeding days, and was not repressed without the aid of the military.'

It seems that the Devon men had been earning more than the Gloucester navvies as they had been put on piece work. Many of them would have come from the tin and copper mines of the south west and were more experienced at using specialist tools to break down rock. Thanks to their expertise, the extra work they were able to achieve was rewarded by being paid at a good rate, while the other navvies were on set wages – hence the disparity. While all this was going on, there was another outbreak of rioting, this time at the opposite end of the line in London, and this was reported alongside the account of the Keynsham riot, quoting 'a London paper'.

'We regret to state that a most desperate and alarming affray took place on the evening of Sunday last, betwixt the English and Irish labourers employed upon the GWR. It was again renewed on Monday and many of the results are anticipated to be fatal. The riot is understood to have arisen in consequence of the Irish party having proposed to work for lower wages than their English fellow-labourers. The atrocities upon both sides have been of the most brutal and unmanly description, and but for the interference of the local authorities aided by a squadron of the 12th Lancers, the most lamentable consequences must have ensued. Twenty-four of the rioters have been committed to Clerkenwell Prison, where they will now remain until a further examination.'

When reading accounts such as these, one can get a false picture of navvy life. One always has to remember that riots are news – 1,000 men getting on with an arduous job day after day is not news. And that was what most of the navvy life was like; living rough and working hard. And although the injuries incurred in riots were widely displayed, those suffered through accidents, even fatal accidents, got scant mention anywhere. The Bristol paper, however, did take an interest in what was happening at their end of the great work. Here are a couple of examples from the period 1838-9, showing how easy it was to lose one's life when working on building a railway.

'On the night of Friday another fatal accident occurred at shaft No. 5 of the Box Tunnel, to a poor man whose name is at present unknown. The deceased had just come up to the brink of the shaft, and was in the act of landing to take some refreshment, when his foot slipped, and he fell to a depth of 260 feet. His body was taken to the Tunnel Inn, on the works, and presented a shocking appearance.'

'A distressing event occurred on Friday at the open cutting at Keynsham Park, on the line of the Great Western Railway, by the falling in of a bank. One of the workmen was killed on the spot, and others were seriously injured. Three were taken to the Bristol Infirmary, viz. Isaac Gibbs, John Smith and Henry Hancock; the latter had sustained a very severe compound fracture of the left thigh, which it was found necessary immediately to amputate; the other leg was also fractured above the ankle. The man's recovery is very doubtful; the other had received lesser injuries, and will probably be discharged in a short time.'

In another report, when brickwork in a tunnel collapsed, leaving three dead, two men with fractured skulls and seven injured, the paper referred to this as 'one of those appalling occurrences which are almost unavoidable in public works of great moment'. The subsequent inquest recorded 'accidental death' and no one it seems enquired who was responsible for seeing that brickwork did not collapse. Even the Bristol Infirmary records are vague, simply recording an 'unusually high' number of accident victims arriving at the hospital. It was a hard and tough life and accidents were indeed accepted as inevitable. No blame for them could be laid at the door of the chief engineer. His responsibilities took in the broad sweep of the whole project, not the day to day work of men spread over miles of countryside.

Much of the work was very straightforward, simply levelling the ground and laying track, but there were many major features that required specialist work, notably tunnels and bridges. The first really major obstacle for the men working westwards from London was the crossing of the Brent valley at Hanwell. Isambard's viaduct design was original. As at Clifton, he designed the piers in what became known as his Egyptian style. Constructed between 1836 and 1837, it is 890 feet long, with eight semi-elliptical arches supported on tapering arches built out of engineering brick with stone cornices. The design is elegant but, apart from the pioneering use of hollow arches, not especially innovative. Both Brunels were fond of nature and would perhaps be pleased to know that the hollow arches have become bat roosts, and the creatures are officially protected. It was named after Lord Wharncliffe, who had presided over the Lords' Committee that had given its assent to the second Bill. His coat of arms adorns the structure. The actual construction seems to have passed with few problems, apart from an altercation between Irish and English navvies at the Stag beer house, which ended with three of the men involved being sent to prison for two months for threatening the local clergyman who had called in the authorities.

The next major river crossing brought a far greater challenge, as the route reached the Thames at Maidenhead. The problem was one that bedevilled many a railway engineer – how to build an economic bridge with as little difficulty as possible while still providing ample space for river traffic. In this case, the Thames authorities were insisting that there should be no more than two spans over the water, which meant arches would need to be 128 foot across. The simplest form of arch is semi-circular, but that would need a height of 64 feet, which would mean the actual track would be over seventy feet above the river. But the land on either side of the river is quite flat and one of Brunel's prime objectives was to keep gradients as gentle as possible: he had no wish to build great embankments to reach the top of a

Hanwell viaduct photographed in the early twentieth century being crossed by a train headed by what appears to be a 47xx class locomotive.

high bridge. He wanted to keep the arches as low as possible – and he knew it could be done. His father had already experimented with flat arches, and in his experimental bridge at Rotherhithe he had successfully constructed an arch that, if it had been completed, would have had a clear span between the piers of 100 feet and a rise to the crown of just 10ft 6ins. This was exactly what Isambard needed, and Marc sent him several sketches of how he might achieve a uniquely flat, brick arch. Would Isambard have found the solution to his problem for himself? We have no idea. What we do know is that he did not need to do so – his father had got there first. It seems only reasonable to describe the Maidenhead bridge as built as a joint effort, with honours shared between Marc and Isambard.

The viaduct had conventional arches on the land at either end, across the towpath, but the interest is all in the river crossing. The central pier was constructed on a small island in midstream, and though the arches to either

The Maidenhead viaduct with its elegant, low brick arches.

side needed to have that span of 128ft, the rise to the crown is only 24ft. The bridge is not quite as solid as it might appear. Internally, there are longitudinal walls and voids, keeping the whole structure light but strong. Many, including several professional engineers, doubted that such a low arch could stand, and when the centering was first removed on the eastern arch, a considerable area of brickwork separated out. The critics were quick to say 'we told you so'. They were premature. The fault was soon discovered. The centering had been eased before the mortar had completely dried. The contractor admitted responsibility, the area was repaired, and the viaduct was complete. It seems, however, that the whole affair had made the company directors nervous and, in one version of events, they ordered Brunel to keep the centering in place until the viaduct had been fully tested. In an alternative version, it was Isambard himself who decided to keep it in place throughout the winter in case of frost damage. One again, the critics had their say – Brunel was afraid to remove the centering because he knew the structure was unsafe. What they did not know was that, although the centering appeared to be offering support, it had in fact been slightly eased and at no point actually touched the brickwork. The ruse was discovered in a winter storm, which swept away the whole of the timber framing leaving the great viaduct standing and undamaged. Isambard had had the last laugh. The bridge we see today is not quite as he designed it. It was later widened to take four standard gauge tracks, but it was done with such care for the original, that what we see is still very recognisably the Brunel design. The bridge appears in perhaps the most famous painting ever made to celebrate the new age brought in by the railways: J.M.W. Turner's *Rain, Steam and Speed.*

As the line moved steadily westward, it encountered the great chalk ridge that sweeps across the country – the long-distance footpath and ancient track, The Ridgeway, follows its route. The same obstacle was being faced further

J.M.W. Turner's famous painting '*Rain, Steam and Speed*' showing a broad gauge locomotive on the Maidenhead viaduct.

north, where Robert Stephenson was battling his way to push the London & Birmingham Railway through the chalk near Tring. On the GWR, the work required a deep cutting at Sonning, sixty feet deep and nearly two miles long. It was a huge endeavour to create such a monstrous gash in the earth, and unfortunately, in the early days the contract had been given to the hapless William Ranger. The work had been taken out of his hands and Brunel himself had the task of supervising the effort. The winter of 1839 brought foul weather, including the storm that had blown away the centering at Maidenhead bridge in the November. Brunel had mustered an army of more than 1,000 navvies and nearly 200 horses, but the foul weather brought everything to a halt as torrential rain filled the cutting. By spring, the weather had improved and the line had reached Reading.

Meanwhile, at the opposite end of the line, the greatest work was the Box Tunnel. Isambard had, of course, had experience of tunnelling when working with his father beneath the Thames, but the methods used in railway tunnelling were very different. It was a technology developed in the canal age and had remained much the same ever since. The first stage was to accurately survey the ground. Today, we have the advantage of excellent maps with contours clearly marked. Railway engineers did not enjoy that luxury. Heights had to be measured with considerable accuracy and plotted. As we know, the tunnel had a slight incline, but it was necessary to have an exact measurement of the distance between the surface and the line of the tunnel. Once this was known, plans could be drawn for the contractors, such as that shown on page 98, and shafts could be sunk to exactly the right depth. Compass bearings taken on the surface could then be transferred to the foot of the shaft to give the direction in which work should be carried out. Men could work from the two ends of the tunnel and outwards in both directions from the foot of the shafts. If everything had been done correctly, then all should meet in a straight line. Unlike the soft chalk at Sonning, the workers here were faced with oolitic limestone, the famous Bath stone. A ton of gunpowder was set off every week in blasting a way through. The *Bristol Mercury* of 27 July 1839 had a very full account of just what work was like in the tunnel. It is too long to quote in full, but this extract is at the heart of it, as their reporter made the trip underground.

'The descent by shaft No. 7, which is 136 feet deep, is effected on a platform, without any railing or other security on the sides attached to a broad flat rope and unwound by a steam engine, and is attended with no inconvenience (if the idea of a fall from giddiness, or from the breaking of the rope, be not allowed to intrude) except the hard bump with which your arrival at the bottom is announced to you. The works are being carried on each way from the shaft and which, every way you go, the same appearance meets you. The dark, dim vault filled with clouds of vapour is saved from utter and black darkness by the feeble light of candles which are stuck upon the sides of the excavation, and placed on trucks or other things used in carrying on the works; these which in your immediate neighbourhood emit a dull red light are seen gradually diminishing in size and effect, till they appear like small red dots and are then lost in the dark void. Taking a candle in your hand you pick your way through pools of water over the temporary rails among blocks of stone, and the huge chains attached to the machinery which every now and then impede your way happy and lucky if no impediment, unobserved in the dull, uncertain light should arrest your progress by causing you to measure your length on the wet and rugged floor. Pursuing your onward course examining by the way the appearance of the works and admiring the solid walls which nature has provided, you notice every now and then a beautiful rill as clear as crystal issuing from some fissure in the rock trickling down the sides of the tunnel, and helping to form the pools and streams with which the floor yet abounds. Not during all this time have your ears been idle, the sounds of the pick and the shovel, and the hammer have fallen upon them indistinctly, but as you advance they increase and the hum of distant voices is heard. The faint illumination, before only sufficient to make darkness visible, now becomes stronger and the lights which had been placed chiefly in line along the walls become more frequent, they dot the whole of the opening, being pretty thickly planted from the floor to the roof. The cause for this is soon apparent, as you advance, a busy scene opens before you; gangs of men are at work at all sides, and the tunnel which to this point had been cut to the full dimension suddenly contracts: you leave the level of the floor and scrambling up among the workmen stepping sometimes on the solid rock 'at others on loose fragments' you wind your way slowly and with difficulty. Having been informed that a shot is about to be fired at the further extremity you stop to listen and to judge its effects. The match is applied, the explosion follows and a concussion such as probably you never felt before takes place; the solid rock appears to shake and the reverberation of the sound and shock is sensibly and fearfully experienced; and with a slight stretch of the imagination you may fancy yourself in the middle of a thunder cloud with heaven's artillery booming around. You pursue your rugged path and having arrived at that part where the junction was made between the two cuttings, you have an opportunity of examining the roof and of admiring the solid bed of rock of which it is formed, and of appreciating the skill which enabled the engineer to keep a true course under all the difficulties of such a work.'

After that, the reporter made his way to the next shaft and was brought back to the surface 'glad to breathe the pure air'. The anonymous reporter gives us a colourful insight into the conditions in the tunnel, though some elements he found romantic were not looked on so kindly by the engineers. The 'beautiful rills' required a steam engine to be kept pumping day and night to keep the workings clear of water. Another author, George Measom in his *Illustrated Guide to the Great Western Railway* (1852), provides the equally impressive statistics of construction: 414,000 cubic yards, mainly stone, were excavated; 54,000 cubic yards of brick and masonry were used; and more than 30 million bricks were laid. A ton of candles was used every week to light the work of around 1,000 men. One statistic is not mentioned – although it is difficult to get accurate figures, it has been estimated that perhaps as many as 100 men died during the work which started in 1837 and was only completed in the summer of 1841. One thing which has been endlessly repeated is that the rising sun shines straight through the tunnel on Isambard's birthday, 9 April. Recent tests, however, have shown that it doesn't – but it does do so on 8 April, the birthday of his sister Emma. Is this a coincidence or a very special birthday present for a sister?

During all this time, Isambard must have had very little time for family life as he rushed around the various construction sites. There are very few letters surviving from Isambard to Mary, and none from her to him. This does not, of course, mean that they didn't write – simply that if they did the letters have not survived. There was one major event in their lives, the birth of a son, also named Isambard, in 1837. He was a somewhat sickly child, with a leg deformity which could perhaps have been improved with surgery, and certainly would have been today. But at this time in the nineteenth century, with no anaesthetics available, the parents were reluctant to put the child through a terrible ordeal. There would be two other children – Henry Marc born in 1842 and Florence five years later. Several writers have dismissed Mary as cold and aloof, but there is no real evidence for this, nor indeed very much information about her at all. Marc and Sophia were known as a very affectionate and loving couple, but they were fortunate in that they were never apart for long stretches of time. One of the few surviving letters from Isambard does give a glimpse of what appears to be a very affectionate feeling towards his wife – and of the hectic lifestyle that kept them apart so often. At this time in 1840 he was working near Wootton Bassett.

'My dearest Mary,

I have become quite a walker. I have walked from Bathfrod Bridge to here – all but about one mile, which makes eighteen miles walking along the line – and I really am not very tired. I am, however, going to sleep here – if I had been half an hour earlier, I think I could not have avoided the temptation of coming up by the 6½ train, and returning by the morning goods train, just to see you: however, I will write you a long letter instead. It is a blowy evening, pouring with rain, my last two miles were wet. I arrived of course rather wet, and found the hotel, which is the best of a set of deplorable public houses, full – and here I am at the 'Cow and Candlesnuffers' or some such sign – a large room or cave, for it seems open to the wind everywhere, old-fashioned with a large chimney in one corner; but unfortunately it has one of those horrible little stoves, just nine inches across. I have piled a fire on both hobs, but to little use, there are four doors and two windows. What's the use of the doors I can't conceive, for you might crawl under them if they happened to be locked, and they seem too crooked to open, the ones with not a bad bit of looking glass between them, seem pretty friendlily disposed.

The window curtains very wisely are not drawn, as they would be blown right across the room and probably over the two greasy muttons which are on the table, giving just light enough to see the results of their evident attempts to outvie each other trying which can make the better snuff. One of them is quite a splendid fellow, a sort of black cauliflower, and I don't like to destroy him, so I send you a picture of him.

I hope this very interesting letter will reach you safely, dearest … There is a horrible harp, upon which really and truly somebody has every few minutes for the last three hours been strumming these chords all the same.

Goodbye my dearest love,
Yours,
I.K. Brunel'

Such were the joys of life on the line. It is little wonder he was tempted to grab a night at home with his wife.

The one thing we do know was that Isambard loved children and liked to amuse them with tricks. One of these led to a famous incident in April 1843, when he was showing off his conjuring skills and accidentally swallowed half a sovereign which stuck in his trachea. His surgeon, Sir Benjamin Brodie, described what happened next in a paper read to the Royal Medical and Chirurgical Society. After he swallowed the coin, Isambard vomited violently and afterwards coughed a great deal. It seemed there were no other symptoms for a while, but a few days later he was off on his travels, spending a great deal of time facing a cold east wind. Now the coughing returned, he vomited again and noticed blood and a small piece of membrane and afterwards had a severe pain in his chest, close to the right bronchus. He continued to have problems, but it was two weeks after the event before he consulted a doctor – and was seen by three eminent men, including Brodie. After examination, they all concluded that the coin was indeed in the right bronchia of the trachea. It was Isambard himself who suggested a way of dislodging it. He was strapped to a board, pivoted at the centre, which was then swivelled so that his body was about 80° to the horizontal with his head facing down. He was then slapped on the back, but all this produced was violent coughing and the patient was in danger of choking. The attempt was abandoned. The doctors consulted about what to do next. They decided to make an opening in his chest and try to remove the coin using forceps. This attempt failed: they never felt the coin and the unfortunate patient was coughing so violently that they abandoned that idea. The next plan was to combine the two previous attempts. Isambard was once again strapped to the swinging board, with the chest kept open. This time with more slaps on the back, Isambard suddenly felt the coin rap against his teeth before it fell out of his mouth. The ordeal was over, a month after he had first swallowed the coin. Three weeks later, he was well enough to make a trip into the country to recuperate. He was inevitably soon back at work, supervising his many concerns.

As work progressed from the two ends, it became essential to start thinking seriously about the locomotives that would use the track. They would be needed both to help in moving the materials needed for construction, and once sufficient lengths of track had been opened, begin providing services that would bring in revenue to help pay for the steadily increasing building costs.

Chapter 12

THE LOCOMOTIVES AND THE WORKS

George Henry Gibbs was a director of the company, and a staunch supporter of Brunel. His diary, edited by Jack Simmons and published in 1971, covers the crucial period from 1836 to 1839 and provides a unique insight into the troubled story of the company in those years. On 7 June 1837, he simply notes that the Committee was to deal with the 'important question' of 'immediately giving out orders for engines'. It sounds very straightforward, but it has to be remembered that no one had built for the broad gauge before. Nevertheless, Brunel took note of what was happening elsewhere and then, as usual, made his own decisions. He laid down two limiting factors on speed and weight in designing the engines: the 'standard speed' should be thirty miles an hour; piston speed should not exceed 280ft per minute; and the weight of the engine, fully fuelled and with the boiler full, should not exceed 5½ tons if carried on six wheels and 8 tons on four. This was quite extraordinary. Other engines were being built with piston speeds of 500ft per minute and in 1830 Robert Stephenson had introduced his highly-successful Planet class of locomotives, which weighed in at 10 tons but were carried on just four wheels. These were of course built for the Stephenson gauge – had they been scaled up to broad gauge they would have been far heavier, but as we shall see, that would not have reduced their performance.

Among the first locomotives to be ordered were *Thunderer* and *Hurricane*, designed by T.F. Harrison and built at the Hawthorn works in Newcastle. It has been suggested that Harrison was the engineer who influenced Brunel's thinking on engine design – if so, he must soon have regretted his advice. To meet the strange design limitations and to gain sufficient power in spite of the slow piston speed, the engines had to be built with massive drive wheels. This inevitably made the locomotive too heavy to meet Brunel's other requirement about weight. The first, *Hurricane*, was built with a separate boiler and power unit. The actual power unit at the front had a 2-2-2 wheel arrangement and a ten foot diameter drive wheel. It was little more than a platform for the steam cylinders and connecting links. The boiler and footplate were coupled on behind, carried on six wheels and superficially looked like a conventional locomotive. Steam passed between the two units down a flexible pipe. When working, there also had to be the addition of a tender behind the boiler. To describe these two engines as freaks seems an understatement. Two other engines were also ordered, this time from the Haigh Foundry in Wigan. They were geared locomotives and though not as odd as the Hawthorn engines, proved hopelessly ineffective. Two more came from the Vulcan foundry – all meeting Brunel's quirky rules and none of them proving a success. Gibbs did take a ride on *Thunderer* and declared himself to be well pleased on the whole:

> 'I went backward and forward on it twice. In some places we had the knocks, which we had observed before at Drayton, but this we were told occurred only when the screws were not completely screwed down. Along the greatest part of the four miles the engine ran beautifully smooth and for some way we cleared sixty miles an hour.'

But the engine was running light, and it soon became apparent that when rolling stock was added, the engine struggled and there was a recurring problem with leakages from the flexible piping between boiler and power unit.

There were grumblings of disquiet among the directors of the company, particularly from what came to be known as the Liverpool group. The Bristol and London investors had bought shares because they saw the line as benefitting their communities and their own business interests. The Liverpool group had simply seen their investment as a means of making a good profit – largely on the basis of the success of their local railway, the Liverpool & Manchester. The Stephenson line being worked with Stephenson locomotives was a success. They tended to regard the broad gauge as an expensive, and probably unnecessary, luxury but were prepared to go along with it, provided the promised results of improved performance materialised. They were never convinced, however, that Brunel would ever produce results as good as those supplied by George and Robert Stephenson. They would have loved an excuse to get rid of their young engineer. It was obvious that the railway needed far more effective locomotives or it would turn into a total disaster. At this point, the story becomes a little less clear, but one thing is certain – at the centre of the change was a young man, Daniel Gooch.

Gooch was born in 1816. His father was chief cashier and bookkeeper at the Bedlington Iron Works in Northumberland, in which his maternal grandfather was a partner. The company dealt with some of the leading engineers of the day, and this was an area which greatly appealed to the young boy. He was educated at a private school until he was fourteen. When his father moved down to South Wales to take over the management of the Tredegar iron works, Daniel was taken on as an apprentice. Looking back on his time there, he described it as a marvellous time, where he acquired his basic engineering skills. Later, he moved to the Robert Stephenson locomotive works at Forth Street, Newcastle. In 1836, when still only 20 years old, he was already working as locomotive superintendent at Forth Street and it was at this time that work was being carried out on two locomotives built for a 5ft 6in gauge line overseas. Here, the story becomes slightly complicated. Gooch in later life wrote that they were built for Russia, but other sources say that they were for the New Orleans & Nashville Railway. The latter seems the most likely. There is then the question of who designed these engines. One thing that at least is clear is that they were firmly based on an existing type of locomotive designed by Robert Stephenson – the Patentee class. They were a development from the highly successful Planet class. The name Patentee derives from a patent taken out by Stephenson for using flangeless drive wheels, which made it easier for the engine to move round tight curves. No doubt many adjustments had to be made in adapting to the wider gauge, and as Robert Stephenson was very busy elsewhere, the work would have been down to Gooch to sort out. He wrote that he was 'delighted in having so much room to arrange the engine'.

As a result of his work on these engines, Gooch became convinced that far better engines could be built for a broader gauge than were already being constructed at Forth Street, a view close to blasphemy in the Stephenson world. He decided that his future lay with Brunel and he tried to set up a meeting. This didn't happen, but he left Forth Street and went to work with his brother Tom on the Manchester & Leeds Railway. But he was still set on joining the broad gauge enterprise and wrote to Brunel. This time he was successful, a meeting was arranged, and Daniel Gooch was appointed locomotive superintendent in August 1836, just before his 21st birthday. It seems incredible to us now that anyone should be given such a position at so young an age, but this was a young man's world. The three engineers who at that time were in charge of the most important railway projects in Britain – Robert Stephenson, Locke and Brunel – were themselves just over thirty. Gooch may have been young, but he was one of the few young men around with practical experience in locomotive design and construction. In any case, Brunel must have been delighted to find anyone who shared his wholehearted enthusiasm for the broad gauge. They were, however, very different characters, Brunel lively and mercurial, Gooch somewhat dour and straitlaced. On one occasion, when Brunel invited Gooch to a party in London at the lively Horsley house, the latter wrote that he only got as far as the staircase, disgusted by what he described as unseemly behaviour.

Gooch's first job was to try and make the existing locomotives work efficiently, a thankless task and one which was never likely to succeed. Gooch did, however, apparently remember that only one of the 5ft 6in locomotives had actually been delivered, before the company that had placed the order ran out of money, a fact that supports the view it was originally intended for America. He suggested that it could easily be adapted to fit the 7ft gauge, and the engine was duly ordered, and renamed *North Star*. The engine had 7ft diameter drive wheels and like all Patentee type locomotives, an outside frame. Gooch was to claim that he had designed the engine and was certainly responsible for bringing it to the Great Western, but the main features were certainly down to the Stephenson original, which in turn had been developed from the earlier Planet class. Whoever was responsible, Brunel was delighted with it, which was hardly surprising since it was the only reliable locomotive he had at work at that time. It was delivered to Maidenhead, where it waited unsteamed until the line reached there from London in 1838.

In spite of a successful opening run to Maidenhead on 31 May 1838, criticism of Brunel, headed by the Liverpool contingent, continued unabated. On 5 July 1838, Gibbs wrote in his diary:

'We had a painful discussion today at the Railway Office, having received an intimation from some of our Liverpool proprietors of their intention to call a special meeting. The Chairman proposed instead that our August meeting should be adjourned a fortnight, to allow time for a consideration of our report. I was unprepared for such a serious measure, and I much fear that it will open the door to many unpleasant propositions from our northern proprietors who are bent upon crushing Brunel and are availing themselves of the fall in shares brought about by the stock-jobbers to accomplish their object. I really believe that we would have done exceedingly well if they had only left us alone. The line is improving daily.'

A few days later, he noted that Brunel himself had suggested that two or three competent engineers should be asked to report on the condition of the line. One of those approached was Robert Stephenson, who wrote back to Brunel with a very frank and responsible letter:

'I find it quite out of my powers to report on your permanent way – I have written to Sanders declining to do so. I have carefully considered what

A replica of *North Star* built in the 1920s and now in the Steam Museum, Swindon.

I saw at Maidenhead and I am compelled to say that my former views as to the increased width of the Rails as well as the plan of laying them remains unchanged, you will I am sure readily see how unpleasant my position would be, if I expressed myself in an unequivocal manner in my report; and to do otherwise would be making myself ridiculous since my opinions are very generally known – To report my opinions therefore would do harm instead of good to the cause in which you are interested and this I am sincerely desirous of avoiding.'

This would be a disappointment to the Liverpudlians who would have been looking for Stephenson to do a thorough demolition job on Brunel and all his works. In the event, the engineers selected were John Hawkshaw, engineer for the Manchester & Leeds Railway, and Nicholas Wood, one of the railway pioneers. Wood decided that he would enlist expert scientific advice and actually selected none other than the man who had so seriously got the Box tunnel wrong, Dr Dionysus Lardner. Hawkshaw's report was first in and was strong on criticism but bereft of constructive suggestions.

Gibbs dismissed it sourly as ill-natured, adding that he could have written the whole thing without bothering to see the line, since it contained little more than generalities. When it was presented to the meeting, Brunel easily dealt with the whole thing, and nothing was decided as they waited for the Wood report. Where Hawkshaw had been brief, Wood was verbose. There seemed to be just one salient point – he felt the vertical piles were superfluous and Brunel readily agreed, pointing out that he had already decided to have them removed. He had discovered from experience that the track was far more stable without them and would now have the necessary 'give'. There were still those who wanted Brunel's head on a platter and put forward a suggestion that he should work with an associate engineer, either Locke or Stephenson. As they were confirmed opponents of the broad gauge, Brunel's position would have been untenable. Now it was the turn of Dr Lardner to present his pseudo-scientific mumbo-jumbo in which he 'proved' that *North Star* was incapable of ever reaching the speeds claimed for it. In fact, early performances had been poor in trials, and though the locomotive had been able to reach 37mph with a load of 33 tons, when the load was 82 tons it dropped to a niggardly 33mph. Lardner's answer to why the performance was so poor was that due to the wide track and size of the locomotive, it was held back by wind resistance – even though he had earlier expected any steam engine to career through Box tunnel at over 100mph because he had ignored wind resistance. What he did not know and nor did the meeting as a whole, was that Brunel and Gooch had been themselves worried about performance and instead of turning to theory took the trouble to examine the locomotive to see what might be wrong. They soon discovered that the blast pipe that took exhaust steam up the chimney, and was essential in drawing air through the firebox, had been wrongly positioned. They enlarged and moved it, with excellent results. On 29 December, they had made a journey from Paddington to Maidenhead with a 43 ton load at an average speed of 38mph. This was the average, one should note, so at times it would have been travelling a good deal faster. As soon as Wood and Dr Lardner's views had been heard, the results of the new trial were produced, demolishing their theoretical pronouncements. After that, although the Liverpool faction still wanted to have their way and insisted on a vote with a view to removing Brunel, the issue was really not in doubt. The shareholders voted by 7,790 votes to 6,145 to preserve the status quo. Brunel had won the battle for the broad gauge, at least for the time being, and for his own career,

The success of *North Star* led to more Star class locomotives being constructed, the first of which, *Fire Fly,* was built in 1840. One of the notable features of the engine was the high, domed firebox, in a style that came to be known as Gothic. In initial trials, it was recorded as reaching a speed of 58mph while pulling three vehicles. It was, however, obvious that the company would need to have its own locomotive, carriage and maintenance facilities and the search began for a suitable site, preferably one near the centre of the line, which would also serve as a locomotive depot. Daniel Gooch found what he considered the ideal spot and explained his reasoning in a long letter to Brunel on 13 September 1840:

'According to your wish I give you my views on the best site for our principal engine establishment, and in doing so I have studied the convenience of the Great Western Railway only. But also I think the same point is the only place adapted for the Cheltenham and Great Western. The point I refer to is the Junction at Swindon of the two lines.

'The only objection I see to Swindon is the bad supply of water. There is also an apparent inequality of distance or duty for the engines to work – but which is very much equalized when the circumstances attending it are taken into account. I find the actual distances are as 76½ to 41 and the gradients for the short distance of 41 miles a rise of 318 feet or 7.75 feet per mile and for the 76½ miles a rise of 292 feet or 3.8 feet per mile.

'Swindon being the point at which these gradients change, the different gradients necessarily require a different class of engine, requiring for the Bristol end a more powerful one than for the London end.

'That power can only be obtained conveniently by reducing the diameter of the Driving Wheels, therefore supposing we work between Swindon and Bristol with 6 feet wheels, and between Swindon and London with 7 feet wheels, there will actually be very little difference between the work required of the two engines when the additional gradients and curves, and the increased number of revolutions per minute are taken into account … a large station at Swindon would also enable us to keep our Bank engines for Wootton Bassett incline at Swindon instead of having a separate station for the purpose at the bottom of the incline, and in addition it would at any rate be necessary to have a considerable station at Swindon to work the Cheltenham line, which would be saved if Swindon was our principal station.'

He continued by pointing out that as the Wilts and Berks Canal was nearby, there would be no problem of bringing fuel to the depot, and that the water problem could probably be overcome by building reservoirs. Finally, he noted that he had not considered the line from Bristol to Exeter in making his decision, as the engines for that section could be kept at Bristol.

The letter is interesting not just in showing how thoroughly Gooch had thought about the problem, but also for the light it shines on locomotive performance at that time. The incline at Wootton Bassett was just over a mile long at a gradient of a modest 1:100, yet it was thought necessary to have a banking engine on hand to provide extra power to get up the slope. By 1848, however, it was noted that it was being worked 'without any extraordinary assistance' – a tribute to the advances being made in locomotive design by Gooch.

At the beginning of the nineteenth century, Swindon was a small market town, with around 1,500 inhabitants. There was a need to recruit skilled workers but nowhere suitable to house them. The only solution was to build homes that would themselves attract the best men and their families to live there. The Company would build New Swindon, and the man who was given the job of designing it was the architect, Matthew Digby Wyatt, a young man just at the beginning of his career. He would later add the architectural embellishments to the new Paddington station. The first houses to be built were laid out as six streets in a regular grid with a square in the centre.

The houses were built to a very high standard, quite unlike the semi-slums that disfigured so many industrial towns in the nineteenth century. They were constructed of the attractive local stone, much of it coming from the excavations at Box Hill. Each house had at least two bedrooms, a small front garden and a yard at the back with a privy. The Company laid on water and supplied gas for lighting from their own plant. Over the years, the town was extended and more facilities added including a church and a school for the children. The Mechanics' Institute was opened in 1845, where the men could be taught subjects useful in their work, such as mathematics, and their wives could receive basic lessons in reading and writing. Land was bought in 1844 and became a park open to the workforce and their families and, most usefully of all, a hospital was built, with a staff that included eight medical officers, a consultant surgeon and three dentists. At the height of its success, the GWR was employing some 10,000 workers, who were enjoying facilities that many other workers at the time could only look on with envy.

The first works buildings to be completed were the main engine house and the smaller engine house for light repairs. The main engine house was a massive 490ft by 70ft. The light repair shed was 290ft by 140ft and was carefully arranged for maximum efficiency.

Locomotives could be run onto a traverser, that could move up and down the length of the shed. On either side were stalls, thirty-six altogether, and

The restored houses of New Swindon, built to a design by Matthew Digby Wyatt.

the traverser would trundle down until it was opposite an empty booth where the engine could be rolled in for treatment. The first locomotive to be built at Swindon went into service in 1846. Gooch developed the Star class of locomotives by increasing the drive wheel to 8ft diameter and when that proved successful, he developed it into a whole new class. The first to be built was *Iron Duke* with a much larger firebox but without the Gothic dome. It proved to be too heavy for the standard 2-2-2 wheel arrangement so was rebuilt as a 4-2-2, though the two pairs of leading wheels were rigid within the frame, not set on a sperate bogie. It was a great success, at once achieving speeds of over 50mph with a load of over a hundred tons, and when working on a 1:100 downward slope reached around 80mph.

Swindon station was duly built with a refreshment room and an agreement was reached that trains would stop for ten minutes to allow passengers to use the facilities. Many must have been glad of the chance to leave the

The engine shed at Swindon, showing a locomotive on a traverser, ready to be wheeled into an empty booth for repair.

A working replica of *Iron Duke* at the National Railway Museum. It is currently at the Didcot Rail Centre.

train, for in the days when there were no corridor carriages, only closed compartments for the first and second class passengers, the chance of what might euphemistically be called light relief would have been welcome. As well as the refreshment rooms, there was a station hotel for passengers wanting overnight accommodation. Unfortunately, the company let out all these facilities on a long lease, with no provision for exercising any control over the quality of service. Brunel famously was scathing in a letter to the proprietor.

'I assure you Mr. Player was wrong in supposing that I thought you purchased inferior coffee. I thought I said to him I was surprised you should buy such bad roasted corn. I did not believe you had such a thing as coffee in the place. I am certain I never tasted any. I have long since ceased to make complaints at Swindon. I avoid taking anything there when I can help it.'

The present refreshment room is nowhere near as grand as that in Brunel's day, but fortunately the coffee at least is better.

Swindon was not the only place along the route that was transformed, at least for a time, by the arrival of the railway. The village of Steventon would hardly have warranted a station, but it had a special significance when the

The first-class refreshment room at Swindon station that looks splendid, but where the offerings failed to match the surroundings.

line was first built. It was here that passengers got off and walked to the local inn to wait for the stagecoach to Oxford. Once the line from Didcot to Oxford was opened, Steventon slid back into obscurity and today trains simply rush past without a pause. There was until recently one reminder of the railway years with a local pub – the North Star.

By 1841, the whole line from Bristol to London was nearing completion. The great Box tunnel was finally completed in March of that year and was an engineering triumph. In spite of the slope, the roof formed a continuous line, and the walls, worked out from shafts and entrances, all met to within 1¼ inches. At first, it was only laid with a single track, and the day after the opening almost brought the first tragedy. Gooch was on the footplate of a locomotive in the tunnel, when it became apparent that another locomotive was entering the tunnel and heading straight towards him. Fortunately, rapid engagement of the reverse gear avoided the catastrophe. On 30 June, the line was officially opened, and the directors left London in a train bedecked with flags, arriving in Bristol four hours later. They then continued as far as Bridgewater, the first section of the Exeter line to be completed. The great work was complete, but there was no rest for Isambard. He had other projects to keep him constantly busy and still constantly on the move.

A train headed by *Fire Fly* emerging from Box tunnel. The driver is being given the 'all clear' hand signal. One of J.C. Bourne's illustrations of the GWR.

Chapter 13

THE *GREAT WESTERN*

Steamships were not a novelty in the 1830s. The first successful paddle steamer had been developed as early as 1783 when the *Pyroscaphe,* designed by the Marquis Jouffroy d'Abbans, chugged down the Sâone near Lyons. The French could well have established a lead in modern shipbuilding had the country not been convulsed by political revolution. Just five years later, the British inventor William Symington built a steam engine which he used to work a small boat on a lake near Dumfries and the poet Robert Burns was one of the first passengers to enjoy this novel form of transport. Encouraged by this success, Symington designed a steam tug for use on the Forth & Clyde Canal. The craft had a modest ten horsepower engine, but in a demonstration in 1802, it hauled two 70-ton barges along a twenty mile stretch of the canal in about six hours in spite of a strong headwind. The company, however, decided that the churning paddle wheels would erode the bank and the experiment came to an end. The next development was the work of an American, Robert Fulton, who actually managed to set up a regular service between Albany and New York with his paddle steamer *Clermont* in 1807. Five years later, the British finally acquired a steamer service on the Clyde and up and down Scotland's west coast with David Napier's little steamer *Comet.*

The early steamers were limited to working in rivers or in coastal waters, but in 1819 the *Savannah* that was being built as a conventional three-masted, square rigged sailing ship was bought by Captain Moses Rogers with the backing of the Savannah Steamship Company. He installed a 90 horsepower engine with the intention of making the first Atlantic crossing using steam. However, it was never intended to steam the whole way – there was simply not enough space for fuel. Instead, she was designed with special paddle wheels, that could be folded up like a fan and stowed on board when not in use. The idea was to carry on under sail, until the wind dropped, then attach the wheels and work under steam until the wind picked up. She set off from Charleston, South Carolina, on 14 April 1819, arriving in Liverpool on 20 June. En route, the captain of the schooner *Contract* spotted what he thought was a ship on fire, and changed course to go to the rescue, only to discover that he was witnessing a steamer out in the Atlantic. Other Atlantic crossings were made with sailing ships fitted with auxiliary steam engines, but up to the 1830s no crossing using only steam had been made. However, it was clear that such a crossing would be made at some time, once someone had worked out how to carry enough fuel without using up so much space that voyages would be uneconomical.

Marc Brunel had been offered an opportunity to design a steamer that could travel from Europe to the West Indies but had declined. However, when at a meeting of the Great Western Railway board in 1835 one of the directors pessimistically surmised that it was simply too great a distance for a railway to go all the way from Bristol to London, Isambard rather jokingly replied – why stop at Bristol, why not go on to New York? Did he mean it seriously? Perhaps not, but one of the directors did, Thomas Guppy, his old friend and supporter. They met after a dinner in October 1835 at Radley's Hotel in Bristol and discussed the idea at length and as a result took their ideas to Christopher Claxton, the former naval officer and another friend of Brunel's, and William Patterson. The latter was a Bristol shipbuilder who had been born at Arbroath in Scotland in 1795 but moved to England where he was apprenticed as a shipwright at Rotherhithe. He made a number of moves, each time to a more responsible position. He became foreman at the William Evans yard, which specialised in steamers. He then moved as assistant to William Scott in Bristol. When Scott went bankrupt in 1830, he took over the yard himself. His first vessel was a paddle steamer for the Bristol Channel trade, but he was equally competent in building sailing ships, including an innovative schooner with very fine lines and a big West Indiaman. His experience was invaluable.

Isambard had carved little model ships as a boy, but that hardly qualified him as having any special knowledge, either of the sea or shipbuilding. On the other hand, his father had an intimate knowledge of what was entailed in Atlantic crossings from his experiences in the French navy, and from his time in America – and had indeed himself designed the paddle steamer for the Ramsgate tourist trade. Father and son would have had a lot to talk about as the project became a reality. The popular view was that steamships would never be able to complete an Atlantic crossing, because there would never be enough space available for fuel. This was backed up by, inevitably, that ubiquitous scientist, Dr Dionysus Lardner. In an address to the British Association for the Advancement of Science, he explained that the power needed to move a ship was directly related to its displacement, so that doubling the size would simply double the fuel needed. He ended with the pronouncement that the idea of steaming from New York to Liverpool was 'perfectly chimerical, and they might as well talk of making a voyage from New York or Liverpool to the moon'.

For an allegedly eminent scientist, Dr Lardner seems to have forgotten basic scientific principles. Two millennia before, Archimedes had shown that a floating vessel displaces its own weight in water – this is the measure used for a ship's displacement or tonnage. In other words, the weight of the ship is supported by the water. Power is needed to overcome water resistance – and to a lesser extent air resistance – and this is dependent on surface area not the volume. A very simple analogy might make the idea easier to understand. Imagine you are trying to push a cube against a resistant surface. Say that the cube has sides of one metre long, then the area of the face pushing against the obstacle is one square metre and the volume one cubic metre. Now suppose this requires one unit of power. Next double everything. The cube has two metre sides, the area pushing forward is four square metres, requiring four power units. But the volume is now eight cubic metres, so there's twice as much space as needed for fuel. In ships, the same idea applies; the force needed is proportional to the area of the hull, etc. – doubling size does not mean doubling the fuel needed.

Guppy set off on a short tour of ports in Britain to assess just how successful steamships were and found that everywhere there was a move towards building larger vessels. Encouraged, he put up £15,000 of his own money towards the project. Soon other shipping men in Bristol followed his lead and the Great Western Steam-Ship Company was formed, with an initial capital of £250,000. The building committee would consist of Guppy, Claxton and Brunel and Patterson would build to Brunel's design. Isambard himself was the consultant engineer. The chairman was Peter Maze, who was one of the supporters of the Great Western Railway. For once, Brunel could be confident that he had the complete support of everyone in power in the new company. Another favourable sign was that Patterson was described by a contemporary as being known as 'a man open to conviction and not prejudiced in favour of other quaint or old-fashioned notions of ship building'.

During Marc Brunel's time at Chatham, he would have been aware of the master shipwright Robert Seppings, who had introduced some new ideas into the conservative world of naval shipbuilding. His two most important innovations were the use of diagonal strappings to strengthen the hull and iron knees to replace the wooden knees that had traditionally joined the deck planks to the sides. Thanks to the diagonal trusses, it had been possible to build longer vessels without the risk of hogging – the tendency in wooden vessels to droop at bow and stern. This method was used for the construction of the new steamer. Another new technology was patented by John Kyan in 1832, which was to use mercuric dichloride to preserve timber and protect against rot. The process came to be known as Kyanisation and was used for the new vessel. Protection against the marine worm was supplied by copper sheathing to the bottom of the hull. Brunel's concern throughout this was to ensure the vessel had longitudinal strength to withstand the buffetings that were unavoidable in Atlantic crossings at some time or other. The vessel was, it is clear, to be made as strong as possible by using all the latest techniques available in the construction of wooden ships.

There was then the task of finding an appropriate engine for the new vessel. Tenders were requested from the leading manufacturer, but the choice went to Maudslay, Sons & Field, a company already well known in the Brunel family, who appreciated their reliability. The accepted design was for a side lever engine. This is rather like a beam engine, except that here there are a pair of beams, below the level of the cylinder, one end being attached to a cross head above the cylinder by a connecting rod, while the other end works a cranked axle. There were a pair of these cylinders, each able to work one or both paddle wheels. This type of engine was common in paddle steamers, because of the low centre of gravity, which aided stability. Steam was provided by four boilers at the very low pressure of just five pounds per square inch, but the engines produced a grand total of 750 indicated horsepower.

The vessel was not the only contender for the glory of being the first vessel to cross the Atlantic under steam for the whole voyage. Work had already begun at the Carling and Young shipyard in London on the *Royal Victoria*, later renamed the *British Queen*. Everything was seemingly going well, until news arrived from Scotland that the manufacturers who were supplying the engine had gone bankrupt with the work only partly completed. There was a rush to find another supplier, and the company turned to Napier, but there was an inevitable long delay and their initial advantage had slipped away. Another vessel, the *Liverpool*, was to be built in that city and was to sail from there. She was not likely to be ready in time either.

No such problems were troubling the yard at Bristol. Everything was ready for the official launch on 19 July 1837 before a crowd of some 50,000 spectators. Captain Claxton broke a bottle of madeira over the figurehead and Mrs. Smith, mother of the Bristol member of Parliament, officially named the ship *Great Western* and she floated out into the Cumberland basin. The ship carried

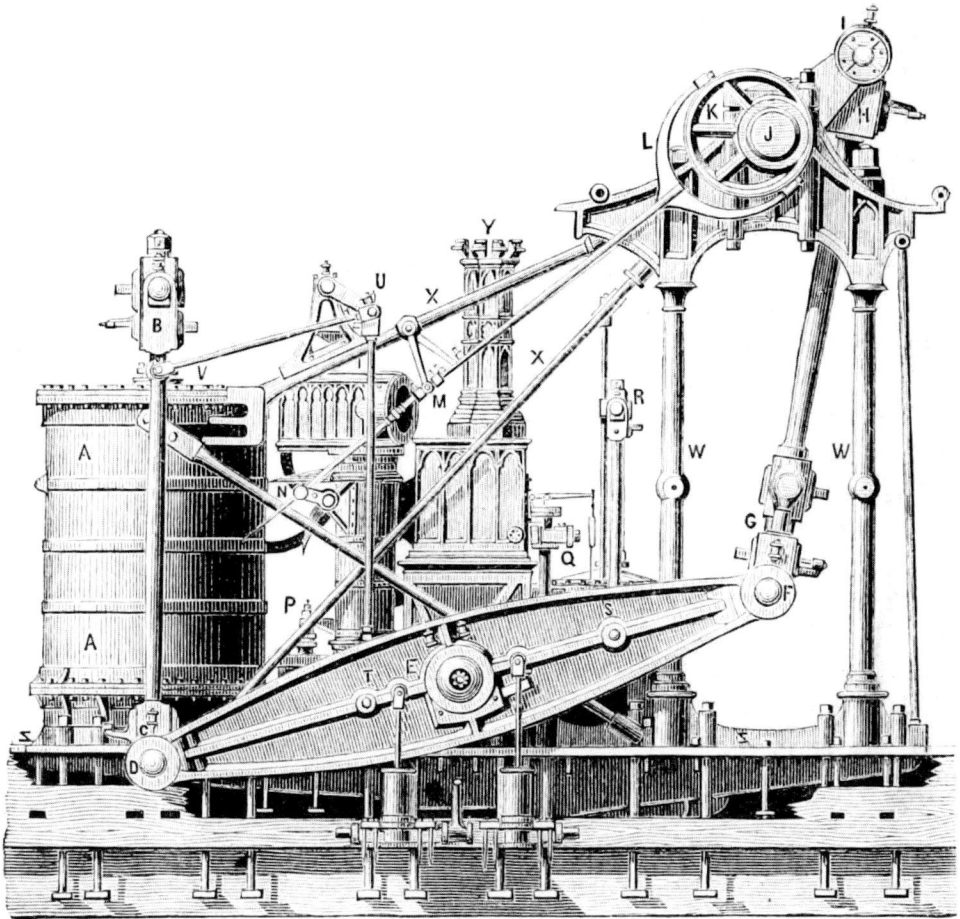

A typical side lever steam engine of the type regularly used in paddle steamers.

sail on four masts and a month later, accompanied by the tug *Lion* and a coastal packet, she set sail for London, where she was to be fitted out and where the machinery would be installed. Once the vessel arrived in London, she attracted huge interest. Outwardly there was nothing, apart from size, to attract attention, but the interior was unlike anything ever seen on a ship before. The centrepiece was the great public room, seventy-five foot long and twenty-one foot wide, and decorated with fifty large, painted panels, described as showing rural scenes, agriculture, the arts, the sciences, landscapes and interiors, while smaller panels had mythological characters, such as cupids and Psyche. The overall style selected by Brunel was in the fashionable Gothic. One commentator noted that it was a room that could 'vie with those of the clubhouses of London in luxury and magnificence'. It was estimated that 1,000 visitors a day came to stare at the wonderful ship, incuding the Duke of Wellington and the Lord Mayor of London. There was, of course, one other interested visitor – Marc Brunel.

Inevitably, as in any Brunel project, there were innovations. One of these was the bell system installed to allow passengers to summon a steward. The passenger pulled a bell rope and the bell in a box in the stewards' room tinkled, and at the same time, it activated a lever that forced up a tin tab with the room number that popped up through a slit in the box. It remained in view until a steward saw it, cancelled it and scurried up to the appropriate cabin. One other innovation was introduced to the engine room. One of the problems that threatened any Atlantic crossing was the supply of fresh water for the boilers – there was water aplenty all around the ship, but salt water and boilers are not happy companions. Fortunately, a patent had been taken out in 1833 by a Nottingham engineer, Samuel Hall, for a new type of condenser. This allowed the pure steam exhaust vapour to be turned back into pure water for reuse. This was an idea that had already been put forward by Marc Brunel.

The only people who were dismayed rather than delighted by the sight of the *Great Western* were the proprietors of the British and American Steam Navigation Company. They had hoped to have the honour of being the owners of the first ship to cross the Atlantic in steam for the whole voyage. Had things gone according to plan, the honour would undoubtedly have gone to the *Royal Victoria* but thanks to the delays in supplying the engine, that was not going to happen. But they were still determined to be the first across the Atlantic. They began looking around for a suitable vessel and they found what they were looking for in a coastal steamer belonging to the St. George Steam Packet Company, the *Sirius*. She was a compact, wooden two-masted vessel of 700 tons, somewhat austere in appearance, apart from her figurehead, which was a dog holding Sirius, the dog star, in its paws. Her normal voyages took her to London, Plymouth and Cork, but now she had to be prepared for an Atlantic crossing. She had none of the grandeur of the Brunel ship and she was to carry just forty passengers on the great voyage, while the *Great Western* was advertising '128 sleeping places for one class of passenger … and good bed places for servants'.

The two vessels were ready at much the same time, but the *Great Western* was out on a sea trial on 28 March 1838, with a group of dignitaries on board, including Brunel, when they were surprised to see their rival steaming out of the Thames, not on a trial run but at the start of her Atlantic crossing. It came as a shock to the Brunel party, but they knew that the smaller vessel was going to stop off at Cork to take coal on board. It certainly brought a sense of urgency to the *Great Western* party, and on 31 March, trials concluded, they set sail for Bristol. Everyone was still confident that, with their greater speed and power, they would still be first to New York. There is no doubt they could have been, but they had scarcely left the Thames estuary and were just passing Leigh-on-Sea when flames and smoke suddenly erupted from the forward boiler room. The chief engineer, George Pearne, took a deep breath and plunged down into the smoke filled engine room. He opened up all the boiler feed cocks and put on a feed plunger. It was soon apparent that the fire was actually caused by the boiler lagging that had been wrapped too close to the furnace flues below the funnel and had become so hot that it had suddenly ignited, setting fire to the deck beams and planking.

Captain Claxton rushed down to help Pearne, by hosing down the burning timbers. Brunel was desperate to see what had happened and started off down the ladder into the boiler room. Unfortunately, the fire had caused a rung to buckle and as he put his foot on it, the rung gave way and Brunel plunged 18 feet to what could possibly have been his death. Instead of hitting the hard deck below, however, he landed on top of Claxton. He was unconscious, but alive, though his head was under the water that was collecting from the attempts to quell the fire. Claxton dragged him clear of the water, called for a rope and had him hauled back on deck. Brunel regained consciousness, but in spite of pain, he insisted on being left alone while all the efforts were concentrated on putting out the fire.

In the midst of all this activity, the captain, Lt James Hosken R.N., decided that to preserve the vessel it was essential to ground her, and headed towards Canvey Island and she came to rest on the Chapman Sands. Isambard was placed in a ship's boat, which was taken across to the island, where he was to stay for several weeks, recuperating. He was to miss being present at one of the great moments in his career, but he never was very interested in the actual crossing – his work had been done. Meanwhile, the vessel floated off at the next high tide. Being bed-ridden and in considerable pain, Brunel was not about to give up all control of events. He sent off a long letter full of instructions about what needed to be done to get her ready for the Atlantic crossing.

Once under way, the ship made good time to Bristol, arriving on 2 April, to the considerable surprise of the citizens who had received alarming reports that she had been destroyed in the fire – and yet when she appeared, all they could see were a few badly charred planks. But the rumours had done nothing to reassure the passengers, most of whom cancelled their reservations, leaving just seven stalwarts ready to make the journey. There was a period of bustle and hurry, as everything was got ready to sail on the 7th, only for bad weather to keep her in harbour until the following day. The bad news reached Bristol that *Sirius* had left Cork on the 4th, which was not merely a four day advantage, but the port was a full day's sailing nearer to New York. The race it seemed had been lost even before the *Great Western* could weigh anchor.

The *Sirius* had at first, it seems, a comparatively uneventful voyage, though eight days out from Cork, she had to hove to in order to refasten some of her floats on the paddle wheels that had come loose. The weather was not always kind. On the twelfth day, there was a violent storm, but Captain Roberts blithely noted the vessel was 'behaving nobly and riding like a duck'. On 17 April, there was what even the unflappable Roberts was forced to describe as a dangerous sea and 'snow to cool our energies', which apparently terrified the few passengers on board. Then on the evening of 22 April, she finally reached land and signalled for a pilot to bring her into New York. There was no reply and no pilot appeared and the captain was eventually forced to put her bows into a mudbank, having already stopped the engines, to prevent her wallowing uncontrollably. The next morning, she floated free and made her way into harbour in New York – very appropriately, it was St. George's Day.

Huge crowds welcomed her, but rumours spread that she had only just made it, having run out of coal just before arrival and been reduced to burning cabin doors to keep going. It was not true, but the bunkers were almost empty. In the meantime, the *Great Western* had been steadily gaining on her rival, though not without difficulties of her own. In his book, *The Sway of the Grand Saloon* (1971), John Malcom Brinnin records the views of some of the passengers as the ship hit the same bad weather that had troubled her rival. 'Sea sickness stalks in stifling horror among us, and the dreadful cry of "steward – steward" – the last ejaculation of despair, comes from a dozen nooks.' Then the nights were disturbed by a terrible racket to add to the tribulations of bad weather: 'The repose of last night might be compared to a tossing in a blanket, and a dance of pot-hooks and frying pans was nothing to the din of the glorious clatter among the moveables that accompanied it.' Much of the row came from bolts having come loose on one of the paddle wheels.

The crew were not much happier than the passengers, and they had the task of moving coal from the bunkers to the boilers in bad conditions. Pearne managed to persuade them to carry on by offering them an extra payment for

THE STEAMER GREAT WESTERN.

The paddle steamer *Great Western*.

working overtime. Everyone agreed except for one stoker called Crooks, who stopped work, got drunk and took to his bunk. The Captain ordered Crooks to be 'secured to the poop', but he resisted, attacked the captain and tried to shove him overboard. He was eventually overcome, but then the stokers warned they would come out on strike in sympathy unless he was released. So, Crooks was let free and left alone with an almighty hangover, which the captain treated with medicine. One can safely assume that the medicine was worse than the hangover. The crisis past, the great ship steamed on. Just after *Sirius* had docked in New York harbour, the *Great Western* dropped anchor off Sandy Hook. Then as she steamed past Ellis Island, she received a 26 gun salute – one for each of the then 26 states of the Union – and the ship replied in time-honoured fashion by dipping her colours. She received an immense reception, as described by James Gordon Bennett in the *Morning Herald*.

'The approach of the *Great Western* to the harbour, and in front of the Battery, was most magnificent. The sky was clear – the crowds immense. The Battery was filled with the human multitude, one half of them were females, their faces covered with smiles, and their delicate persons with the gayest attire. Below, on the broad blue water, appeared this huge thing of life, with four masts and emitting volumes of smoke. She looked black and blackguard, rakish, cool, reckless, and forbidding and sombre in the extreme.'

The papers in New York were full of similar eulogies, but little mention of the facts that really mattered. The big ship had been gaining on the smaller ship at the rate of 2 knots, or roughly 50 miles a day: the smaller ship had almost run out of coal, the big ship still had 200 tons of coal in her bunkers. Bigger really was best. There was one event to cast a pall over this day of triumph. Pearne, who had on arrival at the wharf in New York, at once written to Maudslays to tell them how well their engines had performed 'even beyond my expectations', then went down below to blow out the boilers and released the steam which erupted, fatally scalding him. The man who had saved the ship in the Thames and helped bring it across the Atlantic was dead.

Once the two vessels had made the Atlantic crossing, The *Royal William*, that had been hired to deputise for the *Liverpool* that was still unfinished, finally made it to New York in July, after a voyage of just short of nineteen days from Liverpool. She was the first to make the voyage from Liverpool, which was to become one of the main departure points for Transatlantic liners. She was followed by two others, the *British Queen* and the *Liverpool*, the two ships that had originally been planned for the route. Neither matched the performance of the Brunel ship, but that was immaterial, for Brunel was already beginning to think about how he might develop an even bigger and more powerful vessel. Meanwhile, the *Great Western* began a regular service, and by the end of 1844, she had made 54 voyages, with an average of 15 days 12 hours westward and 15 days 9 hours eastward, very close to the figure that Brunel suggested when she was first designed.

Chapter 14

THE *GREAT BRITAIN*

In September 1838, a notice appeared in the Bristol newspaper announcing that 'the Great Western Steamship Company was to build another vessel of equal size to the *Great Western*; she will be called the *City of New York*. A large cargo of African oak timber has been purchased for this and further ships.' The vessel would have had the dimensions of 205ft on the keel, a breadth of 35ft 4in and a depth of hold of 23ft, but Brunel was not happy simply to repeat earlier successes. Claxton, in his own account of building the ship, published in 1845, noted that the directors 'guided by the suggestion of that superior man' had agreed to increase the size to 254ft by 40ft but with the same hold depth. This was getting very close to the maximum size possible for a wooden hull. This was not the only change being proposed. Brunel was keen to increase the speed of the new vessel from 10.6 to 12 knots, which would require an engine with bigger cylinders. In November 1838, he wrote to Claxton setting out his ideas. He had worked out that the speed could be increased to the new rate by increasing the diameter of the cylinder from 73 to 85 inches. But at the same time, he was looking for more efficient working. This would involve cutting off the steam at about five-twelfths of the stroke and allowing it to expand in the cylinder for the rest of the stroke – a practice that was already common in steam locomotives. This would mean a further increase in cylinder size from 87.5 to 88in. He then asked Claxton if it might be possible to use 84in cylinders if the piston speed was increased to 240 from 220ft per minute.

The drive for a better, faster vessel led to some radical rethinking. It was obvious now to Brunel that size was the key to profitable Atlantic travel, but there was a problem. With the *Great Western* he had arrived very close to the maximum size that was possible for a wooden hull and he was pushing the technology now to its limits. There was, however, an alternative form of construction that had been around for decades. The Industrial Revolution had transformed the iron industry. Coke-fired blast furnaces had replaced the old charcoal variety, but they produced cast iron. That, however, was little use in ship building, but in 1784 Henry Cort patented his puddling furnace that transformed pig iron into wrought iron. Other iron masters were developing the industry. John Wilkinson had introduced a steam engine to provide the blast for his furnace, but he depended heavily on water transport to bring in the raw material and take out the finished product from his Shropshire works. He was an innovator, who not only looked for ways to improve production but also was on the look out for new ways in which iron might be used. He decided to build an iron barge. This was largely regarded as foolhardy. It is certainly counter-intuitive. Throw a piece of wood in the water and it floats, chuck in a lump of iron and it sinks. But Wilkinson was aware that it was the volume of air inside the hull that provided the buoyancy that kept the boat afloat, regardless of the material used. His first vessel, *The Trial*, was launched into the Severn in July 1787. 'It answers all my expectations,' he wrote, 'and it has unconvinced the unbelievers, who were 999 in a thousand'. A river barge is a long way from an ocean-going steamer, but it was a start, and once a start has been made, others will inevitably begin to develop the idea.

Over the next few years, several small iron vessels were built for inland waterways, but the first vessel to take to the seas was built in 1822 just about as far from the coast as you can get in Britain, at Tipton at the heart of the Birmingham Canal network. Charles Manby took out a patent for an iron steamboat and formed a manufacturing company. His first vessel was the *Aaron Manby*, still a comparatively small vessel, 180ft long by 17ft beam and 3ft 6in draught. She was built for the French waterways, but was too wide to fit into the English canal system, so she was sent in sections to London, assembled there and when completed set off down the Thames and made her way across the Channel to Le Havre and then on to Paris. So, iron ship building began to interest several people, including William Laird who set up the Birkenhead Iron Works, with the specific aim of building iron vessels. The first craft to be launched was a lighter for Ireland that took to the seas in 1829. In October 1838, the large iron-hulled clipper ship, the *Rainbow*, sailed into Bristol. It provided the ideal opportunity for the working committee to investigate an iron ship, and Claxton took the opportunity for a thorough survey of its seaworthiness. So, there were precedents for building in iron and it was obvious to Brunel that it was the one and only material that would enable him to build a new and bigger ship. Iron had a further advantage over timber – it took up less space. Claxton explained why in simple terms:

'Suppose all the angle irons or ribs, the shelves, etc were all rolled out flat and added to the thickness of the plates forming her sides, when an average thickness of 2ft of timber would be replaced by an average thickness of 2½ in. of iron, with far better ties, a more compact framework and greater strength, than wood can under any circumstances give.'

The argument was sound; the ship would be built of iron.

There were problems to be solved with the iron ship. Navigation relied on the magnetic compass, and unfortunately as well as pointing to the magnetic north pole, the compass needle is also attracted to iron. But the iron hull doesn't change and so its magnetic effect is constant and could be counteracted by positioning balancing magnets alongside the compass to cancel out the effect. There was also a problem with fouling on the hull and that problem remained with the iron ship for a long time. It was not, however, sufficiently problematic to prevent the development going ahead. By January 1839, a third version of the new vessel appeared, this time with an iron hull, a length of 260ft, breadth of 41ft and a depth of 14ft, and the engines would be as Brunel had suggested, built with 88in cylinders. But the more Brunel thought about the new vessel, the more his ideas changed – and each version he came up with was bigger than the last until eventually the length on the keel would be 289ft, with an overall length from the figurehead to the stern of 322ft, an extreme breadth of 50ft 6in and a depth from keel to upper deck of 32ft. There still remained a question to be answered – who would build and design the engines?

Brunel's first thought was to turn to the experienced and trusted company of Maudslay Sons & Field but it was decided to look at alternatives. There were designs from Seaward & Capel, which were quickly discarded, and from a young engineer who had developed a trunk engine, Francis Humphreys, and it was an engine of this type he was proposing for the new ship. This design of engine was considered particularly useful for ships as it was lower than conventional engines of the time, which both improved stability and saved space. The connecting rod travelled inside a wide, hollow tube – the trunk -which itself moved with the piston. A reproduction of an engine of this type can be seen in the restored nineteenth century warship, HMS *Warrior*, on show at Portsmouth Historic Dockyard. Humphreys first developed the idea with Halls of Dartford, but when the Great Western Company approached them, they showed little inclination to take on the task of manufacture. This, they said, would involve installing new machinery in their works, and they were not convinced, apparently, that if they built this engine there would be a successor, and if not the special machinery would not be needed again. They could, however, install the machinery, provided Bristol paid for it. They suggested an alternative. Perhaps the Great Western Company might consider manufacturing the engines themselves. This idea did have a certain appeal; the Company would be able to develop their own manufacturing capability for future projects. Maudslay had proposed constructing an engine with four 75in cylinders, which he claimed would provide the same power as the two 110in cylinders proposed by Humphreys. Brunel looked at the two proposals carefully. The estimated cost for Maudslay was £45,500 and that for Humphreys £50,700. Brunel, however, was not confident that the young engineer's estimate represented the true cost. 'The items seem to me to be moderate prices only for each article named and I see no allowance for those alterations, damages and a waste of parts and a variety of other contingencies which in a piece of machinery of this magnitude and novelty is certain to amount to a very large sum.' And although he saw the advantages of building in Bristol, he was also clear that there were considerable risks involved:

'The making of the vessel itself is no mean effort and to superadd the construction of the largest pair of engines and boilers yet made and upon a new plan is calculating very much upon every effort being successful and particularly upon the assistance of those who hitherto attended to the subject; as it must be well known to the Directors that if Mr. Guppy for instance should be prevented from giving his time as he has hitherto done or that Mr. Humphreys should from illness or other cause leave us the manufactory would be brought to a stand and the loss would be serious.'

In spite of these reservations, it was decided to go ahead with Humphreys' design, and he was placed in charge of construction. Almost immediately, a problem arose. No one could work out how to forge the immense shaft that was needed to connect the engines to the paddle wheels. At this date, forging was done using tilt hammers, which acted like giant mechanised versions of the blacksmith's arm and hammer. The butt of the hammer was lifted by cams on a rotating drum and then, as the cam was cleared, the hammer head fell back down again onto the iron on the anvil. But no hammers existed that could raise the head high enough to exert the necessary force. Humphreys wrote to James Nasmyth to see if he could help with the difficulty. The letter, in Nasmyth's own words, 'set me a-thinking'. He considered ways in which some force could be used that would raise the hammer vertically, instead of at an angle, and then let it fall from a considerable height. He had the solution, as he explained.

'Following up this idea, I got out my "Scheme Book", on the pages of which I generally *thought out* with the aid of pen and pencil, such mechanical adaptations as I had conceived in my mind, and was thereby able to render them visible. I then rapidly sketched out my Steam Hammer, having it all clearly before me in my mind's eye. In little more than half an hour, after receiving Mr. Humphries' [sic] letter narrating his unlooked for difficulty, I had all the contrivance in all its executant details, before me in a page of my Scheme Book.'

The idea was simple. Steam power would be used to raise a hammer vertically within a stout iron frame, which would then be released to fall under gravity. In later versions, steam would also be used to provide extra impetus to the fall of the hammer. It was a machine that would soon be used in shipyards throughout the country – but it would not be used to forge an axis for paddle wheels for the Brunel ship, which now had a name – *Mammoth*. The name was appropriate as she was by far the largest yet constructed with a length on the keel of 274ft and breadth of 50ft 6in.

Meanwhile, the work on the hull was continuing. The first decision to be taken was how to attach the iron plates of the hull to the ribs. It was going to involve a great deal of work as at this stage only comparatively small plates were available, generally around 6ft long. Brunel went back to one of the oldest construction methods used in wooden vessels, clinker building. In this, the planks that formed the hull were overlapped, and then fastened together. A similar system was used here, with overlapping iron plates. Everything seemed to be going well, but there was to be one other major change of direction.

There was speculation among engineers about the best means of propelling a steamer through the water. Up to this date, the paddle wheel had been the only answer. One could think of the paddle wheel as a mill wheel in reverse. Where the latter is turned by the water hitting it, the former is turned by machinery and forces water backwards, which according to Newton's law that every action has an equal and opposite reaction, propels the ship forwards. There was another device for moving water that had been around since antiquity, named after its inventor, the Archimedean screw. Two men were considering using this device, John Ericsson in America and Francis Pettit Smith in Britain.

Smith was a farmer, who grazed cattle on the Romney marshes, but he had an inquiring and inventive mind. He began by using model boats with clockwork motors to drive screws to act as propellers. He tried a number of different versions, and he was working with one that had a double twist to the screw. Then it was accidentally snapped in half, and to Smith's surprise, the single turn worked far better than the double. He now needed to scale

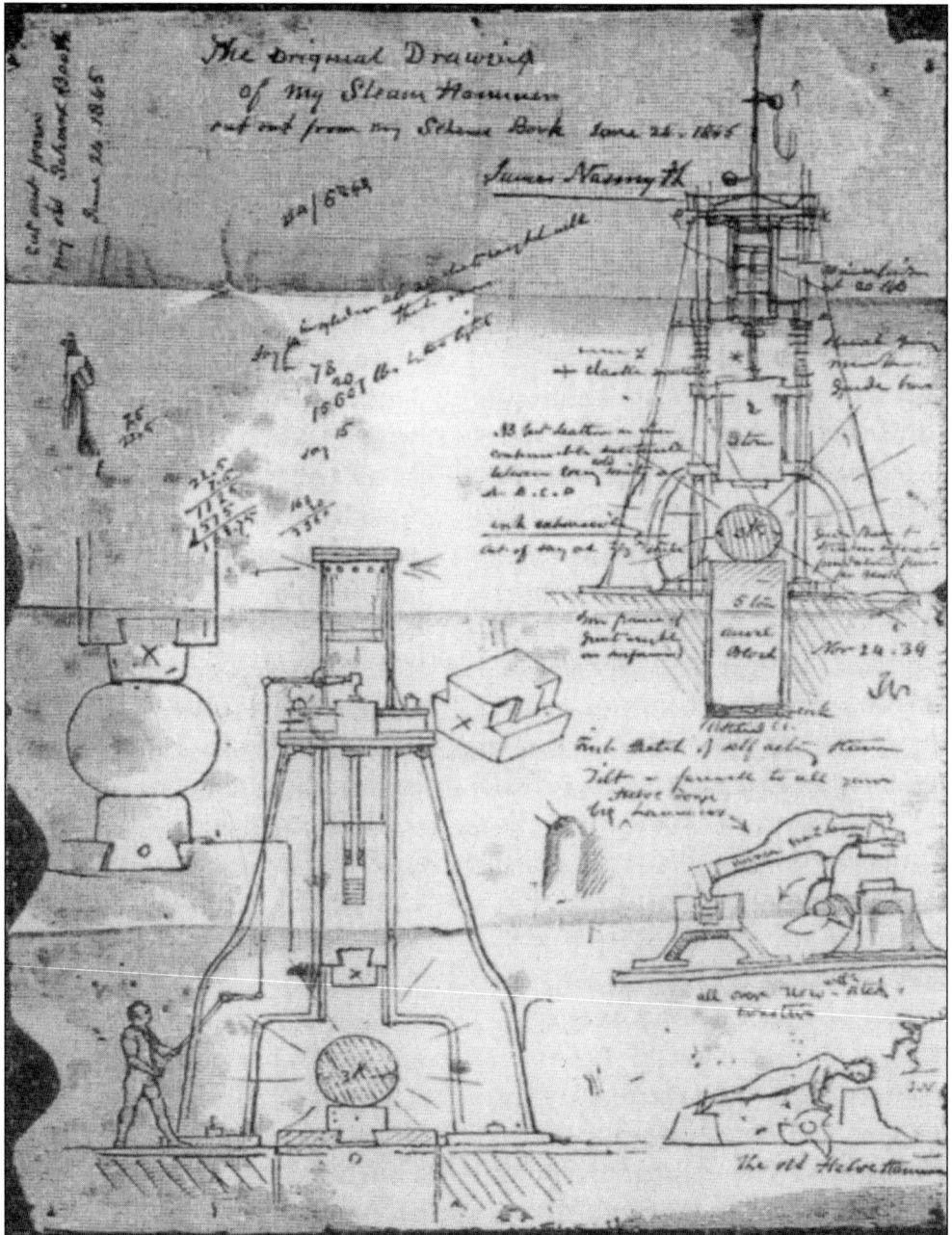

James Nasmyth's original design for a steam hammer, which was intended for use with forging a paddle axle for the *Great Britain*.

up his experiments. He built a launch that he named the *Francis Smith* and when that proved a success, he was able to persuade investors to join him in order to form the Ship Propeller Company and build a sea-going vessel, the *Archimedes*. She was comparatively modest, just 125ft long and 22ft beam and once completed she was sent to tour round Britain's shipyards to persuade shipbuilders that this new form of propulsion represented the future.

In May 1840, the ship arrived at Bristol and made a number of demonstration runs in the floating harbour. The Building Committee were intrigued and Guppy accompanied her when she left Bristol and stayed with her all the way to Liverpool. He was so impressed that he hired the vessel for some months for further experiments. The Building Committee now put all engine construction on hold. They tried eight different designs of propeller before finding the version that would eventually be used on their own ship. Brunel presented his report on 10 October 1840, in which he explained the results of the experiments and strongly advised that the screw propeller would be installed in the ship and the existing plans for the trunk engine and paddle wheels would be abandoned. His recommendations were accepted.

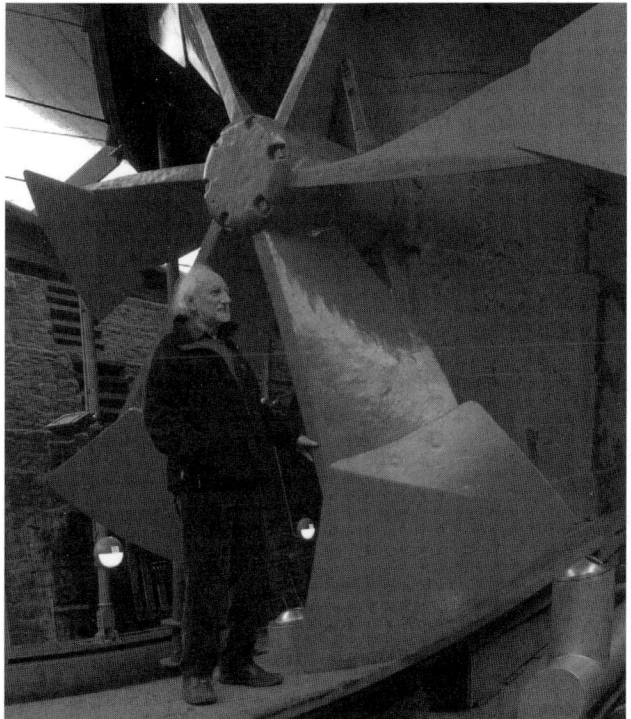

The author beside the replica propeller on the SS *Great Britain*.

This was undoubtedly a wise decision, but devastating news for Humphreys, who saw all his dreams disappear at once. The outcome was sad. Nasmyth described the aftereffects. 'Mr Humphries [sic] was a man of the most sensitive and sanguine constitution of mind. The labour and the anxiety which he had already undergone, and perhaps the disappointment of his hopes, proved too much for him; and a brain fever carried him off after a few days' illness.'

At this stage, the great ship acquired her third and final name. She would be the *Great Britain*. Now, it was necessary to design a quite different form of engine, and although Guppy was nominally in charge of the construction, the design was firmly based not on a new idea of Isambard's but one based on a patent taken out by his father in 1822 for what was called 'the Triangle Engine'. His explanation in the patent is commendably brief, the main points being, 'In the first place, the disposition I adopt to produce the rotary action is by placing the line of the powers in the direction to be at right angles, or nearly so, with each other' and 'the crank is a solid, double crank'. This would be the basis for the engines that were eventually built. There would be two pairs of cylinders, angled at 60°, each 88in in diameter. They operated on a massive crankshaft over two foot in diameter from which the drive was transmitted to the propeller shaft by four chains weighing 7 tons. As well as the engines, the ship was schooner rigged and carried fore-and-aft sail on five masts, and again there was an innovation: the standing rigging was wire, not rope.

The launch was scheduled for 19 July 1843, the anniversary of the launching of the *Great Western*. It was a grand affair at which Prince Albert was the principal guest – and a double honour for Brunel as the Prince travelled to Bristol by train on the Great Western Railway. He did not, however, carry out the actual ceremony, which this time fell to Mrs Miles. There was the usual banquet for the VIPs but thousands of ordinary Bristolians turned out for the event, and nearby Brandon Hill, which provided a good vantage point, was crowded. The great ship was to be hauled from her resting place in the building dock by a small steamer '*Avon*' and to be guided carefully by crews manning ropes to either side. Unfortunately, the *Avon*'s tow rope snapped so that the ship slowed just as Mrs Miles was about to break the champagne over her bows and she missed. At this point, Prince Albert stepped in, grabbed a second bottle and threw it accurately and it duly smashed, showering several spectators. Marc and Sophia were also among the guests – this was the great event for which they had left their Somerset holiday home.

Once out of the building lock, work began on fitting her out and, as with the *Great Western* in London, attracted a great deal of attention. Among the visitors was the King of Saxony, who was given a personal tour of the ship by Brunel

A model of the engines of the SS *Great Britain* made a hundred years ago for the Victoria and Albert Museum.

who, the King's physician noted, spoke German 'very tolerably'. Fitting turned out to take far longer than expected, and it was not until December 1845 that she was ready to leave Bristol. There was, however, a problem – she was too wide to fit in the two locks that connected the floating harbour to the River Avon. Bristol was alive with rumours that getting the great ship out of the harbour would be a disaster – that the waters in the basin were to be raised, flooding half the city, and other equally preposterous ideas were put forward by the public and rapidly refuted. In the event, the obvious agreement was made to widen the locks and on 10 December 1845, she was finally ready to leave the city. But as she was towed into the lock by the tug *Samson*, she stuck. Claxton, who was on the tug, immediately ordered her to be hauled back into the Cumberland Basin. It was an anxious time as Brunel wrote the next day:

'She stuck in the lock. We *did* get her back, I have been hard at work all day altering the masonry of the lock. Tonight, our last tide, we have succeeded in getting her through but being dark we have been obliged to ground her outside. I confess I cannot leave her until I see her afloat again and all clear of her difficulties.'

She now began her initial sea trials in the Bristol Channel, with Brunel, Guppy and Claxton all on board. She proved to be a remarkably handy vessel; steaming a circular course, she turned in less than half a mile. Gradually the speed was increased from 4 knots to 11 knots and a report in the *Mechanics' Magazine* noted that the engine worked smoothly and quietly and 'when going at her best speed there is no swell whatsoever under the bows, her stem cutting through the water'. It was all very satisfactory, and Guppy was able to send an official report to the Board. He began by flattering them:

'Relying upon the opinion of Mr. Brunel, you boldly decided in December 1840 to alter the method of propulsion of the large steamer which you had then commenced to construct from paddle wheels to the then scarcely tried Archimedean propeller. The triumphant result of your decision was ascertained on Thursday last.'

It had indeed been a triumph, with the ship performing exactly as had been calculated. There were then the official trials after which, on 14 January 1845, she was officially registered as being owned by John William Miles and Thomas Bonville Were as Trustees of the Great Western Steamship Company – Miles being the husband of Mrs. Miles whose champagne bottle had failed to hit its mark. It seemed that all the troubles were over and the new ship could look forward to a successful career.

On 23 January she set sail for London, but had got no further than Lundy, when an immense storm blew up: this was not necessarily a problem for the experienced sailors on board, but was a nightmare for the stokers who were more used to shovelling coal into boilers on immovable ground; sea sickness was rife. On the afternoon of the 24th, she was hit simultaneously by two waves, which brought the great vessel to a momentary standstill, before smoothly getting under way again, but with a little damage, including the loss of part of the figurehead. The artist Joseph Walter was on board and later produced a painting of this dramatic moment (page 141). Fortunately, the weather eased; she made good progress and off Beachy Head recorded a maximum speed of almost 14 knots. Her arrival in the Thames caused great excitement and during her stay in London she was visited by the Queen and

Prince Albert. She was not as elaborately decorated as the *Great Western* and when one of the newspapers reported on the extravagance of the carpeting, Claxton replied: 'A large sum of money has not been uselessly squandered in procuring gaudy decoration. Its fitting are alike chaste and elegant.' Which is certainly an apt description of the dining room, where the only elaboration comes with the gilded capitals of the twelve columns that line up down the centre. Compared with the decoration that would be seen on ocean liners just a few decades later, it is positively Spartan. He added a very Victorian statement, when describing the staterooms reserved for female passengers, with boudoir and sitting room: 'Ladies who may be indisposed, or in negligee, will be enabled to reach their sleeping berths without there being the slightest necessity for their appearing in public.'

Things were going well. In July 1845 she set off on her first trip to New York, where she arrived fifteen days later. There was a minor, but embarrassing mishap. Instead of passing Sandy Point for the approach to New York, the ship

The dramatic scene when the SS *Great Britain* was hit by two big waves in the Bristol Channel, portrayed by Joseph Walter.

was found to be actually near the island of Martha's Vineyard, some 35 miles north of where she should have been. She hove to and had to send for a pilot to bring the ship safely into port. A far more damaging navigational mishap occurred the following year. She left Liverpool on 22 September 1846 and set off on a course that should have taken her past the southern tip of the Isle of Man, where she would have turned north to round the Irish coast and set off across the Atlantic. She passed the island but instead of turning north, steamed straight on and grounded at Dundrum Bay in County Down. How could such a major navigational error have occurred? The captain's answer was that the North Point lighthouse near the bay was not on his Admiralty Chart. He in fact believed at the time that he had grounded on the Isle of Man. But he had, in fact, steamed some 35 nautical miles past the island. As conditions were good, she would have actually passed the Calf of Man around three hours before she grounded. Now the simplest navigational calculations, which would have shown the course from the compass bearings, and the speed would have also been known, should have made it abundantly clear that the vessel was nowhere near the island. The story about the lighthouse is irrelevant. As a former navigator myself, I can only conclude that the disaster was down to negligence. Whatever the cause, the effect of the disaster was felt immediately. There was panic among the passengers, but no lives were lost. The reports that came back to Bristol, however, were of a ship irretrievably lost.

Brunel was only able to get to the ship himself in December, but he was furious. He wrote to Claxton, expressing his views:

> 'I have returned from Dundrum with very mixed feelings of satisfaction and pain almost amounting to anger, with whom I don't know. I was delighted to find our fine ship, in spite of all the discouraging accounts received even from you, almost as sound as the day she was launched … the ship is lying like a useless saucepan kicking about on the most exposed shore you can imagine with no more effort or skill applied to protect the property than the said saucepan would have received on the beach at Brighton.'

He went on to list the damage that had been done, none of which was irreparable. He then went on to list what should be done if she was to be saved:

> 'I say "If", for really when I saw the vessel still in perfect condition left to the tender mercies of an awfully exposed shore for weeks while a parcel

of quacks are amusing you with schemes for setting her off, she is in the meantime being left to go to pieces. I could hardly help feeling as if her own parents and guardians meant her to die.'

But Brunel was not going to let her perish. With his usual energy he not only came up with a plan of action, but at once started to put it into operation. Basically, what he proposed was to lighten the ship and remove much of the gear; to divert the currents that were washing away the sand from beneath the hull, to support the damaged stern and, most importantly, to protect the whole vessel from storm damage. To do that, he proposed building a breakwater from faggots, fixed together with iron rods and weighted down with chains. In fact, by the time the letter was sent off to Claxton, he had already started ordering the faggots. Claxton was put in charge of the whole salvage operation, and soon repair work was started to ensure she was watertight. In August, everything was ready to refloat the ship. A cable was passed right round the hull, to which floats were attached and lines ran out to the *Birkenhead* at anchor in the bay. The job of winching her off the shore could begin. At half past eleven in the morning, the ship began to move. Claxton sent a message at once to Brunel: 'Huzza! Huzza! You know what that means'. She was clear of the shore, but only just – only clearing rocks at the fringe of the bay by a paltry five inches. She was towed back to Liverpool for repairs. There was almost another disaster when the towrope snapped near the mouth of the Mersey, but a new line was quickly attached, and the *Great Britain* was ready for restoration. It was a resounding success as far as the future of iron ships were concerned, for it proved the resilience of the material. The vessel had not only withstood such a battering but could actually be repaired and, as the surveyors officially reported, had she been built of timber she would have had to be scrapped. This should have been good news, but the total cost for restoration was put at £22,000 and the vessel that had cost almost £120,000 to build had only been insured for £17,000.

The Great Western Company did not have the funds to carry out the work, and she was put up for sale at auction with a reserve price of £40,000 – only £20,000 was bid. Eventually, in December 1850, she was sold to Gibbs, Bright & Co. for just £18,000 and the Great Western Steamship Company was wound up. That is the end of the story of Brunel's involvement with the ship, but it is not the end of the ship's own history. On the other side of the world, gold had been discovered in Australia and the ship that had been built specifically for the Atlantic trade was now put into service, sailing off to the southern hemisphere. She would later find yet another new route to follow, not to the Atlantic coast of America but to the west coast, a voyage that would include the hazardous passage round Cape Horn in the days before the Panama Canal was built. In 1886, she met heavy weather off the South American coast and was eventually forced to seek shelter in the Falkland Islands. This time she was too far gone to be repaired, but for the Falklanders, she was a blessing. The islands depended on sheep farming for their livelihood, but there is scarcely a tree to be found there. Any ship with a sound hull could be pulled up into shallow waters, stripped down to deck level and used as a wool warehouse – which is why, even today, there are still an astonishing array of preserved hulls around the islands. The *Great Britain* was about to join them. She was scuttled in Sparrow Cove, and that really should have been the end of the narrative. But she was such an iconic vessel, that enthusiasts decided she needed to be preserved and if possible restored. A plan was hatched to bring the historic ship back to Bristol. On 15 April 1970, she was afloat for the first time since her scuttling. She was put on an immense pontoon and the long job of towing her back to Bristol was begun. On 19 July she was back in the dock in which she had been built exactly 127 years after she had been launched. Restoration work has been completed, and today visitors can enjoy visiting one of the most important ships ever to leave a British shipyard. However, there is one piece of the ship on display elsewhere; the mizzen mast remained in the Falklands and is mounted on a plinth at Port Stanley.

There is a coda to this account of the great ship. It was the last big event in Isambard's life at which his parents were present. After the launch, they left for a life in retirement in London. In 1845 Marc had a second stroke, which left him paralysed all down the right hand side, at which point he promptly started to teach himself to write with his left hand. He was still prepared to travel and he and Sophie made a visit to Watcombe, just north of Torquay, where Isambard had planned to build a house, but mostly Marc was happy to stay at home with his wife. Paul Clements, in his biography of Marc, published in 1970, quotes Mrs Crosland and her account of visiting the couple in their later years.

'I believe I was a good listener, and assured of my sympathy they poured out their reminiscences freely, or rather, I should say, Lady Brunel did, for the old man was not voluble, though he often by a nod of the head or some short exclamation confirmed his wife's words. She was a little old lady, with

The restored SS *Great Britain* back in the Bristol dock in which she was built.

her faculties bright and apparently unimpaired; he with a ponderous head surmounting what might be called a thick-set figure. The old couple usually sat side by side and often the old man would take his wife's withered hand in his, sometimes raising it to his lips with the restrained fervour of a respectful lover.'

Marc died on 13 December 1849 at the age of 80 and was buried in the Kensal Green Cemetery. Sophie lived on and moved into Duke Street with Isambard and his family. When she died on 5 January 1855, she was buried next to her husband, with a gravestone that he had designed for her. They lay side by side, just as they had happily sat side by side through their long and loving marriage.

Chapter 15

BRIDGES AND RAILWAYS

One of the problems in trying to provide a coherent narrative of Isambard Brunel's life is that he never had just one project in hand at a time. There was no period when he stopped working on railways to concentrate on ships; both were going on at the same time. And if anything else of interest came up, he was likely to take that on as well. One of these was to design a pedestrian bridge across the Thames in London to link Hungerford Market on the north bank to Lambeth. Perhaps it appealed to him as a chance to put his ideas, that had failed to materialise with the stalled Clifton bridge, into practice. Once again, he chose a suspension bridge, but one with far fewer problems. The four sets of chains, made up of wrought iron links, each 24 foot long and 7 inches deep, were anchored on the banks at either side, then passed over towers, mounted on foundations on the river bed. The towers themselves were brick, with stone trimming. The style was Italianate, with the topmost section looking rather like a campanile. Begun in 1841, it was completed four years later. The bridge was not destined to enjoy a long life. In 1860, it had to make way for the railway bridge from the new Charing Cross station but its main components survive. The towers are still there, and the chains were removed and used to complete Brunel's first major project – the Clifton suspension bridge. Work began in November 1862 and was undertaken by the engineering company, Hawkshaw and Barlow. It is not exactly the bridge that Brunel designed. The height of the towers was increased from 230 to 245 feet and, where originally, there were two chains at each side, there were now three, with the anchor points brought nearer to the towers. The grand decorative effects originally planned never happened, and the towers never appeared in their pseudo Egyptian style but were left plain and unadorned. They have been variously described as ugly or simply monumentally grand. I, at least, hold the second view.

At least while working on the Hungerford bridge he was able to spend some time in London with his family. At this time, he had just two children, Isambard born in 1837 and Henry Marc, 1842 – his third child, Florence's birthdate is uncertain but was probably 1847. Young Isambard's leg was always a problem. His father wrote to him, rather unhelpfully: 'If I could

OPENING OF THE HUNGERFORD SUSPENSION BRIDGE, ON THURSDAY LAST, MAY 1.—(SEE NEXT PAGE.

The Hungerford suspension bridge.

have you under my care for three months, I feel sure I could cure you. I wish I could do it, my dear fellow, but you must try and do it for yourself.' The rare existing letters dealing with family matters show the father to take a very unsentimental attitude towards the boy. When he went away to school at Harrow, his father wrote to Mary: 'I hope the poor little fellow is not very unhappy, but it is what all must go through, and he has infinitely less pain than most boys in beginning.' Young Isambard showed little interest in following his father's career, but Henry at once showed that aptitude that had marked both his father and grandfather. He would go on to have a career in engineering, which was successful, if not as spectacularly so as his forebears. He worked with Sir John Wolf-Barry in designing the Blackfriars railway bridge across the Thames and Barry Docks in South Wales. He also helped design the Creagan railway bridge in Scotland. Florence had a short but uneventful life, marrying an Eton housemaster.

Mary Brunel has not been treated kindly by biographers and commentators, generally presented as a vain, selfish creature, whose main interest was parading around in her finery, with a footman in tow. But when Isambard wrote to her about their eldest son leaving for Harrow, his main purpose was to console her rather than comfort the son. So, perhaps, she was a kind and loving mother after all. There were family holidays down in Devon, where Isambard dreamed of building his perfect house – a dream destined never to be fulfilled. And Mary did accompany Isambard when he went overseas – but as these were all trips concerned with engineering projects, they might not have been very appealing. And, it should be remembered, her husband was away most of the time, leaving her in the house in Duke Street. It was, however, a house of considerable grandeur.

In 1848, Isambard bought the house next door, Number 17, and doors were knocked through to create a single dwelling. There was a considerable domestic staff of some dozen servants and some sumptuous rooms. The Organ room was home to a chamber organ, where the family could gather for musical evenings. In the days before the arrival of the gramophone, any self-respecting wealthy Victorian family would be expected to make music for themselves – and, of course, the Horsleys were at the heart of London's musical life. The drawing room was hung with paintings by the Horsley family, including two by Mary's brother John. The most elaborately decorated room was the great dining room. This reflected Isambard's taste for the Tudor style as exemplified in the Bristol station. The walls were covered with paintings representing scenes from Shakespeare, some once again by John Horsley, but also with works by other leading artists of the day, including Landseer. There was a crystal chandelier, curtains of scarlet silk and solidly imposing furniture. There were other works of art in the house – for Isambard collected a great deal on his travels and had, according to his brother-in-law, a good eye. If Mary was noted for ostentation and display, it has to be said that her husband matched her. This was a house intended to impress and Isambard was, it seems, equally keen to show off his beautiful wife and was never reluctant to spend money on the latest fashionable clothes and jewels. Domestic life, however, was strictly limited for the engineer. The Great Western empire was beginning to spread, but so too was the rest of the network being built to the Stephenson gauge.

In the battle of the gauges, it did seem that there were some areas where the Great Western empire was secure, and nowhere was apparently safer than the routes into Bristol. But there was one obvious link to be made; a direct line from that city to Gloucester. A first tentative move had been made with the little Bristol & Gloucestershire Railway, but it was only with the formation of the Bristol & Gloucester Railway Company that the junction could be made. The original line had been the old colliery route, built to the narrow gauge, and it seemed only sensible to continue it to Gloucester, providing a through route from Birmingham. The Company was faced with a dilemma, under pressure from the narrow and broad gauge interests. The Great Western empire was being expanded by taking over the line to Cheltenham and the small company was in danger of simply being engulfed. A decision had to be taken – they went with the broad gauge and that was how the track was constructed, track that reached Gloucester in 1844. But it was still an independent company. It was always a small concern, and a takeover was all but certain, and the odds were on the Great Western. They saw it as a sensible route in itself, but also as a chance to extend on to Birmingham. They made an offer for the two companies – the old Bristol & Gloucestershire and the new Bristol & Gloucester. It was considered, but the two companies wanted £5 more per share than was on offer. The GWR board went away to consider the matter at their leisure. Saunders, negotiating for the GWR, probably thought he had such a strong case, he had no reason to offer more. At this point, John Ellis, deputy chairman of the newly formed Midland Railway, stepped in with a good offer that was accepted. To the absolute horror of the Bristol board, the narrow gauge had penetrated to the heart of their empire. The Great Western would not get the route it wanted to Birmingham. The battle was on.

The two systems now collided at Gloucester, where the broad gauge arrived from the south, while the narrow gauge Birmingham & Gloucester came in from the north. This caused a degree of chaos, though not perhaps quite as bad as that shown in an illustration of the time (see page 150). But it did mean not only that passengers had to change trains – a common enough experience even today – but everything had to be moved, parcels, baggage, all kinds of freight – basically anything on a goods or passenger train had to be transhipped. It was not a happy situation, and with both the GWR and other companies planning to extend, it was decided to set up a Royal Commission in 1845 to investigate the situation. Three commissioners were appointed. The first was an obvious choice, the former Inspector General of Railways, Sir Frederick Smith. The other two are perhaps more surprising – George Biddell Airy, the astronomer in charge of the Greenwich Observatory, and Peter Barlow, Professor of Mathematics at the Woolwich Military Academy. But these two were highly qualified scientists, who could be assumed to take a rational view of the problem and they had the added advantage that, unlike almost every railway engineer in the country, they had no partisan bias before they started.

When the Commission was set up, Brunel had recently returned from Italy, where he had been asked to survey a line from Turin to Genoa. Things did not go well. One of his assistants was the son of his friend, inventor of the first computer, Charles Babbage. The young man was at work in his office when

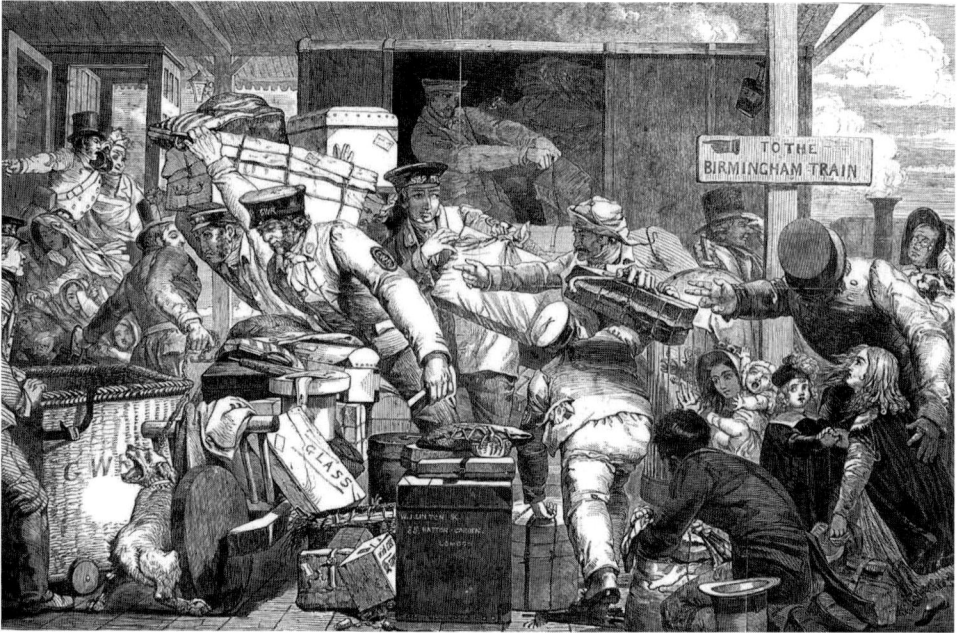

A cartoonist's view of the confusion caused by the break of gauge at Gloucester station.

two Italian engineers appeared who proceeded to tell him what to do and how to do it. If there was one thing guaranteed to get Brunel's temper rising, it was outsiders telling his staff what to do, especially as one of them was 'not even of the Sardinian Court, but a foreigner'. That was bad enough, but he discovered dealing with governments was resulting in him being inundated with a flood of bureaucratic demands. He wrote to Count Pollin, who had first invited him to Piedmont, to explain why he was withdrawing from the scene:

> 'The unexpected difficulties I find to exist by the (to me) extraordinary complicated forms to be gone through, the detailed reports to be made upon each separate piece of work were enough to deter me from proceeding, but these difficulties I found bound to meet. I do not feel bound to attempt the impossibility of satisfactorily conducting the work when the principal & most essential condition of entire confidence & absence of interference is not carried out.'

The difficulties he encountered in Piedmont were probably not helped by his own rather arrogant attitude towards the government staff. In a letter to Babbage, he described the government committee set up to oversee the railway construction as 'contemptibly childish', and then went on:

> 'They go to work as if I had been an operative employed by them to furnish sections & plans of the various lines of Country for them to select and direct …instead of the case being that I was called as a person assumed to be *more experienced & competent* than they are, and their business only to see on the part of the Govt. that the proposed line is acceptable.'

His trip was not, however, entirely wasted; he brought back several works of art to adorn Duke Street.

On his return, when he appeared to give evidence before the Royal Commission, he was asked, quite reasonably, why he had not recommended building a broad gauge track for the Italian project. He replied that he did not think it was necessary, simply because he thought it would be many years before that country would need or have high speed trains. He was also concerned that the railway from Milan to Venice was already under construction to the Stephenson gauge, and he did not want to create problems with future mergers. It is perhaps worth pointing out that at this time Italy did not actually exist, but the country was made up of individual states under a variety of different controls. The railway for which he briefly acted would be provincial, not national. He was also asked if he considered it 'injudicious' to adopt the 7ft gauge, to which the engineer jauntily replied, 'I should rather be above than under seven feet now'. He then made a proposal; why not see which system is best by staging a trial to see which offered the faster ride – 'broad' or 'narrow' gauge. The Commissioners thought this was a good idea and agreed.

This is really quite surprising, for it is difficult to see what could be gained by such a trial. It was certainly possible to find track of the same lengths and gradients. Brunel's original suggestion had been a test over the whole run from London to Exeter, but this was a stage too far. Eventually, the two sections chosen were Paddington to Didcot, 53 miles and Darlington to York, 44 miles. Yet, whoever won, what would it prove? The argument was about the track, but the trains would be hauled by very different locomotives, designed by two different engineers. Whichever came out best, there was no way of assessing whether it was due to better track or superior locomotives. But the trial went ahead.

The locomotive chosen to carry the Great Western colours was one of Gooch's Firefly class *Ixion*, built in 1841 by Fenton, Murray and Jackson.

She made three round trips between Paddington and Didcot with 60, 70 and 80 ton loads. With 60 tons, the engine averaged 50mph on the down journey and 53.9 on the return to Paddington. The 80 ton load run actually hit the highest top speed of 60mph. This was all very satisfactory. The Stephenson camp sent in two contenders. One was Robert Stephenson's latest design, a 4-2-0 long boiler locomotive that had not yet been named. In spite of several slightly dodgy attempts to improve performance, including installing a portable boiler at Darlington to give an extra blast for the return, the top speed obtained was just under 54mph with a modest 50 ton load. A second run was abandoned after the first leg because of the weather conditions. The second engine not only carried the Stephenson hopes but had the same name as well. *Stephenson* ran off the rails halfway down the first leg and rolled over. It was a clear victory for Gooch and Brunel, and they certainly saw it as a vindication of the broad gauge.

The trial proved nothing and was largely ignored. The truth of the matter was that there was never really any doubt about the outcome if common sense prevailed. What would have happened if the Commissioners had decided that Britain should have only broad gauge? It would not just be a matter of putting rails further apart, every structure on the line would need to be widened as well – every bridge, tunnel and viaduct – not to mention the fact that every station would have to be rebuilt. Even if that was considered desirable, there was at the time almost 2,000 miles of narrow gauge track in existence as opposed to just 274 of broad gauge. Converting the latter required very little extra work. The broad gauge could even be allowed to stay, as all that was needed was a third rail between the other two to allow the track to be used by narrow gauge locomotives. The Commission was decisive; from henceforth a law should be passed forbidding the construction of any more broad gauge – the narrow gauge would henceforth simply be the standard gauge for Britain.

It seemed that the fight was lost when Parliament passed a Gauge Act in 1846, forbidding the future construction of any railway to a gauge other than 4ft 8½in or 5ft 3in in Ireland. But there was a curious clause that exempted 'any railway constructed or to be constructed under the provisions of any present or future Act containing any special enactment defining the gauge or gauges of such railway'. Reading this convoluted clause several times, the meaning appears to be that railways could be built to any gauge if the company concerned could get approval from parliament. That was more than a loophole in the Act; it was a yawning gap. The Brunel camp were delighted, the opposition livid. They began a rather vitriolic campaign against Brunel and all his works. In one of them, the anonymous author wrote: 'He has not been able to find a single independent railway engineer to back his eccentricities, for we cannot regard Mr. D. Gooch of the G. W. as but Sancho to Don Quixote'. This is hardly a convincing argument as the vast majority of other engineers were employed by companies building to what we can now call standard gauge. Brunel did not deign to reply in kind. The unpleasantness, however, never extended to the two chief engineers concerned. Brunel and Robert Stephenson may have differed professionally, but it never affected their personal friendship and mutual respect.

The rivalry between the two systems was not a matter of one side trying to prove it was better than the other. At the heart of the argument was the whole question of the rapidly expanding rail system. How far could the different systems expand? The broad gauge enthusiasts were keen to advance into Wales and north towards Birmingham and possibly Liverpool. The standard gauge companies were equally enthusiastic about cornering the trade in southern and western England. One of the main battlegrounds would be the fight over the Midland routes. It all came to a head in the convoluted story of the Oxford, Worcester & Wolverhampton Railway.

The Great Western had already extended its line from Didcot up to Oxford, and now was proposing to extend up into the Midlands via the Oxford, Worcester & Wolverhampton and the Oxford & Rugby lines. This was bitterly opposed by the London & Birmingham Railway in alliance with the Midland. They proposed an alternative route, the London, Worcester & South Staffordshire. The big question was – which would provide the better service, the narrow gauge or the broad gauge routes? A Parliamentary Committee of five, known as 'the Five Kings', was set up to look into the matter. They came down on the side of the standard gauge on the grounds that the standard gauge trains were running a faster service. This stirred Brunel into action. The case for the broad gauge would be made by creating a new class of locomotives that would run at previously unprecedented speeds. Daniel Gooch set to work on designing this new breed of engine.

The first locomotive, *Great Western*, was not only a new design, but the first locomotive to be built at Swindon. There was a huge rush to get the work completed as quickly as possible and it was completed in just thirteen weeks. This was a most imposing engine, with a tall firebox and 8ft diameter drive wheels. On the first run on 1 June 1846, she completed a round trip of 194 miles each way at an average running speed of over 55mph. There were problems, however, and when the second engine came from the works it had been modified, by the addition of an extra pair of leading wheels and an improved boiler, producing steam at the then very high pressure of 100psi and the firebox no longer towered over the boiler. The engine was *Iron Duke,* described in Chapter 12. The new class were a triumphant success, but still left the question unanswered – was it Gooch's skill or an inherent property of the broad gauge? Whatever the answer, the Five Kings now changed their mind. They decided in favour of what would be the Oxford, Worcester & Wolverhampton Railway, but with the proviso that there should be an additional third rail to allow the track to be used by standard gauge stock. It was a very British compromise.

The London and Birmingham faction felt cheated and were prepared to do battle before the Bill went to parliament, but then a new, and as it soon turned out ruthless, player appeared in the game – Captain Mark Huish. His captaincy came from the East India Company, but now he was general manager of the Grand Junction Railway, the line that linked Birmingham to the Liverpool & Manchester. He was not an advocate for the broad gauge, but he saw an opportunity to use the Great Western to further his own interests. He offered the GWR a very tempting deal. They would be offered running rights to link into the lucrative trade of Liverpool and Manchester, by the addition of an extra rail to allow their trains to use routes controlled by the Grand Junction. In return, the Grand Junction would be able to make a new line to take them to Oxford, and again an extra rail would allow them into Paddington. This spread alarm among the London & Birmingham shareholders and, to protect their interests, they readily agreed to go into partnership with the Grand Junction and others to form the London & North Western Railway, which unsurprisingly would have Huish as its manager. He had got what he wanted and all thoughts of a joint project with the Great Western were slung out of the window. Huish had been devious if not downright dishonest, and now it was the turn of Brunel and his colleagues to feel cheated and prepare to fight back.

The struggle to win this part of the network went on for years until eventually the Great Western bought up the Birmingham and Oxford Junction Railway that had been abandoned to its fate by Huish. In 1848, the GWR now had that line together with the Birmingham, Dudley & Wolverhampton – a grandly named line which didn't quite live up to its title; it stopped short of Wolverhampton itself by a mile and a half. This, with the Oxford, Worcester & Wolverhampton Railway, gave them the access to the Midlands. It seemed a triumph, but it was all to prove a bitter disappointment and presented

Isambard Brunel with a challenge and a dilemma that was to lead to one of the most notorious and controversial episodes in his career.

The Oxford, Worcester & Birmingham suffered from the earliest days with financial problems, and with just one major engineering work, the mile-long tunnel under Chipping Camden at Mickleton. The work was proceeding at a snail's pace. The first contractors only lasted four months before their funds ran out. The next set on the site lasted a little longer, but when they had to start borrowing money for equipment, their days too were numbered. Next on the scene was a partnership between William Williams and Robert Mudge Marchant. Brunel must have hoped that this pair would prove more competent than their predecessors, for Marchant had been one of his own assistants, but he did warn him that he was entering a dangerous business. Some railway contractors were making fortunes – rather more were going bankrupt. The new partnership had scarcely got going when work stopped. This time the company, not the contractors, were short of funds.

Work restarted in December 1850, and Brunel urged everyone to make an effort to get the tunnel completed, so that the company could finally start running trains and start earning money instead of just spending it. But the tunnel continued to be the bottleneck, and the following June, Brunel demanded that the contactors must either find extra men to do the work, or give up the contract. It was now that the situation deteriorated rapidly.

In July it was decided that the company would take over control of the work themselves. Marchant, who claimed the company owed him £30,000, barricaded himself in and prepared to resist the sub-contractors when they appeared on site. He rather cunningly called on two local magistrates to warn them that he was likely to be threatened with violence and they agreed to go to the scene and swore in special constables – including Marchant himself, scarcely a disinterested party. When the company's agent, Varden, arrived with his workmen, it seemed trouble was likely. Brunel himself now arrived on the scene, but negotiations achieved nothing. The Riot Act was read, and Brunel agreed to withdraw. He was not a man ever likely to take such a setback lightly, especially as he considered he was legally in the right to ensure the work went on.

The Local magistrate, James Ashwin, heard that Brunel had only made a temporary withdrawal, and was planning to advance on the tunnel with some 3,000 navvies. He set off for the tunnel very early and came across the navvy army, who seemed to be uncertain exactly where the tunnel was. He helpfully offered them directions – the wrong way. As a result, he was at the tunnel when Brunel and his men finally arrived. It was never going to be a peaceful meeting, and though it has since been described as the Battle of Mickleton, it was never more than a minor skirmish, and the presence of the magistrates ensured that things did not get too bad. But the outcome was never really in doubt – the Brunel thousands against the Marchant hundreds. Eventually, it was agreed that the differences between Marchant and the company would be settled by arbitration. Marchant lost and, as Brunel had warned, was ruined. But it was an event from which no one emerged with credit. The law was with Brunel but, as Henry Waddington of the Home Office wrote to the railway company directors, that did not justify what happened: 'However clear the right to the possession of property may be the law will not allow the party claiming it to assert such right forcibly and in a manner calculated to endanger the peace.' And that seems reasonable judgement on the whole sorry affair. Brunel resigned shortly afterwards. He discovered that the company was not actually laying the extra broad gauge track where needed, and was laying standard gauge where broad gauge had been specified. He must have wished that he had never heard of the Oxford, Worcestershire and Wolverhampton.

The battle between the Great Western and the London and Birmingham might have led to antagonism between the two engineers responsible for the lines, Robert Stephenson and Isambard Brunel, but that was never the case. They disagreed professionally on several points but respected each other. They were friends, though there were few opportunities in their busy lives for them actually to meet. The situation was perfectly summed up by an entry in Brunel's diary for 1846, referring to a meeting of the two men when the battle of the gauges was well under way: 'It is very delightful in the midst of our personal professional contests, carried to the extreme limit of fair opposition, to meet him on a perfectly friendly footing and discuss engineering points.' Their common interests also meant that they understood the stresses that could be caused when attempting something entirely new, which Robert Stephenson was to do when faced with a complex problem.

He was the chief engineer for the Holyhead Railway, which would link mainland Britain to the principal port for the Irish mails at Holyhead. There was one major obstacle in the way: the Menai Straits. This had first been crossed by Telford's suspension bridge, but that type of structure was not considered suitable for a railway. Eventually, Stephenson came up with a solution. There would be what were in effect two giant box girders that would run from the two sides to a central pier built on the Britannia rock. Before reaching the Straits, the rails had to pass across the River Dee at Conwy.

This could have been a simpler form of bridge, but Stephenson used it as a test for the greater challenge at Menai. This would have two tubes side by side, for travel in both directions. The tubes would be prefabricated on the shore, then floated out on pontoons and jacked up into position. Nothing of the sort had ever been attempted before, and the engineer would have been more than a little nervous. But the man chosen to supervise the floating of the tubes was Captain Claxton, just returned from Dundrum Bay and with him was Brunel, who had arrived to give moral support and encouragement to his friend. In February 1848, the first tube was floated out, ready to be lifted and things did not go perfectly at first. One of the pontoons carrying the tube fouled on a rock, but the tube was eventually fixed in place. The first train crossed in April and the line was later opened to single track traffic, while the second tube was being got ready. Stephenson now faced the far greater challenge of the Menai Straits, and once again, Brunel took time off from his own hectic life to turn up on site to lend his support. Brunel was also about to attempt to develop a radical new railway system.

Chapter 16

NEW IDEAS

The one thing guaranteed to hold Isambard Brunel's interest was a new and original idea. In the early days of the GWR, signalling was comparatively primitive. Needless to say, the system used was unique. At the top of a long pole were a disc and a bar at right angles to each other. When the disc was turned so that it faced the driver, then he was clear to go ahead. When the bar showed, he had to stop. Safety was preserved, in theory at least, by allowing a time interval between trains. There was a problem with this. It worked on the assumption that nothing disastrous happened to one train, unknown to the following one. On a clear day that might not be a problem – the oncoming driver might see what had happened and stop. But if an accident happened at night or in a tunnel, then things could go badly wrong. The problem was exacerbated by the fact that signalmen had no means of communicating with each other. That was a problem that was about to be solved by science.

Physicists had discovered that an electric current flowing in a wire would deflect a magnetic needle placed close to it. The idea was developed in Germany as a means of long distance communication by using the needle as an indicator – an electric telegraph. Baron Schilling was able to demonstrate just such a device in the laboratory and one of the many who came to see it in 1836 was an Englishman, William Fothergill Cooke, who had recently been retired from the army in India due to ill health. He at once saw the commercial possibilities of the device and returned to England and devoted his time to perfecting it. He had seen that it was exactly the sort of thing that was needed to enable railway signalmen to communicate with each other. He took his idea at first to the Liverpool & Manchester Railway, who agreed to a demonstration, but there were technical difficulties. What had worked in the lab did not work over a long distance. Cooke approached various scientists who understood electricity, including Faraday, and was eventually to meet Professor Charles Wheatstone of King's College, London. It turned out Wheatstone had already been experimenting with the same idea and had solved the problem, but he had no time to develop it commercially. As a result, they went into partnership and took out a patent in 1837 for a five-needle

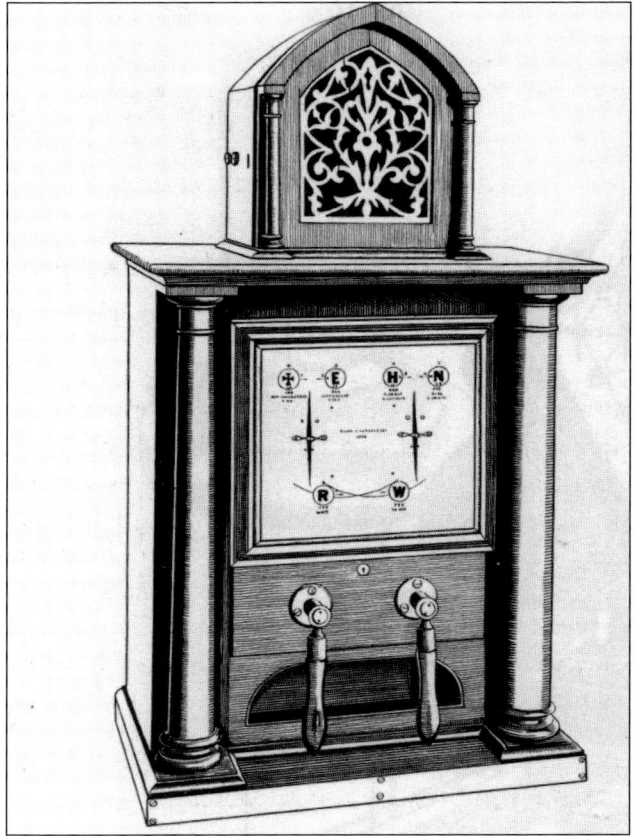

Above left: **A GWR** signal installed by the broad gauge section of the Didcot Railway Centre.

Above right: **The Cooke** and Wheatstone two-needle telegraph of the type first installed on the Great Western Railway.

telegraph, which could point to all the letters of the alphabet to spell out a message. This was now demonstrated to the London & Birmingham Railway, who showed no real interest in it. So, the inventors approached Brunel and the Great Western. The system was simplified to a two needle system and the world's first working electric telegraph was installed in 1838 between Paddington and West Drayton, later extended to Slough.

It was an event of little interest to the world at large until 1845, when a murder was committed in Slough and the suspect was spotted boarding a train for Paddington, hoping to escape among the crowds. But a full description was sent by telegraph and when he arrived in London, the police were waiting. But the importance of the telegraph to improving rail safety was its main function, not catching criminals, and it was to be vital to railway signalling for many years to come. No doubt, it would have been accepted anyway, but the honour of first seeing its potential goes to Brunel and the directors of the Great Western.

Back in the 1820s, there had been a long discussion on whether railways were best run by locomotives or by hauling trains from engine house to engine house by cable. There was another idea being suggested in the early nineteenth century, using a combination of a vacuum and air pressure – a pneumatic system. The first atmospheric engines were designed by Thomas Newcomen at the beginning the eighteenth century, in which steam was condensed in a cylinder below a piston, creating a partial vacuum, allowing air pressure to force the piston. A similar system could be considered and would work just as well if the cylinder was horizontal. Then, if some form of carriage could be attached to the piston, it would move along with it. The idea was proposed early in the nineteenth century but was developed into a practical idea by Jacob and Joseph Samuda, working with Samuel Clegg. The first successful experimental version was completed in 1840 as Mr. Clegg's pneumatic railway. The Birmingham, Bristol & Thames Junction Railway had a grand name and great ambitions but fewer resources. They had a 1½mile length of track available and it was here that the innovative railway was installed. A pipe was laid between the rails, with a slot in the top. This was closed by a valve consisting of a metal flap covered with short metal plates. One side of the flap was fastened to long metal rods attached to the tube that acted as a hinge. At the opposite side of the slot was a groove filled with tallow and wax. The sticky mixture held the flap firmly against the tube. The leading carriage on the train had a piston attached beneath it by a bent metal support. The piston was then introduced into the open end of the tube with the metal support pushing up through the slot. At the opposite end of the tube, a steam engine began pumping out air, creating a partial vacuum, and air pressure drove the carriage along, the vertical metal support pushing the valve aside as it went along. The idea was to have a system with stationary engines situated at suitable distances along the line to move the train. It succeeded in moving a considerable load up a 1:20 gradient.

Several interested parties came to view the experiment, including George Stephenson, who dismissed it in his usual blunt manner as 'a great humbug'. Others saw it as a viable proposition. The directors of the Dublin and Kingstown Railway, Ireland's first steam railway, were hoping to extend their line from Kingstown – modern Dún Laoghaire – to Dalkley. It was only thirteen miles, but there was a considerable rise to overcome, mainly at a modest 1:115 but with one section at 1:57, which was beyond the capabilities of any steam locomotive then built. The atmospheric railway seemed the answer – the train could travel uphill using pneumatic power, returning under gravity. The system was installed and continued successfully in use for many years. One passenger had an unexpected demonstration of just how powerful the system was. Frank Ebrington was sitting on the forward truck attached to the piston when it was started up before the train had been attached. He shot off and reached the unprecedented speed of 80mph. It was, in its own terms, a success. Brunel travelled to Ireland to see the system at work

There was a good reason why the Irish chose the system as it solved a specific problem for them. Brunel considered it equally appropriate for the extension of the existing line by the South Devon Railway, from Exeter down to Plymouth. He had first surveyed the route in 1836. His original plan had been for a route that would pass close to Torquay, and then head for a crossing of the Dart. This proved too expensive, so an alternative route was selected that followed the west bank of the Exe, then ran along the coast from Dawlish to Teignmouth, before turning inland for Newton Abbot, and then heading for Plymouth via Totnes. This was difficult country for railway construction, and in the section between Newton Abbot and Plymouth, he planned for three sections with heavy gradients at Dainton, Rattery and Hemerdon. Of these the most formidable was Dainton at three miles long, with the steepest section at 1:57. This was the route that was now to be operated by an atmospheric railway, and he would never have allowed for such gradients if he had been planning a conventional railway. The new route had broad gauge rails with the pipe in between and would involve building pumping stations at roughly three mile intervals. When the proposal to run the Liverpool & Manchester Railway using cable haulage was being debated, Robert Stephenson and Joseph Locke were given the task of writing a pamphlet to make the case for locomotives. In it, they pointed out that if just one of the many stationary engines failed, the whole system would stop until it was repaired, whereas if a locomotive failed, it simply had to be towed away. Exactly the same argument applied to the atmospheric railway, but Brunel went ahead anyway.

There were problems from the start in getting accurate castings for the pipes, an essential if the system was to work smoothly. By 1846, the section between Exeter and Teignmouth was being worked by conventional locomotives, but by February 1847, the first piston carriage had arrived and was taken on a test run, as described by one of the engineers on the line, P.G. Margary: 'Started at 6.0 p.m. for Turf, towing a locomotive behind. Went on very slowly to Turf, there being a large quantity of water and dirt in the pipe.' It was not the most promising of starts, but a year later the system was operating between Exeter and Newton Abbot. Press reports at the time were enthusiastic:

'The novelty of the thing begins to disappear; passengers go in and out with the same indifference and confidence they would manifest towards a stagecoach. Master Piston is getting a general favourite. Indeed many prefer this noiseless track to the long drawn out sighs of "Puffing Billy".'

Brunel must have been delighted by this reception, though Gooch may have been less pleased to hear his mighty engines described as 'Puffing Billies'. But the sense that all was going well did not survive the arrival of winter. The leather valve froze solid and could only work when it was thawed out. Worse still, the leather itself was deteriorating at such a rate that it was obvious that it would need replacing at regular intervals and at huge cost, with inevitable disruption of services. Brunel had to admit defeat. The atmospheric railway was

The atmospheric railway at Dawlish, showing the Starcross pumping station.

A drawing of the leading carriage and driver on the atmospheric railway.

dismantled, and the line was built as a conventional railway. Very little remains as reminder of those days, but three of the engine houses survive at Starcross, Totnes and Torquay. The former is the best preserved and was for a time opened as a museum, where the system was demonstrated, not with a steam engine but with an ordinary domestic vacuum cleaner. Even that had enough power to send a visitor whizzing down the pipe. It was an impressive demonstration.

One can see why Brunel was drawn to the idea of an atmospheric railway, given the difficulties of the terrain and, of course, it would have appealed to him simply because it was out of the ordinary. He was always on the look out for something new to try. But in the end, it was an expensive failure, and Brunel himself was among the losers, for he had invested in the system. Now he had a new problem. He had relied on the atmospheric system to conquer the steepest sections. On 20 July 1847, the first train left Newton Abbot for Totnes, heading for the Dainton incline. Just how challenging the bank can be was brought home to me when I was on a steam excursion behind a Castle and a Hall. It was obvious that there was trouble with the Hall, and unfortunately the train was stopped at the foot of the bank, and after several attempts to get started the effort was abandoned and the enthusiasts on board suffered the ultimate indignity of having to be rescued by diesel. One can imagine why Brunel was concerned, when even these locomotives struggled. Daniel Gooch wrote:

'I never saw Mr. Brunel so anxious. Relying on the atmospheric transport he had made these steep inclines and he feared there might be difficulties in working them. These difficulties disappeared with the day of opening.'

There was another problem that came to light when the atmospheric railway was scrapped. Brunel had planned for a number of viaducts along the route but based his design on the premise that they would only be needed to support a light piston car rather than a heavy steam locomotive. The grandest of these was at Ivybridge and stood 104 feet high, and was carried on eleven arches, each 61 feet wide. The supports were slender masonry piers, but the arches were constructed from timber with laminated timber for the bridge deck. It had to be strengthened when the atmospheric adventure ended. Later, when the line was converted to standard gauge, the old viaduct was replaced by the current structure, but the piers of the old still remain standing.

The late 1840s were a time when great expositions became popular. Prince Albert was an enthusiast for exhibitions that in his own words would 'wed mechanical skill with high art'. There were successful exhibitions in London and Birmingham, but the most impressive was a show held not in Britain but in France, the Paris Exposition of 1849. It was decided that anything France could do, Britain could do better and plans were laid for a grand exhibition to be held in 1851. The site was London's Hyde Park and a Building Committee

The Exeter and Plymouth Railway was run by locomotives following the failure of the atmospheric railway: the scene between Dawlish and Teignmouth.

was appointed, with both Robert Stephenson and Isambard Brunel among its members. They invited the public at large to submit plans, but must have been overwhelmed by the response, when 245 of them appeared – overwhelmed but not over-impressed. They rejected the lot. The decision was then taken to invite one of their own committee to draw up a plan and the job fell to Brunel.

The design that he produced was for a vast sixty-foot-high brick building, topped by an immense iron dome. The building was roughly 2,000 feet long and 50 feet wide, while the dome was 150 feet high and 200 feet in diameter. It was dark and foreboding and although the Building Committee accepted, as soon as illustrations appeared, there was a storm of public protest, summed up by *The Times*.

'By the stroke of a pen our pleasant Park – nearly the only spot where Londoners can get a breath of fresh air – is to be turned into something between Wolverhampton and Greenwich Fair. The project looks so like insanity that, even with the evidence we have before us, we can scarcely bring ourselves to believe that the advisers of the Prince have dared to connect his name with such an outrage to the feelings and wishes of the inhabitants of the metropolis. Can anyone be weak enough to suppose that a building erected on such a scale will ever be removed?'

As we all know, it was never built. Instead, the Great Exhibition was housed in Joseph Paxton's airy construction of iron and steel, the Crystal Palace. It was not Brunel's finest hour, but to give him credit, as soon as Paxton's design was presented to the Committee, he was its enthusiastic supporter. There was one consolation for Brunel and his friends – pride of place in the railway section went to the Iron Duke class locomotive, *Lord of the Isles*.

In 1854, Britain declared war against Russia, and the troops marched into the Crimea. There were early gains, but everything came to a halt in front of the great Russian fortress of Sevastopol. The war was carried on with less than competence by the British generals, and many back in Britain were frustrated at the lack of progress, including Isambard Brunel. He devised an extraordinary floating siege gun. The hull, largely submerged, could be manoeuvred by steam jets to bring the gun to bear. The gun itself was housed in a hemispherical armour-plated shield. The vessel was to be brought to the site, towed by a specially built screw steamer,

Brunel's rejected design for the hall for the 1851 Great Exhibition.

with opening bows that in the engineer's words were 'made to open at the bows and its contents floated out ready for action'. He had invented the landing craft. He sent details to Sir John Burgoyne, then a senior officer in the Royal Engineers. He was impressed by the idea, and passed it on to that conservative body, the Admiralty. There was no response. Brunel, given his father's experiences with that body, was not surprised as he wrote to Sir John:

> 'You assume that something has been done or is doing in the matter which I spoke to you about last month – did you not know that it had been brought within the withering influence of the Admiralty and that (of course) therefore, the curtain had dropped upon it and nothing had resulted? It would exercise the intellects of our acutest philosophers to investigate and discover what is the powerful agent which acts upon all matters brought within the range of the very atmosphere of that department. They have an extraordinary supply of cold water and capacious extinguishers, but I was prepared and proof against such coarse offensive measures. But they have an unlimited supply of some *negative* principle which seems to absorb and eliminate everything that approaches them.'

Eventually, a messenger was sent to the Admiralty to retrieve the model of the floating gun that had been sent to them. At first no one seemed to have any idea what was being asked for until somebody at last remembered having seen – 'the duck shooting thing'.

The Crimean War is better known for failure and incompetence than for British enterprise. The best-known example was the infamous Charge of the Light brigade, where the cavalry were misdirected to the wrong site and then ordered to charge straight at a well defended gun battery, with huge loss of life. But even more lives were lost when any soldiers unfortunate enough to be injured or fall seriously ill were sent to the 'hospital' at Scutari. In the winter of 1854-5, of the 25,000 British troops in the Crimea, 12,000 were in hospital. Their chances of recovery were slender, due to the atrocious conditions in the makeshift hospital. The plight of the soldiers was famously publicised by Florence Nightingale, and harrowing accounts of the conditions were sent back to Britain by the correspondent from *The Times*.

Florence Nightingale's chief complaint was that she was unable to get any response from the Permanent Under-Secretary of State at the War Office, who she described as 'an autocrat, irresponsible to Parliament, quite unassailable from any quarter.' This reviled gentleman was none other than Sir Benjamin Hawes, Isambard Brunel's brother-in-law. But he did react and contacted

Brunel in February 1855 to see if he could design some form of prefabricated hospital to send out to the Crimea. The engineer replied immediately:

> 'This is a matter in which I ought to be useful and therefore I need hardly say that my time and my best exertions are entirely at the Service of Government'.

He at once set about designing not just a hospital with wards for patients, but included a nurses' room, water closets and outhouses. The ward areas were roomy enough to allow plenty of space between beds and a fan kept them well ventilated. He made arrangements for a water supply to feed hand basins and invalid baths. Most of the buildings were built from wood, but the kitchen, bakehouse and laundry were iron to avoid fire risk. By April, everything was ready and the sections of the hospital were sent off for assembly, complete with staff, and a full set of instructions from Brunel.

> 'By steamer *Hawk* and *Gertrude* I shall send a derrick and most of the tools, and as each vessel sails you shall hear by post what is in her. You are most fortunate in having exactly the man in Dr. Parkes that I should have selected – an enthusiastic, clever, agreeable man, devoted to the object, understanding the plans and works and quite disposed to attach as much importance to the perfection of the building and all those parts I deem most important as to mere doctoring.
>
> 'The son of the contractor goes with the head foreman, ten carpenters, the foreman of the WC makers and two men who worked on the iron houses and can lay pipes. I am sending a small forge and two carpenter's benches, but you will need assistant carpenters and labourers …Do not let *anything induce you to alter the general system and arrangement that I have laid down.*'

Brunel had been scrupulous in his attention to detail – right down to the provision of toilet paper. He had expected that the military authorities would either supply soldiers to help with the construction or make some sort of arrangements with local craftsmen and labourers. They did nothing, so the little group from England had to do everything themselves, yet they did the job and within seven weeks the first patients were being treated. Something like half the patients who were admitted to the old Scutari hovel died. It has been estimated that some 1,500 were admitted to the new hospital, of whom only 40 died. It is a great tribute to Brunel and his meticulous planning that so many men returned safely to Britain. Florence Nightingale, who had railed against Sir Benjamin Hawes, called the field hospital 'those wonderful huts'.

Chapter 17

THE SYSTEM EXPANDS

The Great Western's ambitions to forge links with the north culminated in their attempts to reach the Mersey, bringing yet more conflicts with Captain Mark Huish, who had been in charge of the Grand Junction, but which had now merged with other lines to become the London & North Western Railway (LNWR). There was a route from Wolverhampton to the Mersey through three standard gauge lines, the Birmingham & Shrewsbury, the Shrewsbury & Chester and the Chester & Birkenhead railways. The LNWR, however, also had agreements with lines in the region – the Stour Valley and the Shropshire Union railways – and was doing its best to deprive rivals of traffic and profit. The two Shrewsbury lines responded by cutting their fares and the reaction was immediate. Huish was not a man to engage in subtleties, nor was he in favour of long, expensive legal actions. The Chester station was a joint holding, and it was now attacked. The Shrewsbury booking clerk was hauled out of his office, his tickets were removed, timetables torn down and access obstructed. Everyone knew who had ordered the assault, but proving it was a different matter. Other obstructive measures were taken, including blocking the canal in which the railways had a share. Unfortunately for the Shrewsbury interest, the Chester & Birkenhead decided to come in with the LNWR and refused to accept any 3rd class tickets from the Shrewsbury lines. All this went on for two years, during which time the latter were losing money. Their only hope was to find a big company on their side to prop up their finances and to lend a weighty presence to counteract Huish and his plots. They turned to the Great Western.

As a result, the Great Western agreed on mutual running rights with the Shrewsbury lines. Huish employed his usual bullying tactics. He bought up as many Shrewsbury shares as possible. He employed a device he had used before, using a forged Shrewsbury seal to issue false documents and calling meetings that were packed with his own supporters. None of it worked, and now the tactics began to tell against him. They were costing his company money, not just the opposition. By 1854, the Shrewsbury lines were formally merged into the Great Western empire. But it was something of a pyrrhic victory, as the vital link to Birkenhead was not included in the deal. Brunel's hopes of bringing the broad gauge to the Mersey were dashed.

The gauge battles in England had been fought, but there was still a potentially highly profitable area for railway development. South Wales had become one of the vital areas of growth in the Industrial Revolution, thanks to its iron and coal industries. Now it was more important than ever as the demand for coal to fuel the railway locomotives and the increasingly large fleet of steamers was accelerating at an unprecedented rate. Equally important was the connection with Ireland. The prospectus was published and advertised in newspapers. As originally proposed, it was planned to leave the Gloucester line at the tiny village of Standish, just north of Stonehouse. From there it would head directly west to first cross the Gloucester & Sharpness Canal via a swing bridge and then cross the Severn between Frethherne and Awre. The route would then run down the Severn valley to cross the Wye at Chepstow before crossing into South Wales through Cardiff and Swansea to Fishguard with a branch to Pembroke Dock. From the two Welsh ports, ferry services would run to five Irish ports.

It seemed straightforward, but Brunel's old bête noire, the Admiralty, immediately objected on the grounds that any bridge would interfere with shipping. As this stretch of the Severn was notoriously difficult to navigate and had already been by-passed by the ship canal, it seemed a little pointless. Brunel hoped to satisfy their criticism by offering them something to their advantage. Close to the proposed line at Frampton on Severn, the river goes through a huge U-bend. He offered to build a navigable cut across the narrowest part, but the Admiralty were adamant. As a result, the line was authorised by parliament in 1846, but only from a starting point at Chepstow. Now a minor railway development suddenly assumed a crucial importance. The Gloucester & Dean Forest Railway was authorised to join the Monmouth & Hereford Railway in 1846. All that was needed now was a short extension to a point just two miles south of Awre and a direct connection could be made with the South Wales. The GWR agreed to take over construction of the little railway and when that was agreed, it became possible to start work on running the broad gauge into Wales.

Everything seemed set fair for a successful project, when a disastrous potato blight struck Ireland in 1845. It was the staple food for many families and famine spread through the land, while the laissez-faire government in Whitehall did absolutely nothing to relieve the suffering. The country went into a deep financial depression, and the investors who had been needed to establish the ferry services no longer had the resources to support the scheme. The Great Western had offered financial support, with substantial sums to be

paid over once the line reached Fishguard, but now that seemed increasingly
unlikely to happen. The SWR suggested that the money should be paid when
the lines reached Swansea, but the proposal was turned down. The South
Wales supporters felt badly let down, and eventually it was agreed to start
construction, but to end, at least temporarily, at Swansea.

Brunel was the chief engineer for the South Wales Railway, and his first
great challenge was the crossing of the Wye at Chepstow. There were physical
problems to overcome. On the Gloucestershire side was a limestone cliff,
but on the Welsh side of the river there were just mud flats. His first design
involved constructing a timber arch, but once again the Admiralty stepped
in to scupper his plans. An arch was unacceptable – the river must be
crossed by a flat bridge to allow a minimum of fifty feet clearance above the
whole river at high tide. He needed to find a new solution to the problem. It
seemed obvious that some form of iron bridge would be needed, but there
were doubts about the best way in which such a material should be used.
Robert Stephenson had used wrought iron for a bridge to carry the Chester
& Holyhead Railway across the River Dee near Chester. On 24 May 1847, the
bridge collapsed as a train was crossing, resulting in five deaths and several
injuries. At a subsequent inquest, it was claimed that the accident had been
caused by the derailment of the locomotive damaging the bridge. Several
leading engineers spoke up in Stephenson's defence, including Brunel, and
he was not charged. In fact, we now know that the design was fundamentally
faulty, and that Stephenson was lucky to escape with his reputation intact.
Faced with this new challenge, Brunel made sure that nothing of the kind
happened at Chepstow.

There was one idea that he had already tried successfully, when building
a bridge to carry the branch line across the Thames to Windsor. He had built
a wrought iron bow and string bridge, where the bow was actually three
graceful wrought iron tubes, connected to the deck by the supporting iron
'strings'. He was to adapt that design for one part of the bridge at Chepstow.
On the Welsh side, the bridge was approached by an embankment to bring it
level with the cliffs on the far side. It was then constructed as a conventional
span, carried on rows of pillars, the first next to the embankment, the next on
the shore, then a set positioned one quarter of the way across the river. These
were sunk down through the mud to reach solid foundations. The last was
expanded upwards as part of the new construction. This was to be in effect a
cross between bow and string bridge and a suspension bridge. The support
in the centre of the river was matched by a tower on the bank, between which

circular iron tubes were fitted. The deck below was suspended from chains, but also had rigid ribs between the two parts. At three hundred foot long, it provided ample room for ships to pass up the Wye. It was a bold design and before embarking on it, Brunel showed his idea to Robert Stephenson, who by then had enjoyed a more successful venture crossing the Menai Straits, and he gave his approval. The bridge remained in use until the 1950s, when the increased speed and weight of trains started to cause problems and speed over the bridge had to be restricted to 15mph. It has now been replaced.

The Wye was not the only obstacle to be overcome. Wales is a hilly country, but there was an obvious route that could be taken by staying close to the coast. Even so, there were river crossings to be made and Brunel opted for the comparatively cheap construction methods he had used on the line between Exeter and Plymouth of a wooden superstructure mounted on masonry piers. The grandest of these was the Landore viaduct across the River Tawe, north of Swansea. This involved building a straight approach on the eastern side with a gradient of 1:109 while on the west, the lines curved away with a 1,320 ft radius and a 1:109 gradient. The viaduct itself had 37 arches of varying size. The largest crossing the river was 110ft wide with a bow and string construction. It was the most imposing of all Brunel's timber viaducts but has

The original viaduct that carried the South Wales Railway over the Wye at Chepstow.

suffered the same fate as the rest, replaced by a structure better adapted to modern rail traffic, leaving only stone stumps behind.

By 1852, the Chepstow bridge was ready for traffic and the route to Swansea was open. At the same time, work commenced on extending the line towards Fishguard, but with Ireland still in a state of depression, money was short and at this stage it was simply built as a single track line. Swansea had grown in importance thanks to its links with the tin and copper mines of Cornwall. The latter had the ore but no coal, while South Wales could supply the coal. As smelting the ore requires a lot of coal, it was economic sense to ship the ore across to Swansea. When the South Wales Railway arrived, the town – not yet designated as a city – was frequently submerged under blankets of smoke. Now the valuable tin and copper it produced could be sent by rail throughout Britain. Meanwhile, the railway interests were busy in the area where the ore originated, across in Cornwall.

The route from London to Plymouth involved separate companies, starting with the Great Western and then ending with the South Devon, and all had employed Brunel as their chief engineer and all had been broad gauge. It was therefore anticipated that what was, in effect, the Great Western empire would extend its bounds westward to the end of the peninsula at Penzance and that Brunel would be in charge. It was not quite that straightforward. The first railways to be built in Cornwall were horse-drawn tramways, serving the mining regions and connecting them to the coast. Then, in 1832, the Bodmin and Wadebridge Railway was authorised, a curious isolated length of track, but the first in Cornwall to be worked by steam locomotives. It was followed by the Hayle Railway of 1839, which, although it was primarily intended as an industrial line, did carry passenger traffic. Both of these lines were built to the Stephenson gauge. If they had not been built, then the Great Western could have made a sound case for their own route being the logical extension. But they were there, and there were other companies prepared and eager to offer alternatives. Another gauge war was about to break out, if not quite on the scale of previous conflicts.

As early as 1835, Falmouth businessmen were promoting the idea of a Stephenson gauge line running up through central Cornwall to Launceston and then via Okehampton and Salisbury to London. It was rejected by the House of Lords, but reappeared in 1845, this time with the substantial backing of the London & South Western Railway. At the same time, the Great Western put their backing behind a broad gauge line from Plymouth that would run closer to the south coast. In the event, the decision in parliament was made less on the merit of the proposals than on party politics. The Whigs favoured the central route but were outvoted by the Tories and Brunel now had the task of completing his great line that would stretch all the way from London to the western tip of England at Penzance. It was something of a switchback route that he chose. Crossing the Tamar near Plymouth, it rose to a summit of 435ft, then dropped down to sea level, before climbing again to a 350ft summit beyond Liskeard before descending back to sea level again at Truro. The line then rose once more to a 420ft summit on the line to Redruth, before continuing on a more or less level last section to Hayle and Penzance. Along the way there were many valleys and estuaries to cross – requiring many bridges. In the section from the west bank of the Tamar to Truro there were no fewer than 34 bridges in 53 miles. For these Brunel followed the pattern established on the South Devon railway, designing timber upper sections carried on timber or masonry piers. There was one bridge, however, that needed to be on a very different scale.

An old postcard showing the original masonry and timber viaduct at Truro.

The entrance to Cornwall involved crossing the estuary of the River Tamar at Saltash near Plymouth, and an all too familiar problem arose – the demand by the Admiralty that the deck must be 100ft above the high-water mark. It seemed impossible to cross in a single span, and Brunel needed to discover if there was submerged rock in mid-channel that could support a pier. He arranged for an 85ft long and 6ft diameter iron cylinder to be floated out between pontoons into the middle of the river. This was then pumped out and used as a space in which test borings could be made to see if the rock was suitable to support a massive pier. There were to be 175 of these tests before Brunel was satisfied that the solid foundation he needed was there, and once found it needed to be accurately mapped. It was good, hard solid rock and Brunel put in his design, which was very much based on his experience with the Windsor and Chepstow bridges. It was too costly for the company, so he was forced to reduce it in size to take just a single track and to reduce the length of the two main river spans.

The whole bridge would have a total length of 2,187ft. There were 17 spans built in a conventional way at either side of the river and two central spans of 455ft each. They followed the idea used at Chepstow, but here instead of horizontal tubes to support the deck, the immense iron tubes arched high above in an elegant curve. As before, there were chains that acted as in a conventional suspension bridge – and in this case many of them had been manufactured for the Clifton bridge, but never used there. As well as the chains, there was cross bracing. The plan involved building the central pier and approach piers and prefabricating the spans and floating them out to be raised into position. This was the system he had watched at work when he went to support Robert Stephenson at the Menai Straits. The contractor was Charles John Mare of Blackwall who had worked with Stephenson on the Britannia Bridge, so seemed the ideal choice. Unfortunately, it turned out he had underestimated the amount of work involved, and had to withdraw before the work was completed, leaving Brunel to finish the job with direct labour employed by the company.

Once work began, one of the first jobs was to confirm that the rock was able to withstand a solid structure. So, the tube was now used as a coffer dam, inside which a trial masonry foundation was constructed. Everything went well, but then a problem arose, that was all too common in railway programmes – the money ran out. It was not until 1852 that work could be resumed. The central pier was always going to present the real challenge, and Brunel designed a vast iron caisson, 37ft in diameter and 90ft long that was lowered down to sink through the mud and sand to the rock. The test borings had enabled Brunel to construct an accurate profile of the rock, and the bottom of the caisson was shaped to fit snugly. Once in place, it was securely moored between two pontoons. The basic coffer dam was actually a double tube. The centre section acted as a diving bell, while the outer ring was pressurised to keep the water at bay. While workmen worked to clear away the mud and sand, the masons could get on with the construction of the pier.

Meanwhile, on the bank, the great central spans were being prefabricated, including the oval shaped tubes, 12ft 3in high and 16ft 9in wide, from which the vertical chains would drop to the bridge deck, when everything was in place. After a difficult time, coping with the very hard rock on which it rested, the great central pier was completed to a point close to high tide level at the end of 1856. Brunel was now ready to float the sections into place. He had seen the problems that Stephenson had faced at the Menai Straits with swirling currents and unpredictable tides, so he devised his own tide meter to get an accurate picture of the movement of water up and down the Tamar. He was also aware that the one essential for success was keeping everything under tight control. Shouting orders across the water was not an efficient way of doing that, so he planned to use a very different system. First of all, he worked out that he was going to have to move about a thousand tons and that he would need four pontoons, each 100x20x10ft. To move these into position and steady them would require a small army of men, and instead of shouted commands he proposed using flag signals. He made a note of the flags and signals he needed:

Heave in – red
Hold on – white
Pay out – blue
Waved gently means gently
Waved violently means quickly.

On 1 September 1857, Saltash on the Cornish bank was en fete with flags flying from every house and boats crowding the upper Tamar, ready for the first great lift. Two docks had been cut in the bank beneath the great truss. The pontons were filled with water, then manoeuvred under the truss and the water gradually pumped out. As they rose, the giant structure was seen to rise gradually from the ground. It was afloat. Now it had to be moved into position. Brunel was now the master of ceremonies. From a platform built

The Tamar bridge under construction.

high on the truss, he waited with his array of flags and called for silence. The whole crowd was hushed, as Captain Claxton 'in charge of the boats' began the operation to move the pontoons into place. Slowly and majestically the pontoons and their load moved forward and the load rose with the incoming tide until the truss was on the level of the stumpy piers. It was then slid into position and secured. Over the following weeks, it would be steadily jacked up as the masonry rose. Brunel's tidal meter had not let him down. It was later reported that the operation had been accurately carried out to within an eighth of an inch. As soon as it was settled into place, the silence was broken by the cheers of the crowd and a band playing, inevitably it seems on such occasions, *Hail the Conquering Hero Comes*. Throughout the whole proceedings, the hero himself seemed the calmest person there. The second span was installed in July 1858. On 2 May 1859, Prince Albert took the royal train to Plymouth for the official opening for what would be known as the Royal Albert bridge. But it is not his name that can be seen on the bridge, but that of its innovative engineer, I.K. Brunel. Sadly, the man himself was not there. He was seriously ill and was travelling abroad, hoping to restore his health. On his return he was still very weak, but made the trip to Plymouth, where a special truck had been set up with a comfortable couch. The train set off and slowly carried the engineer across the Tamar for his first and only sight of the completed bridge.

The line from Paddington to Penzance was complete, but at the start of the Fifties, London was still being served by the miserably inadequate temporary station. Brunel began planning for an altogether more imposing terminus. Fresh in his mind was Paxton's new idea for a Crystal Palace to house the Great Exhibition. The new station would be a cathedral of iron and glass. There would be no grand entrance: the train shed was in a cutting, approached down sloping carriageways. The unimposing entrance only serves to make what is revealed all the more spectacular. Three great glass curved roofs cover the platforms, like a nave and its side aisles. The central section is 102ft wide, the side sections,40 and 38ft. To continue the cathedral analogy, there are two 'transepts'. The supporting iron pillars are varied. Every third ribbed arch is supported by octagonal piers, and the rest by simpler, plainer versions.

All this is based on sound engineering. The design, however, is jointly shared with the architect Matthew Digby Wyatt, who added architectural

The Tamar bridge, now named Royal Albert Bridge, in the steam age.

Paddington station as it appeared shortly after its opening.

Paddington today, looking along one of the transepts, with the 'Moorish' office windows to the right.

The Brunel statue at Paddington.

embellishments. You can see his handiwork by looking at the decorative details on the ribs and columns, on the elaborate wrought-iron work above the entrance to the station and most notably in the buildings alongside the present Platform One. Especially notable is the ornate window to the offices, in the 'Moorish style', which is rather attractive if anachronistic. When it opened in 1854, the *Illustrated London News* reporter wrote: 'The principle adopted by them was to avoid any recurrence to existing styles and to make the experiment of designing everything in accordance with the structural purpose of the nature of the materials employed.' That is a fair summary, and that is the building's attraction. It does what was needed, and does it with elegant simplicity. The area beyond the tracks was known as 'the lawn', though it is doubtful if any grass ever grew there, and it became an area that was originally largely used for sorting out parcels and freight. It has subsequently been developed as an area of shops, bars and cafes.

Paddington has been my station for visits to London for many decades, and I never cease to be struck by its grandeur. Because it is all down in the cutting, the fact that the station hotel that provides the frontage on Praed Street is frankly dull in no way detracts from the station itself. It has been enlarged over the years, but the essential Brunel station remains intact. Fittingly, there is a statue to its engineer, but Brunel might have been surprised to find he shares the honour with a duffle-coated bear from Peru.

This period of Brunel's life was only partly occupied with railway matters, for he was also embarking on his greatest engineering adventure – designing the biggest ship the world had ever seen.

Chapter 18

THE GREAT SHIP

By the 1840s, Britain was in the grip of railway mania. From modest beginnings at the start of the decade, there was a rush of new bills before parliament that peaked in the middle of the decade, when an astonishingly large number of Acts were passed. Over 4,000 miles of track were agreed. Some were sound schemes, others doomed to fail. Many were destined never to be built at all. It did mean that the promoters were all desperate to find a competent engineer to bring their ambitious ideas into reality. There were three men who, at this time, were pre-eminent: Robert Stephenson, Joseph Locke and, of course, Isambard Brunel. There were many hopefuls knocking at their doors, but the engineers scarcely had enough time for the work they already had, without having to concern themselves with new schemes. All three men were put under a great deal of stress. Stephenson found some relief by having a yacht built in which he could sail away – his cabin on board was 'the door with no knocker'. Brunel did not enjoy that luxury. He wrote to his friend Adolph d'Eichtal in 1845:

> 'Here the whole world is railway mad. I am really sick of having proposals made. I wish it were at an end. I prefer engineering very much to projecting, of which I keep as clear as I can'.

The pressure to get work done in a hurry, particularly where rival schemes were competing to cover the same ground, meant that engineers were constantly being rushed.

One of the leading figures in the mania years was the 'Railway King', George Hudson. He had created one of the great companies, the Midland Railway, by amalgamating smaller companies. In one such amalgamation, when joining the Newcastle & Berwick and the Newcastle & North Shields he managed to illegally pocket nearly 10,000 shares for himself. Eventually, his dishonesty was found out and shareholders turned on him. His fall was dramatic, and it brought home to the investing public a realisation that a railway share was not an automatic entry ticket to a world of wealth. Investment in railways plummeted as fast as it had risen. Railway companies that had relied on raising money whenever it was needed, now found themselves strapped for cash. As we have seen, one of the victims of the crash was Brunel's Cornish railway development and he was forced to lay off some of his assistants. At least it gave him time to think about other aspects of his work – he turned again to consider big ships, in particular ships that could go to Australia.

There were good reasons for thinking about ships that could reach the far side of the world. For a long time, Australia had, for most people in Britain, simply been the place where convicts were sent as a punishment. That all changed when gold was discovered and many from England, especially Cornwall, went to try their luck. There was, however, a more lasting source of wealth, as was made apparent at the Great Exhibition in the Crystal Palace. The country was a valuable source of high quality wool. The problem with getting to Australia by steam power was the inability of any vessel then afloat to reach the Antipodes without stopping several times en route to take on coal. This was true of the largest vessel then built, the SS *Great Britain* when she was taken off the Atlantic run. Her new owners had to arrange for coal to be shipped out from Wales to Cape Town to refill her bunkers for the remainder of the voyage. So, Brunel was well aware that his ship was not up to the task of making a full run to Australia and it is natural that his thoughts began to turn to the idea of designing a ship that could do so.

He had already been approached by the Australian Mail Company in 1851 for his ideas, but when he suggested ships of between 5,000 and 6,000 tons, they baulked at the idea of having anything on that scale. They turned instead, at Brunel's suggestion, to John Scott Russell to build two smaller vessels, the *Victoria* and the *Adelaide* at the Millwall yard he had recently taken over from Fairbairns. Each vessel was 3,000 tons and carried 200 passengers. They were both to prove successful, but that did not stop Brunel from continuing to think about the problem of the non-stop voyage. In a notebook entry for March 1852, he sketched out a vessel that he labelled the 'East India Steamship' and jotted down the dimensions 600ft x 65ft x 30ft. To understand just what a huge advance this would have represented, compare those figures with those for the *Great Britain* – 322ft x 50ft x 16ft. The new ship, if built, would have four times the capacity of its predecessor – more than enough space for fuel to reach Australia. The question was – would anyone commission such a huge vessel?

There was no question of building a vessel of this size in Bristol, for it would have been far too large even to get out of the harbour. Brunel turned to John Scott Russell to see if he could interest him in the scheme. He also had the support of that stalwart friend of his, Captain Claxton, but his other great supporter Thomas Guppy had left Britain for good and settled in Naples, where he had his own engineering business. The Australian Mail Company had already shied away from Brunel's suggestion for a big ship, so there was little point in approaching them. Russell suggested going to talk to the Eastern Steam Navigation Company, that had been formed in 1851 to trade with the Far East and Australia. They had hoped to win a share in the valuable mail carrying business, but the government had granted a monopoly to the P & O – Peninsula & Orient. That had been a blow, but they were open to hear about a venture that would give them an advantage over their rivals, by having the only ship on the run that did not need refuelling along the way.

A partnership with Russell seemed ideal in many ways, as the two men had a lot in common. The former was, like Brunel, an innovative engineer. He had not started out in that way, as after taking a degree at Glasgow University, his early career had been spent teaching, culminating in a temporary post as Professor of Natural Philosophy at Glasgow – 'natural philosophy' was simply the term generally in use at that time for any science. But already he was showing his engineering skills and in 1834, he designed and built six steam carriages, that carried six passengers on a service between Glasgow and Paisley, but, like other steam carriage builders at that time, fierce opposition led to the service being withdrawn. He then turned his attention to steam on the water. He began working for the company that was operating a passenger service on the two canals linking Edinburgh and Glasgow, the Forth & Clyde and the Edinburgh & Glasgow Union. He began practical experiments on hull design to see which was the most efficient. As a result, he developed what was called his 'wave theory' of hulls. The theory was wrong, but the practical results were satisfactory, as he was able to design some fine craft, notable for their shapely bows. When he went into business himself as a ship builder, one of his commissions was to design and build the yacht *Titania* for Robert Stephenson. The engineer was delighted with this craft, and probably enthused about it to his friend Brunel, which must have encouraged him to put his faith in Russell as a suitable builder and partner in the venture of constructing the world's biggest steamship. In the event, they were to prove to be perhaps a little too similar. Both were strong-minded characters, with their own views on how things should be done. This was fine as long as they agreed but was to cause problems whenever they differed.

Problems began to appear right from the start of the project. Brunel's design called for a ship that would use both paddle wheels and a screw propeller. The reason was due to necessity not choice. The Company had specified that the ship had to be able to enter the Hooghly River to reach the port of

Calcutta, now Kolkata. That limited the draught of the ship and inevitably affected the size of propeller that could be used. Given that the engine used to drive the propeller would be working at the comparatively low pressure of 15psi, there was simply not enough power for a propeller alone. Brunel consulted the ever-reliable company of Maudslay, Sons & Field and between them they decided that 60 per cent of the power needed to move the ship would come from the screw, and the rest through the paddle wheels. This was not disputed, but what did cause a fuss was Brunel's choice of the Screw Propeller Company that had originally been formed by Francis Pettit Smith and used to create the pioneering vessel, *Archimedes*. It turned out that several of the Steamship Board had an interest in another concern, The General Screw Company, and when Brunel refused to change course, several members resigned in protest. This, however, only provided an opportunity for Brunel to recruit men he knew and trusted and who trusted him, onto the Board. The process was completed in December 1852, when Goschen, described as 'the only doubtful director remaining', resigned and Thomas Geach took his place. Brunel and Geach then set to work to raise the necessary capital and by December 1853 they had sold 40,000 shares and raised £120,000. Interestingly, among the list of those who had taken a thousand shares each were three great railway contractors, Edward Betts, Samuel Morton Peto and Thomas Brassey, who presumably knew little about shipping but had faith in Brunel. Among the other major shareholders was Brunel himself.

The whole project had taken Brunel into uncharted territory. Never before had he been in a position where he had personally persuaded men he knew to act as directors or to invest in the project on his personal recommendation. He felt the responsibility strongly:

'The fact is that I never embarked in any one thing to which I have so entirely devoted myself, and to which I have devoted so much time, thought and labour, on the success of which I have staked so much reputation, and to which I have so largely committed myself and those who were disposed to put faith in me; nor was I ever engaged in a work which from its nature required for its conduct and success that it should be entrusted so entirely to my individual management and control.'

It had been suggested by the directors that he might appoint a resident engineer, and he made it plain that there would only ever be one engineer in charge, who would be responsible for everything and that would be himself.

If the Board thought that he should be answerable to anyone else when it came to the construction of the great ship, then he would be forced to leave the project. As the Board well knew that without Brunel there would be no project, they hastily retreated.

Brunel was making it very clear that this was his ship, his design and decisions would all be his alone, which is important, given later events. Having said that, there were elements in the design that were developed from work done by other engineers. Russell, in his own experiments with ship design in the 1830s, had shown that the strength of the hull was improved by using longitudinal stiffeners with closely spaced bulkheads rather than the traditional shipbuilding technique of relying on ribs for strength. This was the system that would be used in the great ship, which at this stage was known as the *Leviathan*. The process of construction began by estimating the likely building costs, and Brunel came up with figures of £275,200 for the hull, £60,000 for the screw engine and boiler and £42,000 for the paddle engine and boilers, with an extra allowance for auxiliary steam engines. The work of building the hull was not put out to tender, but offered directly to Russell, who not only accepted Brunel's figure but even offered to build the hull for less. He would do it for £258,000 provided he also got a contract to build a planned sister ship. In the event, the contract was his for the initially agreed sum, but it would have made little difference which figure was accepted. There was always the possibility, even the probability, that the initial estimated cost would be overshot. Russell may well have thought that with his experience, he could make his own accurate estimate of the costs. But up to this time, he had been his own master. Now he was subject to the demands made by the chief engineer and this was made quite clear in one of the clauses in the contract:

> 'All calculations, drawings, models and templates which the contractor may prepare shall from time to time be submitted to the Engineer for his revision and alteration or approval. The Engineer to have entire control over the proceedings and the workmanship'.

Other clauses specified that all vertical joints should be butt joints and double riveted if necessary, that wrought iron be used throughout, with obvious exceptions such as slide valves and that bulkheads should be built at 60ft intervals. Everything had to be made watertight before launching and that if any defects were found during sea trials, they would be made good at the contractor's expense. One clause was destined never to be applied – the requirement that the ship should be built in a dock. What is not clear is who should be responsible for providing a dock large enough to hold the *Leviathan*, for nothing on the Thames at that time was big enough. And there was one clause which must have seemed harmless enough, but which was to prove crucial; the cost of the launch was to be carried as part of the contract, but there was no mention of the form the launch should take.

The contract did not include the supply of the engines, which needed to be massive; the screw engine specification called for an engine that could produce 4,000 indicated horsepower at 45 revolutions per minute and 2,600ihp at 17rpm for the paddle engine. One change that was made from the SS *Great Britain* was the drive mechanism for the propeller. The chain mechanism was abandoned in favour of a crankshaft. The biggest problem was the crankshaft for the paddle wheels. It was as well that Nasmyth had already come up with his steam hammer, for without it, the piece could never have been forged. As it was, it proved difficult to find a company prepared to take on what was then the largest single forging ever attempted. The job eventually went to the Lancefield Forge in Glasgow, and they only succeeded in producing a faultless version at the third attempt. When completed, it weighed a massive 41 tons. The cylinders for the engines were cast at the Boulton & Watt Soho works in Birmingham, but the engines were assembled on site. As well as the engines, the ship was to have six masts, and could carry over 4,500 square feet of sail. However, because of the heat from the funnels, the sails and engines could not be used at the same time without the risk of the sails catching fire. As the ship was expected to steam the whole route, the sails were more of an insurance policy than a practical aid on the voyage.

The ironwork for the hull was supplied by a company of which Charles Geach was a director, Parkgate Ironworks of Rotherham. The plates were a standard length and width, 10ft by 2ft 9in, but came in three separate depths: one inch for the bottom of the ship; three quarters of an inch for the sides; and half an inch for the bulkheads. The numbers involved are staggering. In total 30,000 plates were needed, and each plate was held by a hundred rivets. In other words, 30 million rivets had to be hammered into place by hand.

There was one unique feature. The hull had a double skin, with a gap of 2ft 10in between the two sets of plates. For the riveters who had to work between the two, the racket must have been almost intolerable. With its longitudinal stays, bulkheads and iron deck plates, the whole of the hull was as stable as a giant girder.

As work progressed, Russell found that the clause mentioning Brunel's intention to scrutinise everything he did was no idle threat. The engineer himself seems to have taken a gleeful pride in finding anything that was either wrong or capable of improvement.

> 'I found for instance an unnecessary introduction of a filling piece or strip such as is frequently used in shipbuilding to avoid bending angle irons – made a slight alteration in the disposition of the plates that rendered this unnecessary and found that we thus saved 42 *tons weight* of iron, or say £1,200 of money in first cost! And 40 tons of cargo freight – at least £3,000 a year.'

Delighted Brunel might have been, but it was probably a constant irritation to Russell, the experienced shipwright, to be corrected time after time. The first hint that all might not be well came with the publication of a newspaper article about the great ship, which not only seemed to suggest that the man ultimately responsible for the amazing vessel was Russell and that Brunel's role was little more than rubber-stamping the ideas he produced. One sentence made it quite explicit: 'Mr. Brunel, the Engineer of the Eastern Steam Navigation Company, approved of the project, and Mr. Scott Russell undertook to carry out the design.' Where did the anonymous reporter get his facts and who in the organisation supplied them? Not surprisingly, Brunel was livid and wrote a long letter of complaint that ended:

> 'And lastly, I cannot allow it to be stated, apparently on authority, while I have the whole heavy responsibility of its success resting on my shoulders, that I am a mere passive approver of the project of another, which in fact originated solely with me, and has been worked out by me at a great cost of labour and thought devoted to it now for not less than three years.'

It was apparently never discovered just who had been behind the briefing, but when Prince Albert visited the site shortly afterwards, Russell was at great pains to point out to Brunel that 'I took the opportunity of explaining what I supposed he and everybody else knew, that you are the Father of the great ship and not I'. Rolt in his biography of Isambard Brunel hints that this was a piece of back-pedalling by Russell, who was himself the source of the story and had become alarmed by the furore. It could equally be argued that Russell, knowing how infuriated Brunel had been by the article, simply wanted to make it clear that he had done his best to refute it.

Before any building work could begin, two important, closely connected decisions had to be taken – just where was the ship to be built and how would it be launched? The initial contract had specified it being built, as the *Great Britain* had been, in a dock. There was clearly not enough space in the existing yard, but fortunately the adjoining yard was lying empty. It had belonged to David Napier, the pioneer responsible for the first excursion steamer, *Comet*. He had realised that the future for shipbuilding did not lie in London and had moved to the Clyde. So, the Company bought the yard, and it was here that the ship would be laid down, with the original yard mainly used for manufacturing, for example building up the vast engines. Russell wanted to build the ship in the conventional way, at right angles to the river for a straight launch, but Brunel objected that the necessary long slope would make building difficult. Instead, he proposed a sideways launch. He even invented a patent slip on rollers that could be moved and used again at another site when necessary if the ship needed repairs. But it was declared to be too expensive, though in the event it could well have proved a first-class investment.

The ground now needed to be prepared for building the flat bottom of the hull. Massive oak piles, 12 by 15 inches and up to 38ft long, were sunk into the ground at intervals of five feet and left with four feet protruding above ground as the foundation for the hull. The work was completed by the end of May 1854. The old Fairbairn yard now took on something of the appearance of a factory. The engines for the paddles were to be constructed on site, which involved digging pits in the foundry floor for the casting of the cylinders and building a new shed for erecting the engine which, when completed, would stand forty feet high. There was the usual array of machine tools for punching and bending metal.

The screw engine that was being built by Boulton & Watt was of a new design, and Brunel was in constant correspondence with Blake, who was supervising the work in Birmingham, making suggestions and consulting over problems. For one important aspect, he returned to an idea of his father's. In Marc Brunel's patent of 1822, which covered various aspects of marine steam engines, he introduced a new design for a governor, the device that ensures a regular supply of steam from the boiler to the engine. In the patent specification, he pointed out that the normal governor used on steam engines on land was not suitable for use at sea, because of the motion. The governor, as used in Boulton & Watt engines, consisted of a pair of rotating heavy balls linked to the throttle. As the speed of the engine increased, the spindle to which the balls were attached also moved faster, causing the balls to move outward by centrifugal force, and that in turn worked through a linkage to close the throttle down by the required amount. In Marc Brunel's description of the new device in the patent specification in his own words, with references to figure omitted:

'it is indispensable that all effect of gravitating or any other power, except centrifugal force, is eliminated … and as a substitution for gravitation, which in the land engine is used to close the balls, I make use of a spring. Thus, when the balls are extended, the plug will close the orifice to the utmost degree required, which is such as to counteract the whole of the power of the engine, even if both wheels were out of the water, and thus the action of the engine will be regulated.'

This was the regulator that would be used on the new ship. An idea of Isambard's own was to have the boiler feedwater passed through a system wrapped round the funnels, which served the dual purpose of cooling the funnels where they passed through the public rooms and preheating the water before it reached the boiler, saving on fuel costs.

At first, things went comparatively well, but at the beginning of 1855, Russell had to write to Brunel to say that he had run out of funds and his bank, Martin's, refused to advance him any money. It was then agreed that he would be paid ten instalments of £8,000 each when an agreed amount of work had been done in each period. This kept the bank happy, but it also marked a turning point in the relationship between Russell and Brunel. To Russell, it seemed that he was being made subject to rules laid down by Brunel, who set the hoops through which he had to jump before he could get his money. To Brunel, it was mere prudence to make sure the company got value for the money it was handing out. This was when relations between the engineer and the ship builder began to deteriorate.

A major difference now separated the two men – the question of how the vessel was to be launched. Brunel had received a letter from Buffalo, in which the writer, having heard about the 'mammoth steamship', gave an encouraging report on the experience of launching ships sideways into Lake Erie. 'Two large steamers [the *Plymouth Rock* and the *Western World*] 330ft keel have been launched here last summer with their boilers and nearly the whole of their engines in place and hurricane deck cabins all complete'. He told Brunel that all their vessels were being launched this way and it was considered completely safe. This was encouraging news, but the American boats were being launched freely into a vast lake. Brunel's ship was far greater in size and was to slip into the comparatively narrow waters of the Thames. He was convinced that he needed to have a controlled launch, with the ship being lowered down gently. Russell completely disagreed. His view was not entirely unprejudiced, as a controlled launch would cost far more and in the contract he had signed, he was responsible for the launch. One can sympathise with Russell insofar as he was now realising that he had made a bad deal when he signed the contract, with no room for extra payments for any contingencies that might occur. On the other hand, Brunel was surely right that an uncontrolled launch was a recipe for disaster.

This was more than a mere argument over technicalities, but an increasingly personal clash, between two men who were both utterly convinced they were right and unwilling to yield. Co-operation that was essential for the smooth running of the whole operation could no longer be relied upon. There were a series of niggling complaints, such as the time when the directors had asked for photographs of the work in progress and none were forthcoming. Russell's letters to Brunel became increasingly stiff and formal, while Brunel's replies were more and more tetchy: 'Your reply this morning to my long list of complaints is an admirable specimen of an Under Secretary's reply in the House to a Member's motion – it does not satisfy one single honest craving for information and for assurance of remedy.' Money was at the heart of most of it. According to Russell, Brunel kept making design changes, which had not been allowed for in the estimates, and which in Russell's opinion required

The building of the *Great Eastern* by John Wilson Carmichael.

extra payment. But the biggest problem was still with the launch, which Russell claimed would cost £37, 673 18s. The question of who would pay the sum – if, indeed, the figures were accurate - was not resolved. So the arguments continued and, after one particularly acrimonious exchange, Brunel finally snapped – where once Russell had ended letters quite informally, he now signed them 'Your obedient servant'. To which Brunel replied – 'I wish you were my obedient servant, I should begin with a little flogging.'

Throughout the second half of 1855, the situation continued to deteriorate. Brunel was constantly having to ask for vital information that he needed to plan for the launch of the ship – and seldom getting a satisfactory or on occasions any answer at all. At the same time, Russell kept running out of funds. He complained that he was keeping many hands employed and unless he got more money, he would have to start laying them off. What he did not mention was the fact that not all those hands were at work on the *Leviathan*, but on other vessels being built at the yard, some of the work actually being carried out in the Napier yard, which was strictly reserved for the owners, the steamship company. Russell was still arguing over the method of launching, and claiming extra money on the grounds that this was a new system that Brunel was introducing at the eleventh hour.

The argument between the two had been kept within bounds, but now Brunel felt he had no option. He needed to make plain to the directors just how matters stood. He stated quite firmly that to allow Russell to go ahead with his idea of simply letting the ship slide into the water was totally unrealistic 'unless the vessel were well insured and you wished to get rid of it'. He finally laid out the shortcomings that had not been dealt with – the shortage of over 1,000 tons of iron and the small ships Russell was building apparently illegally on Company land, which were impeding work on the great ship. He then came to the nub of the matter.

'Mr. Russell, I regret to say, no longer appears to attend either to any friendly representations and entreaties or to my more formal demands and my duty to the Company compels me to state that I see no means of my obtaining proper attention to the contract otherwise by refusing to recommend the advance of any more unless and until those terms are complied with'.

This was a clear ultimatum. Brunel was well aware that without the advances, Russell would be bankrupted. There was an attempt to come to some form of agreement, by which Russell would continue with the work, but under the scrutiny of independent inspectors. But as matters were investigated, more and more problems appeared. Russell owed money all over the place, and although he had received considerable sums from the Company, the money had not always gone to the source for which it was intended. He had received payments for 1,200 tons of iron, but it had never arrived. When the Company contacted the suppliers, they discovered not only had the money for that shipment never materialised, but he was in debt for the iron already delivered. Russell put forward proposals for future payments based on work in hand, but the Company were reluctant to agree, largely because he seemed unable to say how his estimates for the work he would do to earn the money had been arrived at. The unhappy Russell had reached a dead end, and he dismissed the entire workforce. The yard stood silent and idle.

Worse news was to follow as the extent of Russell's debts became clear. The Company had assumed that if Russell was unable to carry out the contract for lack of funds, they would take over the work themselves, but now it appeared that the Fairbairn yard had been mortgaged off and was now in the hands of the creditors, Martin and Stevens. They were already at work, earmarking items that they could take possession of as part of the debt collection process. Unfortunately, as Brunel discovered, that included items which belonged to the Steamship Company. He asked for an inventory of items but Dixon and Hepworth, Russell's two assistants, refused to co-operate. It seemed that there was now only one course of action available. The Eastern Steamship Company would have to negotiate some sort of deal with Martin and Stevens to allow them to finish constructing the ship. It was obvious that if the negotiations failed, the ship would simply be left where it was, unfinished and left to rot. This was really in no one's best interest. Martin and Stevens would have their yard blocked and unusable. The steamship company would have spent a fortune and would have nothing to show for it. That did not mean that there was not a great deal of haggling, with the yard's new owners eager to get every penny they could by leasing it out. Eventually, agreement was reached, and the Company had use of the yard and its machinery until 12 August 1857.

It was May 1856 when the men came back to work, including some of the foremen who had worked for Russell, and who now received new contracts to work for Brunel. He had some trusted helpers at his side, including Captain Claxton and Daniel Gooch, and work progressed well. By June the following year, the ship was almost ready for launching, with only the sternpost, screw and screw shaft needing to be fitted. But it was the launching that had always been a bone of contention and for it to be successful it needed careful preparation. An order had been placed for the launching cradles and tracks in January that year, but it was clear that they would not be in place by August when the lease on the yard expired. There was nothing for it but to go back to Martin and Stevens and ask for an extension. This was granted up to 15 October, but with a charge of £2,500, roughly a quarter of a million pounds at today's prices. They were doing rather well from the deal. Even then all was not ready, and a new launch date was set for the spring tides at the beginning of November.

Brunel may have been impetuous when taking decisions, but he was scrupulous when it came to preparing for important events, such as the launch. But there was no time for carefully testing everything before the great day of the launch. Further delays were simply out of the question. It was a far from ideal situation. That things had gone badly wrong was obvious, but who was mainly to blame? L.T.C. Rolt in his excellent biography of Isambard had no doubts on the matter and laid the blame entirely at Russell's door. Adrian Vaughan in his later biography tended to blame Brunel for making unreasonable changes throughout the building period. My own opinion is rather different.

In a way, Russell was the victim of his own enthusiasm. The chance to build the world's largest ship must have been an irresistible temptation and, in his eagerness, he signed a contract, which was vague in parts and which made no allowances for contingencies. It was unrealistic to think that in such a huge operation, and an operation on a scale never previously attempted, there would be no changes as things progressed. And even if there hadn't been, Russell should surely have been aware how rarely major engineering projects came in within the first estimate. But although he was a very successful builder of ships, he was no businessman and all too soon it became apparent that as the days went by his chances of making a profit were dwindling and were to reach a point where he would be likely to make a loss. It was then that he began desperate attempts to keep the enterprise afloat, borrowing money where he could and mortgaging the yard. He took on extra work with the other steamers on site to try and bring in extra funds. He was like a juggler who starts confidently with one or two balls in the air, but who keeps being thrown more and more balls, until one proves to be one too many and all come crashing down. One can now see why he was adamant that the launch should be free not controlled; the extra money was simply not there. For his part, Brunel was a demanding master, who certainly wanted everything done his way and done promptly. If Russell had been more open about his predicament, things might have turned out differently, but that was not to be. So it was, that there was a desperate scramble to get work finished and all Brunel could do now as launch day approached, was pray that everything went well.

Chapter 19

THE FINAL YEARS

To launch a vessel of this size was always going to be difficult. The ship at launch weighed 12,000 tons and keeping that mass under close control was the challenge Brunel had set himself. He had amassed all the necessary figures for the hull – its weight, centre of gravity and centre of flotation. He conducted several experiments with cradles running down inclined planes before deciding that the ideal slope for the actual launch would be one in twelve. He needed to concern himself with two very different problems. The first and most pressing was how to prevent the whole ship getting out of control and thundering into the water at speed. The other was what was to be done to shift it if for any reason it stuck on the slope before hitting the water.

The whole ship was supported on two 120ft cradles, which left 180ft projecting towards the bows and 150ft towards the stern. The cradles were to run on rails down to the river on a launch way constructed of timber baulks laid over a two foot thick concrete foundation. On top of this a track of typical GWR rails was laid, that connected with iron plates on the bottom of the cradles. When the hull was released, the iron plates on the cradles should, in theory, ride smoothly over the rails. The whole progress down the slope would be controlled throughout by chains wound round immense checking drums at the head of the slipway. There were tackles at bow and stern, with lines fed out to barges moored in the river, which, in turn, were connected to steam winches on the shore. If the ship stuck halfway down, these could be used to get her moving again. Hydraulic rams were available should the ship not move at all when the supports were removed. Brunel had hoped to test everything thoroughly before launch day arrived, but time had simply run out.

He made all the preparations he could to ensure that everything went smoothly. The first day was to be spent gradually easing the great ship into position at the top of the slipway, and there it would sit until the actual launch the following day. He had learned at Saltash that the best way to ensure everything went well was to bar all but essential workers from the launch site, insist on absolute silence and command operations through a flag system. He made this absolutely clear in a letter to the company secretary, Yates:

'I must have sole possession of the whole of the premises on the day of the launch, no men, even of our own, still less strangers, in any part of the yard except those regularly told off for their respective duties and everybody must be completely under my control.'

We can only imagine Yates' reaction when he received this note, for unknown to Brunel he had already sold 3,000 tickets to the general public, inviting them to the yard to watch the great event. He would not have looked forward to meeting Brunel on launch day, when the engineer discovered that his plans for a quiet orderly launch had been sabotaged, and the whole yard was filled with spectators. To add to Brunel's worries, the press had been alerted to what was going ahead, and the banks of the Thames were equally crowded with men, women and children expecting to see the ship slide into the water for the first time. The fact that nothing of the sort had actually been planned for that day had not been mentioned. At least Brunel had one old reliable supporter. Samuel Smiles recorded the event in his biography of George and Robert Stephenson.

'The author remembers being with Mr. Stephenson one evening at his house in Gloucester Square, when a note was put into his hands from his friend Brunel, then engaged in his first fruitless efforts to launch the *Great Eastern*. It was to ask Stephenson to come down to Blackwell early next morning, and give him the benefit of his judgement. Shortly after six next morning Stephenson was in Scott Russell's building yard, and he remained there until dusk. About midday, while superintending the launching operations, the baulk of timber on which he stood canted up. And he fell up to his middle in the Thames mud. He was dressed as usual, without greatcoat (though the day was bitter cold), and with only thin boots upon his feet. He was urged to leave the yard, and change his dress, or at least dry himself; but with his usual disregard of health, he replied, "Oh, never mind me - I'm quite used to this sort of thing"; and he went paddling about in the mud, smoking his cigar, until almost dark, when the day's work was brought to an end. The result of this exposure was an attack of inflammation of the lungs, which kept him in bed for a fortnight.'

Unfortunately, Smiles did not date this encounter, but it appears as if it might have been in the period at the beginning of November, when Brunel was working day and night finalising the arrangements for the launch, rather than on the day itself. Whether Stephenson was with him on the first launch day or not, Brunel was faced with chaos instead of the silent order he had envisaged. Nevertheless, he had no option other than to start the proceedings and hope that the flag signals would ensure the correct proceedings would be followed, for there was no chance of his voice being heard above the hubbub of sound. The directors had insisted on having a naming ceremony at the start of proceedings, instead of waiting until the ship was actually ready to be floated out. The chairman's daughter cracked the customary bottle of champagne over the bows and named her *Leviathan* – a name that would soon be changed to the *Great Eastern*.

At first, all went well. The chocks holding the cradles in place were hammered away, and the order was given that the men on the barges should take the strain, while the steam winches were started up. For a while nothing much happened, and though eventually the hull seemed to be juddering on its cradles, there was no movement down the slope. Brunel had anticipated this might occur, and the two hydraulic jacks were brought into play and the ship moved three feet down the slope. Now Brunel ordered the two checking

Preparing for the launch of the *Great Eastern*. One of the great checking drums is in the foreground.

drums to be started up. The crew on the barges were, it appears, horrified by the sight of the great vessel hurtling down towards them, and one of the crew simply abandoned ship, jumped in a rowing boat and headed for safety. But the crew of the forward cable drum were quickly in action, and the ship was brought to a halt. This should have been a concerted effort from both crews on the drums, but the aft crew seem to have been paying very little attention to what was going on. In fact, they were so lackadaisical that one labourer was actually sitting on the drum. Then it started up, hurling his mutilated body high in the air, as he was caught by the rapidly rotating winch handle; he never recovered.

Brunel had no option but to postpone any further attempts to continue the launch until later in the afternoon, by which time torrential rain was falling on the site. Captain Harrison, who had been in charge of the men on the barge, reported that they were in a state of some panic and were unlikely to be much use, until they had a chance to collect themselves and calm down. The last thing Brunel needed was another horrendous accident, so he ordered the ship to be made secure and brought the day's proceedings to a halt. It was clear that there were major problems to overcome and that an actual launch would not be possible until the next high spring tide on 2 December. But, ideally, he would have liked to get the whole ship down the slipway to the river bank, ready for floating off before then. He decided to revise his plans. The winches that had been placed on barges were now securely fastened on the shore, and he had installed two extra hydraulic presses. Everything was made ready for a second attempt to ease the ship down the launch way on 19 November. It did not go well, and yet more adjustments were needed. The ship was skewed on the slipway, with the stern lower down the slope than the bows. So, the tackle and presses were concentrated on shifting the bows to even up the vessel. The strain, however, proved to be too much for the hauling tackles, which snapped. However, by the end of the second day the ship had been moved, mainly due to the hydraulic presses, a distance of fourteen feet. Over the next few weeks, numerous attempts were made to get the great ship to the bottom of the slope, but always hampered by breaking tackle. It crawled slowly along in fits and starts. Brunel consulted Stephenson, and the two men were agreed that if the whole operation was to be completed then there was no point in relying on the tackle, and extra hydraulic power was the answer.

The job of supplying the new presses went to a company that had only started in the manufacturing business in 1857 – James Tangye and Bros of

The unmistakable figure of Brunel, with his usual cigar, at the launch site of the *Great Eastern*.

Birmingham. It is not known why Brunel chose this particular company. Rolt suggests that he knew them from Cornwall, but although the brothers were all born there, they had never worked in the region. Whatever the reason, it was a move that cemented their reputation, advertising the fact that 'we launched the *Great Eastern* and she launched us'. As Brunel waited, the press that had lauded him, now turned against him, mocking his inability to get the *Leviathan* moving. *The Field* magazine was the cruellest, though as a magazine specializing in field sports it was hardly a beacon of engineering know-how.

That, however, did not stop the editor from voicing his opinion and took the opportunity to have a go at Isambard's father as well:

> 'Why do great companies believe in Mr. Brunel? Is it because he really is a great engineer? If great engineering consists in erecting large monuments of folly at enormous cost to shareholders, then is Mr. Brunel surely the greatest of experts? There is his and his father's great work, the Thames Tunnel, which our uncles and aunts used to look upon as the eighth wonder of the world. With what an expenditure of treasure, labour and blood, was the most stupendous and useless of 'bores' created!'

Such sarcasm could only have added to the stresses on the engineer, battling to get the job done. The new presses arrived and by 10 January, operations had gone so smoothly that the ship was down at the bottom of the slipway, with the water lapping round her at high tide. The last big test was to get the ship out into the narrow river, and it was here that Brunel came into his own. For many of even the greatest engineers of the day, tackling such a job would be down to experience or, lacking that, inspired guesswork. Mathematical calculations rarely came into it. For example, if one looks at the great book produced shortly after the opening of the Telford bridge across the Menai Straits, there are pages of formulae and graphs, but they were all produced after the event, not before it. Telford himself had worked things out using models. But Brunel had all his calculations ready; he had finally got all the information he needed – the weight of the ship, its centre of gravity and its flotation centre. Now he needed to make sure that an unexpectedly high tide did not carry the ship off in an uncontrolled manner. She was carefully secured and a fire float pumped thousands of gallons of water into the hull to act as ballast and keep her sitting firmly on the cradles. The day set for the final stage was 30 January, and Brunel arranged for his son Henry to leave school to join him for the great day. The engineer had done all he could to ensure things went well, but there was one element he could not control – the weather. Dawn broke that day with a howling gale and pouring rain. It was all too clear that nothing could be done that day, and there was nothing to do but wait. And the weather changed. He had arranged for reports from Liverpool on the conditions, as the storm was being carried on a westerly wind. Although London was still enduring the driving rain, a report came in that it was now clear in the west. He decided that it looked as if the launch might occur the next day, and he made everyone aware that this was to happen.

The dawn of the 31st saw a clear day, with blue sky and light winds. After all the delays and problems, the final stage went quickly and smoothly. There were no crowds to bother him this time, but Henry went and fetched his mother and Sophia Hawes to witness the event. The wedges holding the cradles in place were removed. The hydraulic presses were set in motion and began pushing the stern towards the water and by twenty past one, the stern was afloat. The steam winch then rapidly hauled the bows into place and twenty minutes later the whole vessel was safely afloat, and the Brunel family went aboard. There were a couple of minor hitches. The stern line was let loose a little too soon, and the ship had to be manoeuvred carefully to clear the timbers of one of the cradles. Then one of the paddle wheels fouled a barge, which Brunel dealt with promptly and dramatically by simply sinking the barge. Now the four tugs that had been standing by took charge and towed the vessel to a safe mooring at Deptford. The job was done. The delays had been expensive; the company was still paying an exorbitant rent for their prolonged stay at Millwall, and perhaps some of the directors may have thought that if they had listened to their engineer's plans for using hydraulic power in the first place, instead of dismissing them as too expensive, they might have saved themselves a great deal of money. There was no great jostling crowd to watch the launch and Brunel would not have welcomed it. But as he left the ship as it floated in the Thames, he was greeted by the cheering that he could appreciate; the salute from the men who had worked alongside him and made the whole day a success.

The strain of the last few months had told on Brunel, and his brother-in-law John Horsley wrote him a serious letter, imploring him 'to reflect upon that hour of death which must come upon you sooner or later and whether, at that awful moment, you will be able to look with satisfaction upon your life, which has been one of almost unparalleled devotion to your profession, to the exclusion, to far too great an extent, of that which was due to your God and even to your family'. Hardly a cheerful message for a sick man, but Horsley was grieving, having recently lost both his wife and two of his children to scarlet fever. And he was certainly right to show concern. The need to see the launch through had kept Brunel going and now it was over, his strength was fading. He consulted his doctors, who insisted that he needed to get away, preferably somewhere warm, where he could relax and recuperate.

He and Mary finally left England in May for the health resort and spa town of Vichy and then on to Switzerland, eventually getting a boat home from Holland. He was not exactly idle during his absence, as he had work to do on the plans for the Eastern Bengal Railway. One of the reasons for the *Great Eastern's* reduced draught had been the necessity of navigating the Hooghly River. The railway was part of this grander scheme, linking the east bank of the Hooghly to the interior on a 110 mile route. The Act was passed by the British Parliament in 1858 and was part of a deal between the railway company and the powerful East India Company. Although Brunel was involved, it was very much not a broad gauge line, but part of the developing metre gauge system in the sub-continent. In his absence, the hard-pressed steamship company was desperately trying to rake together funds to complete the ship. When these failed to materialise, there was even a proposal to simply auction off the hull. Fortunately, an alternative suggestion was put forward. A new company would be set up that would purchase the hull and take the project through to completion. Nothing had happened to the ship while Brunel had been away, and now in November 1858, the Eastern Steamship Company sold the hull for £165,000 to the newly formed Great Ship Company and a month later the old company was wound up.

Brunel was now given the task of preparing estimates for completing the project. He agreed, but only on condition that he should prepare detailed specifications of everything that needed to be done and that any contract should be absolutely watertight and insist on complete adherence to the plans he had drawn. There had to be some savings. The original plans had called for two large steam launches to be kept on board for use as tenders, since there were no harbours then built to accommodate the monstrous ship. They were cancelled. Otherwise, the designs were thorough and carefully prepared. Ideally, he would have stayed, as he had always done, close to the works, keeping an eagle eye on all that went on. But by now it was clear that his health was deteriorating. He consulted two eminent doctors, Sir Benjamin Brodie and Dr Richard Bright. The latter had recently diagnosed a kidney complaint, that then became known as Bright's disease, but now as nephritis. This involves swelling of the kidneys and can lead to other symptoms including swelling of the veins in the neck and high blood pressure. The latter would not have been helped by the extreme stress he had been enduring throughout the long period of the attempted launches – nor would his habit of continually puffing on one of his famous big cigars have done anything to improve matters. The two doctors agreed, Brunel must not stay in London for another winter, but should head off for somewhere warm. He and Mary decided to go to Egypt and took Henry along as well.

They were accompanied by a young doctor, who according to Mary was more obsequious than useful. She wrote to her elder son, 'He is most obliging, but such a toady to your father! And I wish you could hear Henry's droll imitations of him at night when we go to bed.' The party travelled across France to Marseilles, where they took a paddle steamer across the Mediterranean. It was a stormy passage and all the passengers huddled down below except Brunel. He may have been weak and sick, but he could not miss an opportunity of seeing how a steamer coped in really rough weather. In Cairo, they were joined by Robert Stephenson, who had arrived in his yacht, and the two great engineers had Christmas dinner together. Soon afterwards, Stephenson set off to sail back to Britain, while the Brunels left for a journey up the Nile.

Their iron boat took them as far as the first cataracts on the Nile at Aswan. Brunel, however, was determined to go on further and acquired a wooden boat, and with a party of local workers built up three cabins for his family and the doctor. In this they continued up the cataracts, which are not quite the fearsome rapids that the name suggests; sailing up them is today a popular tourist excursion. Mary it seems found it all a bit alarming, but Isambard and Henry thoroughly enjoyed the experience. They eventually made their way home, arriving first at Naples and spending some time in Rome. On his return, Brunel's first thoughts must have been on the progress that had been made – or not made – on the great ship. He might have expected many things, but one thought would probably never have crossed his mind. The contracts had been put out to tender – and had been awarded to none other than John Scott Russell. The other contender had been Wigram & Lucas and Brunel wrote to the board pleading with them to accept the latter's offer but to no avail. The Company must have been all too aware of their engineer's failing strength, and whatever his faults may have been, Russell knew the ship intimately, and his two right hand men had stayed with the project, even after Russell himself had left.

The grand saloon was ready in August 1859 and the décor was the epitome of Victorian taste, with elaborate decoration and heavy, stuffed furniture, but was undeniably impressive. The Company decided to hold a great banquet for the Lords and Commons. Brunel was again now so ill he was unable to attend, so the honour of hosting the assembly and making a speech fell to Russell. On reading the widely publicised account of what he said, all traces of sympathy for the man must evaporate. He quoted what he claimed as a conversation in which Brunel said: 'Now, I am not a ship builder, nor am I an engine-builder, and now I come to see if you will devote your mind attention to carrying out of this problem to a successful issue.' It seemed all Brunel had was a rough idea that he wanted a big ship and everything else was to be left to the true master, Mr. John Scott Russell. Now this is such obvious arrant nonsense that one can hardly credit anyone believing it. That the man who already had been responsible for the two most important and revolutionary ships of the nineteenth century, and who, as we know, had been meticulous in overseeing every single detail of their construction, should now present himself in this way is just unthinkable. If Brunel had been his old robust, healthy self he would never have tolerated it. As it was, he did nothing, either because he was simply too weak to cope or he thought it beneath his dignity to reply. It was a sorry business.

Brunel recovered his strength to some extent and was able once again to assume at least some control over the fitting out. 7 September was the date set for the first sea trials to test the engines. Brunel went on board on the 5th but was suddenly overtaken by a stroke that left one side of his body completely paralysed. He was taken back to Duke Street and was destined never to see the ship on which he had exerted so much effort moving under her own power. So, on the 7th she set out for Weymouth. At first, everything seemed to be in perfect order and she travelled along at a respectable 13 knots in spite of a heavy sea. But there was a problem that no one on board was even aware of. Brunel had used the same annular system for heating the boiler feed water as he had on the *Great Britain* where it had worked well. From the top of this system was an open-ended standpipe that rose to the top of each funnel. This gave a good head of water that allowed gravity to provide the force to allow the water to enter through the boiler valves. The system had been subjected to a hydraulic test up to a pressure of 55psi and to make the test possible, two stop cocks had been inserted to isolate the annular pipes. Once the test was completed, they served no useful purpose and should either have been removed or fixed permanently open. Somehow, in the course of the voyage, the stop cocks that provided the water for the paddle engine boilers were closed. How or why this happened is a complete mystery. Now the water was being heated and turning to steam, but there was no outlet and the end was inevitable. Just as the ship was passing Dungeness light, there was a huge explosion. The event was described by *The Times* correspondent, who was covering the voyage.

'The forward part of the deck appeared to spring like a mine, blowing the funnel up into the air. There was a confused roar amid which came the awful crash of timber and iron mingled together in frightful uproar and

THE EXPLOSION ON BOARD THE GREAT EASTERN STEAM SHIP,
OFF HASTINGS, ON THE 9TH SEPTEMBER, 1859.

An artist's somewhat dramatic illustration of the explosion on the *Great Eastern*.

then all was hidden in a rush of steam. Blinded and almost stunned by the overwhelming concussion, those on the bridge stood motionless in the white vapour till they were remined of the necessity of seeking shelter by the shower of wreck – glass, gilt work, saloon ornaments and pieces of wood which began to fall like rain in all directions.'

The explosion had ripped right through the grand saloon, but fortunately the passengers had been on deck admiring the view. The stokers in the boiler room were not so fortunate. The scalding steam had done its worst. They scrambled up on deck. One man, unable to stand the agony, simply jumped overboard and was instantly killed as he hit the churning paddle wheel. A passenger tried to help one man, only to find when he grasped his arm that the flesh pulled away. Three firemen died that day, two more lingered on in agony for a further twenty-four hours. On this occasion it was one of Russell's men who saved what could have been an even greater disaster. He recognised at once what had happened and sent a man to open the cocks on the feed to the screw boilers. At once a plume of steam blasted up the standpipe, a terrifying indication of just how close the ship had come to a second explosion. Amazingly, there was no real structural damage to the ship.

There is no record of whether or not the news was brought to Brunel in Duke Street. He was so obviously a dying man that it would have been a kindness to keep this final, unlooked for tragedy from him. But it would have been hard to fool such an astute brain, even when he was weakened by a stroke. In any case, he had no time to brood over the disaster. He died on 15 September.

Chapter 20

ASSESSMENT

The working lives of father and son overlapped, but their achievements were very different. Marc was far more of an inventor than his son, as can be seen by the fact that he took out a grand total of eleven patents, covering a wide range of subjects: a duplicating machine; trimming fabrics; making ships' blocks; timber sawing; veneer cutting; circular saw; making boots and shoes; sawmills; making leather durable; tunnelling; printing plates; copying presses; marine steam engines; and a gas machine. Isambard's entire working life was devoted to large scale engineering projects. Yet in spite of these differences, there was also a certain similarity in their dogged determination, in the way in which they pursued their objectives, and a refusal to let any obstacle deter them. They were men who went their own way – and held their own opinions, regardless of what others might think. Marc as a young man had been recklessly outspoken in his opposition to the French Revolution, even to the point of risking his life. Isambard was equally forthright in stating his opinions and following his own path. Both had great achievements, yet one has a name so widely known that he regularly appears in popular lists of the greatest Briton of all time. Indeed, many would be hard pressed to name another engineer of the past apart from Isambard Brunel – though some might come up with George Stephenson, often quite wrongly naming him as the man who built the locomotive *Rocket*. It helps that he is instantly recognisable – the little man with the tall hat and the big cigar. Few would name Marc Brunel or be able to say what he had done. In this final chapter we shall look at what the two men did and its lasting importance.

Marc Brunel's first great achievement was designing the block mill at Portsmouth. It was something entirely new and represented an original way of tackling a specific problem. For centuries, craftsmen would have made a variety of blocks for sailing vessels of all sizes, each man being responsible for the task of starting with the raw materials and fashioning them into the finished product. Marc broke the production down into stages and for each stage he designed a specific machine. This was the basis for mass production then and is still so today. This was a major advance in technology. Above all, it was immensely useful. Marc took out his block making patent in 1801. Just sixty years later, the Royal Navy received its first ironclad, steam powered battleship, HMS *Warrior,* but even she carried a full suit of sails on three masts that would have required hundreds of blocks to manage them. Even in the age of steam, Marc Brunel's block mill was kept busy. Similarly, the saw mill he built for Chatham dockyard was being used in shipbuilding for decades – and is still in use today. If, as is generally agreed, Britain really did rule the waves through much of the nineteenth century, Marc Brunel had a small but far from insignificant part in helping to assure that ascendancy.

It is sometimes forgotten by those who praise Isambard as a great Briton that his father arrived in this country as a French refugee and as a refugee, he was very conscious of the debt he owed to his adopted country. A patent for making better boots may sound trivial, but Marc was driven to develop the system not to make money for himself but to relieve the suffering that he had seen among the soldiers returning from the Peninsular War on account of the wretched footwear with which they had been issued. They, at least, had every reason to bless his name. A similar feeling of altruism led Isambard to design the prefabricated hospital for the troops in the Crimea.

Marc Brunel's greatest achievement was undoubtedly the completion of the tunnel under the Thames. This was a task that had earlier defeated another great engineer, Richard Trevithick. It seemed that just a few years after it was built, that the tunnel had been a monumental mistake, as it never attracted the traffic it was expected to carry. But it was to prove of lasting value. In 1865, the East London Railway Company bought the tunnel and four years later, instead of pedestrians, the tunnel echoed to the sound of the steam locomotive. In 1913, as part of the Metropolitan Railway Company system, steam was replaced by electric trains and a year later it was incorporated into the London underground system and it remains a vital link to this day. The original shaft is still in regular use at Wapping station, while on the Rotherhithe end, the shaft has now been incorporated into a fine museum telling the tunnel story. The tunnel itself ultimately became a success, but rather more important was the shield he designed, which became the essential method for tunnelling in soft ground from then on, though much modified over the years.

These were the major achievements for which Marc was solely responsible, but as we have seen, he was always experimenting with other new ideas – many of which were to be used by his son in his own work, the flat arch of the Maidenhead viaduct being the classic example. But arguably his greatest gifts to Isambard were the care he took in giving him the sort of education that set him up for the rest of his career and setting an example of following through his own ideas, despite how alleged experts might deride them. Inevitably, not everything worked – the gas engine cost him a great deal of time and money, and was never a viable idea.

At the start of Isambard's career, he was very much the junior partner in what was, in effect, Brunel engineering. It was in this role that he had the chance to design the Clifton suspension bridge, which remains one of the most distinctive of all Bristol landmarks. But there is a question mark over just how much of the bridge we see today can actually be attributable to Isambard Brunel. He had planned for rather elaborately decorated piers in an Egyptian style, but when work was abandoned, they were left unadorned. The bridge was actually completed by the firm of Hawkshaw and Barlow after Brunel's death, and they made several important alterations. The height was increased from 230 to 245 feet, the suspension chains were increased from two to three, the girders were all iron instead of a mixture of wood and iron and the anchorage points on the land were brought nearer the piers. These are all quite substantial changes. Had Brunel been able to complete the bridge himself, it would have looked quite different in many ways. He does, of course, have the credit for having persuaded the authorities to build a suspension bridge that would span the whole gorge, but in planning for a bridge on this unprecedented scale, he undoubtedly made use of his father's experiences in bridge construction in different countries.

For many, Brunel's name will always be associated with the Great Western Railway. No other railway company has ever attracted such ardent followers, whose enthusiasm has remained undiminished, even though the company itself ceased to exist at nationalisation in the 1940s. In part, this is because the company energetically promoted itself, and also it was the one company that retained its identity from inception to the day it was wound up. The one point of contention is the use of the broad gauge. Was it brave or foolish of Isambard to set himself apart from the rest of the railway world? One can see why he did it. It was all part of his independent spirit, his determination to take what he saw as the better path. It was not just the gauge that would be different, but the whole method of laying the track would be unique to the GWR. He was absolutely convinced that his system would provide a smoother, faster ride than what he referred to as the narrow gauge. He was equally convinced that when the world saw how much better his system was, others would follow his lead. We now have no real means of knowing if the broad gauge would have been far superior to the alternative, and comparing running times provides no answer, as the locomotives and rolling stock on the different version were themselves different. Certainly, locomotive engineers would have found working with the extra space provided on a broad gauge locomotive much easier. That was one of the factors that led Daniel Gooch to seek to join Brunel in the first place. We do know, however, that his original track proved too rigid and he was forced to modify it. But what is undeniable is that the Stephenson gauge was already too well established for anyone to even contemplate the huge cost of converting it. Isambard did not live to see that fateful day in 1892 when the last of the broad gauge was lifted and the whole system converted to standard gauge. Brunel might well have been right that his system was better, but he had quite simply started too late. That does not, however, detract from some of the magnificent features of the routes, such as the Maidenhead bridge, the Tamar viaduct and Paddington, one of the world's great railway stations.

There was, however, the one huge blot on his railway engineering reputation – the atmospheric railway. It says a great deal for his reputation that he was kept on as chief engineer for the line, even after the debacle.

Although he is generally spoken of in terms of his railway work, his contribution to the world of ship building was of far greater importance. He did not need to invent any new technology; his genius lay in seeing what others had missed and acting on his insight. He was the first to recognise that the future for long-distance steamer travel lay with big ships that could carry enough fuel for the voyage. It seems obvious to us now, but it was not at all obvious then – and there were quite eminent scientists, such as the egregious Dr Lardner, who declared the whole idea quite wrong. Brunel saw what the supposedly learned mathematician had missed, that the opposition to the motion of a ship was a function of hull area not volume. Having proved his point with the *Great Western*, he then tackled the next problem – how to build a far bigger ship. Iron ships were not new, but it was Brunel alone who saw that they represented the future. And, although not a great inventor himself, he saw the value of what others were doing and was quick to follow through. So, as soon as he heard of Pettit Smith's experiments with the screw propeller, he at once saw its potential. The result was the *Great Britain* – the first iron-hulled steamship to be driven by a screw propeller. It set a pattern that would be followed right through to the twentieth century, when the diesel engine finally ousted steam power.

No project gave him more trouble than his last vast ship, the *Great Eastern*. She has been described by one author as Brunel's 'greatest folly', and in the

The *Great* Eastern in New York.

sense that the ship never actually went into service travelling to the Far East and Australia, she might be thought a failure. Yet, in many ways, she was a remarkable craft, and the value of Brunel's double hull, in particular, proved to be a life saver. In her early days, the ship was employed on the New York crossing. She struck an uncharted reef at the entrance to Long Island Sound, which tore a huge hole 85ft long in the outer hull, but the inner hull remained sound and the ship sailed on safely into harbour. But the repairs proved costly, and the Company decided to auction it off. Daniel Gooch approached two other influential figures, Thomas Brassey, the railways contractor, and John Pender, who was the financier who was backing a company to lay a transatlantic cable for telegraphy, with the suggestion they bought the ship and chartered it for cable laying. They agreed to bid up to £80,000 but to their amazement purchased the ship for a paltry £20,000. After refitting for cable laying, she left Bantry Bay in Ireland with cable and in July 1866 she had successfully laid the world's first transatlantic cable. It was fitting that the man on board in charge of these operations was Brunel's old friend and colleague from Great Western days, Daniel Gooch. As a passenger ship, she never fulfilled her potential, but she was to go on to lay cables around the world. There was probably not another ship afloat big enough to take on the job at that time. Ultimately, the great failure was to prove a triumphant success, even if the triumph was not what was intended when she was built. Brunel, one feels, would have been delighted to find his ship being involved in a new technology. The greatest driving force in his life was the search for the new and interesting, not in following old, well-worn pathways.

Harold Bagust titles his biography of Marc - *The Greater Genius?* – leaving the question open. Can a choice be made between father and son? I don't believe it can, for their talents lay in different directions. Both were innovators, but Marc was the inventive genius while Isambard's genius lay in seeing the wider picture and adapting existing technology in new ways. Both had their failures, which is not too surprising given that they were always pushing at existing boundaries. Both had their triumphs. What I hope their story shows is that they do not need to be measured against each other, because their lives and careers were so intimately entwined. From the time he was a young boy, Isambard benefitted from a father who understood the value of an education that would fit him for the practical life. As he grew up, he worked with his father and learned many valuable lessons, and even when he branched out on his own, he was able to draw on Marc's experience and practical experiments to further his own work. There is no need to choose between them, but rather praise two innovative geniuses who together helped change our world.

SELECT BIBLIOGRAPHY

Bagust, Harold, *The Greater Genius*? Ian Allan, 2006

Beamish, Richard, *Memoir of the Life of Sir Marc Isambard Brunel*, 1862

Booker, Frank, *The Great Western Railway*, Atlantic Transport Publishers, 1977

Brindle, Steven, *Brunel: The Man Who Built the World*, Phoenix Press, 2006

Brunel, Celia, Noble, James, *The Brunels father and son*, 1938

Brunel, Isambard, *The Life of Isambard Kingdom Brunel, Civil Engineer*, 1870

Clement, Paul, *Marc Isambard Brunel*, 1970

Corlett, Ewan, *The Story of Brunel's SS* Great Britain: *The Iron Ship*, Conway Maritime Press, 1974

Kentley, Eric et al., *The Brunels' Tunnel*, ICE Publishing, 2006

Macdermott, E.T., *History of the Great Western Railway* (2 vols) 1927-31

Rolt, L.T.C., *Isambard Kingdom Brunel*, 1957

ACKNOWLEDGEMENTS

The author wishes to thank the following for permission to use illustrations: British Museum, p. 72; Clem Rutter, p. 27; Daderot, p. 5; David Ingham, p. 118; Dsikar, p. 180; Ironbridge Gorge Museum Trust, p. 56; Martin Stone, p. 113; Metropolitan Museum of Art, p. 147; National Portrait Gallery, p. 37; Network Rail Archive, p. 98; Nonan, p. 102; Peter Twyman, p. 91; Popular Graphic Arts, p. 73; Royal Museums Greenwich, pp. 129, 141, 191; Science and Society, pp. 145, 15 (right); Shadowsettle, p. 24; Spudgun, p. 00; SS Great Britain Project, p. 145; Totonvdr 59, p. 2; University of Bristol Library, p. 64; US Libraryof Congress, pp. 10, 94; Victoria and Albert Museum, p. 139; Walter Dandy, p. 178.

INDEX